Rotary
magic

Rotary magic

Easy Techniques
to **Instantly** Improve
Every Quilt
You Make

Nancy Johnson-Srebro

RODALE

RODALE

WE INSPIRE AND ENABLE PEOPLE TO IMPROVE
THEIR LIVES AND THE WORLD AROUND THEM

For any questions or comments concerning the editorial content of this book, please write to:

Rodale Inc.
Book Readers' Service
33 East Minor Street
Emmaus, PA 18098
Visit us on the Web at www.rodale.com for the best quiltmaking news you can use.

Editor: *Sarah Sacks Dunn*
Interior and Cover Designer: *Karen Coughlin*
Layout Designers: *Susan P. Eugster, Dale Mack, and Jen Miller*
Illustrators: *Sue Gettlin* (Techniques) and *Mario Ferro* (Projects)
Photographer: *John Hamel*
Photo Stylist: *Jodi Olcott*
Photography Editor: *James A. Gallucci*
Copy Editor: *Erana C. Bumbardatore*
Manufacturing Coordinator: *Melinda Rizzo*
Indexer: *Nanette Bendyna*
Editorial Assistance: *Jodi Guiducci*

Rodale Home and Garden Books
Vice President and Editorial Director: *Margaret J. Lydic*
Managing Editor, Quilt Books: *Suzanne Nelson*
Director of Design and Production: *Michael Ward*
Associate Art Director: *Carol Angstadt*
Production Manager: *Robert V. Anderson Jr.*
Studio Manager: *Leslie M. Keefe*
Copy Director: *Dolores Plikaitis*
Book Manufacturing Director: *Helen Clogston*
Office Manager: *Karen Earl-Braymer*

The photographs of the projects were taken at the Georgetown Manor, Ethan Allen Home Interiors, 5064 Hamilton Boulevard, Allentown, Pennsylvania.

On the cover: Blocks from Ferris Wheel Flowers, page 156

Library of Congress Cataloging-in-Publication Data

Johnson-Srebro, Nancy.
    Rotary magic : easy techniques to instantly improve every quilt you make / Nancy Johnson-Srebro.
        p.   cm.—(Rodale home and garden books)
    Includes index.
    ISBN 0–87596–783–3 hardcover
    ISBN 0–87596–988–7 paperback
    1. Patchwork—Patterns.   2. Rotary cutting.
3. Machine quilting.   4. Patchwork quilts.   I. Title.
II. Series.
TT835.J634   1998
746.46'041—dc21   97–33817

Distributed to the book trade by St. Martin's Press

    4 6 8 10 9 7 5 3   hardcover
2 4 6 8 10 9 7 5 3   paperback

To Ralph Waldo Emerson, who understood
and wrote about real success and happiness.

What is success?

To laugh often and much;

To win the respect of intelligent people and the affection of children;

To earn the appreciation of honest critics and endure the betrayal of false friends;

To appreciate beauty;

To find the best in others;

To leave the world a bit better, whether by a healthy child, a garden patch, or a redeemed social condition;

To know even one life has breathed easier because you have lived;

That is to have succeeded.

—Ralph Waldo Emerson

Contents

No-Fail Rotary Cutting xii

No-Fail Piecing 54

No-Fail Pressing 92

No-Fail Finishing 100

Projects 116

Introduction

I've spent countless hours in my sewing room (in all its various forms) throughout my quilting lifetime. Over 1,200 miniatures, wallhangings, and bed quilts have passed through my sewing machines, and believe me, I have made every quiltmaking mistake possible. But I never let that slow me down—through trial and error (and a lot of research), I got to the point where I was confident enough to actually enter a quilt in a show. Over a two-year period I won over a dozen national awards, and I'm asked to judge at quilt shows around the country on a regular basis!

With these experiences, I became a firm believer that I can improve on almost anything. And the bigger the challenge, the more I love it! Now, every time I make a mistake, I stop and analyze why I made it. Was I inaccurate? Were the directions wrong or incomplete? Is there a faster, easier, or more consistent way to do a particular technique and still get excellent results? I continuously challenge myself to improve my quiltmaking because I have a personal need to feel in my soul that I've done the best I can. (Also, I just can't resist a challenge—even one I set for myself!) In most cases, I have found that there are better, more accurate, more reliable ways to get the results I want. So I work and think and tinker and cut and sew until I find a way to achieve them.

And that's what I share with you here. I've combined the results of my mistakes, my research, and my expertise into my standard set of No-Fail techniques that I use on every quilt I make and that I teach all over the country. Every time I teach, I get so much gratification from students who look up at me with wide eyes and say, "I can't believe I just did this!" Whether that new technique is cutting a square or setting in a seam, each student gets help with an essential quilting skill—self-confidence.

"My quiltmaking classes are always full of quilters who want their work to look like mine. And now everybody can do what I do because I have put all my secrets, tips, tricks, and favorite time-honored techniques in this book."

It's easy to make great-looking quilts. My No-Fail techniques—cutting, piecing, pressing, and finishing—are the four basic steps to great-looking quilts. I firmly believe that almost all of the problems people experience in their quiltmaking can be totally eliminated by knowing the best ways to cut accurate shapes, piece them correctly, and then press them so they fit together to make the quilt you've always dreamed of. So if you follow my step-by-step No-Fail methods, you'll make a great-looking quilt, too!

Over the years, I have tried virtually every piece of quiltmaking equipment that's out there. I keep a special eye out for ergonomically friendly equipment, since I have had surgery for carpal tunnel in both my wrists. So in this book I include information about comfort—as well as safety features—for all kinds of equipment, from straight pins to sewing machines. And I have recommendations for equipment, supplies, and notions as well—considerations that will make you more confident, more accurate, and more successful in your quiltmaking. Scattered throughout the book you'll find "My Favorite Things" boxes—these are about my special set of tools and supplies that I would never be without.

Quilters have common bonds (a love of fabric and chocolate are the two immediate ones that come to mind!), but we also have different preferences for ways we like to do things. My No-Fail methods are based on my years of experience. I've found that they have helped many students get over the frustration of not having quilts turn out exactly as they wanted. But I also realize that some techniques might not suit certain quilters as well as they suit me—and that's OK! Just keep trying until you find the best way for *you* to do it.

In all my travels and in all my classes, I've come to recognize that each and every quilter is different. That's what makes quiltmaking so wonderful! We form long-lasting relationships with other quilters, and this is the special gift of quiltmaking. Teaching my No-Fail methods has enabled me to touch, change, and enrich many people's lives, and for that I am grateful. Remember: What's really important in the end is how happy you are with yourself and your quilts.

Nancy

"You can beat frustration in your quiltmaking once you master the three crucial steps in quiltmaking: accurate cutting, accurate piecing, and accurate pressing." ❀

"Slow down! Take the time to learn the best way, and do it right the first time. The time you take up front will save you time when you don't have to rip out and redo your work. If you do this, the process of making a quilt will be enjoyable, and the fine quality of the finished product will follow." ❀

How to Use This Book

This book is divided into two basic sections: No-Fail Techniques (Cutting, Piecing, Pressing, and Finishing), and No-Fail Projects. I have included numerous cross-references from the projects to the techniques so that you will know which of my tech-niques to use so your quilts will turn out perfectly. Below, I highlight the special features in each of the sections and show you how they relate to each other. Here are a few additional tips for you when you're making any of the projects in this book.

Technique Section

Techniques used in the projects are shown here in easy-to-follow, step-by-step format. Throughout the projects section techniques are cross-referenced by name.

Step-by-step photos and illustrations show you techniques you'll use in your quiltmaking.

Pressing arrows on illustrations show you which direction to press your seams.

Tip boxes give you ad-ditional information on techniques, equipment, and special tricks.

Piecing 45 Degree Shapes

Pinwheel

The Pinwheel block is one of the many blocks that have eight 45 degree points that must come to-gether perfectly in the center. The secret to getting perfect center seams and sharp points is in the pressing and pinning of each unit—always press your seam allowances toward the *darker* triangle, and master the butting and pinning technique (page 69) before beginning this block.

1. Pin the two halves of the pinwheel together at each end to ensure that the outside edges of the block will stay even.

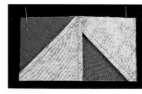

2. Fold the top unit down by ½ inch. If you pressed correctly when making the halves, the light points are slightly recessed, and the dark points are

slightly raised. Align the units so the raised dark points fall into the recessed light points.

3. "Walk" the top unit closed with your fingers, rolling your fingers and thumbs toward each other. Make sure the four points all come together in the center.

4. Pin the units a hair (about ⅛ inch) ahead of the butted seams, *not* directly in the butted intersection (page 69).

5. Sew the seam, stitching a hair above the middle of the X formed by the stitching. (If you sew directly through the middle of the X, you will cut a small amount of the point off on the front of the piece.)

Making Flying Geese

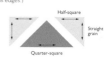

Flying Geese

Sewing two half-square triangles to a quarter-square triangle produces a unit known as Flying Geese. This is such a versatile unit that there are hundreds of ways you can use it. You can combine Flying Geese units to make a block, or you can make other distinctive-looking blocks using one Flying Geese unit with other shapes. There are a few tricky parts to making this pieced unit. First, you have to work with all the bias edges of the triangles. Second, you need to align the triangles correctly to sew them together. Remember that you should always try to keep the straight grain on the outside of all your piecing units (page 24) so that they are less likely to stretch out of shape and will join to other piecing units accurately. By using both half-square and quarter-square trian-gles in this unit, you can position them so the stable straight grain is always on the outside.

1. Position half-square triangles and quarter-square triangles as shown to keep the straight grain on the outside edges of the Flying Geese unit. This will prevent the block from stretching out of shape. (Keep in mind that half-square triangles have only one bias edge, while quarter-square triangles have two bias edges.)

Half-square

Straight grain

Quarter-square

2. Align the bottom outer corner of the half-square triangle with the bottom outer corner of the quarter-square triangle, as shown. Notice that the

bias edges are in alignment, and one dog ear hangs over the top edge. Stitch along the bias edges.

Dog ear

Align bias edges and bottom corners

3. Press the seam allowances (page 98) toward the half-square triangle.

4. Repeat to align, sew, and press the second half-square triangle in the same way.

Align bias edges and bottom corners

5. Trim the dog ears (page 77). You will have a ¼-inch seam allowance between the top of the quarter-square triangle and the top of the block.

Trim dog ears

¼" seam allowance

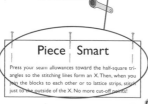

Piece Smart

Press your seam allowances toward the half-square tri-angles so the stitching lines form an X. Then, when you join the blocks to each other or to lattice strips, stitch just to the outside of the X. No more cut-off points!

All measurements are based on 40-inch-wide fabric, after prewashing. Your fabric may be wider after prewashing, but I would much rather have too much fabric than not enough!

Read through the Materials and Cutting Chart footnotes and all the step-by-step instructions for each project before you begin cutting any of your fabric.

Project Section

Everything you need to make the quilt is shown here in one table.

Fabric amounts are generous—just in case of an "oops," and to allow for squaring up your fabric.

The shapes used in the project. The page numbers listed indicate where to find information on rotary cutting specific shapes.

Fabric tip gives you ideas for fabric selection or substitution.

The shapes and techniques used in the project. Techniques used in every project are not listed here. They are referenced by page number in the step-by-step instructions.

Block Diagram shows a completed block, with the outside seam allowances included.

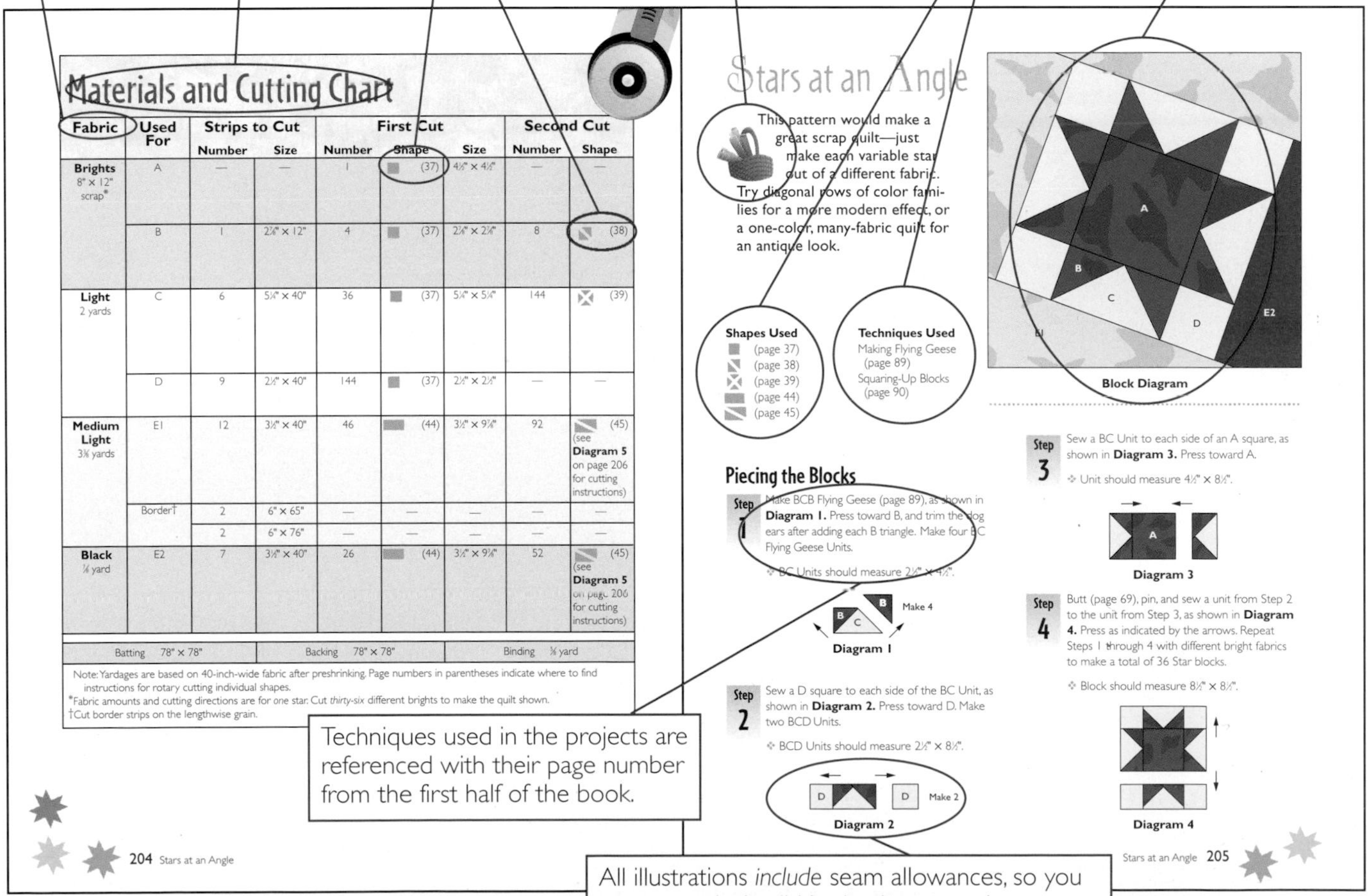

Materials and Cutting Chart

| Fabric | Used For | Strips to Cut | | First Cut | | | Second Cut | |
		Number	Size	Number	Shape	Size	Number	Shape
Brights 8" × 12" scrap*	A	—	—	1	(37)	4½" × 4½"	—	—
	B	1	2¾" × 12"	4	(37)	2¾" × 2¾"	8	(38)
Light 2 yards	C	6	5¼" × 40"	36	(37)	5¼" × 5¼"	144	(39)
	D	9	2½" × 40"	144	(37)	2½" × 2½"	—	—
Medium Light 3¼ yards	E1	12	3½" × 40"	46	(44)	3½" × 9¼"	92	(45) (see Diagram 5 on page 206 for cutting instructions)
	Border†	2	6" × 65"	—	—	—	—	—
		2	6" × 76"	—	—	—	—	—
Black ⅛ yard	E2	7	3½" × 40"	26	(44)	3½" × 9¼"	52	(45) (see Diagram 5 on page 206 for cutting instructions)
	Batting 78" × 78"			Backing 78" × 78"			Binding ⅝ yard		

Note: Yardages are based on 40-inch-wide fabric after preshrinking. Page numbers in parentheses indicate where to find instructions for rotary cutting individual shapes.
*Fabric amounts and cutting directions are for one star. Cut thirty-six different brights to make the quilt shown.
†Cut border strips on the lengthwise grain.

Stars at an Angle

This pattern would make a great scrap quilt—just make each variable star out of a different fabric. Try diagonal rows of color families for a more modern effect, or a one-color, many-fabric quilt for an antique look.

Shapes Used
(page 37)
(page 38)
(page 39)
(page 44)
(page 45)

Techniques Used
Making Flying Geese (page 89)
Squaring-Up Blocks (page 90)

Block Diagram

Piecing the Blocks

Step 1 Make BCB Flying Geese (page 89), as shown in **Diagram 1**. Press toward B, and trim the dog ears after adding each B triangle. Make four BC Flying Geese Units.

❖ BC Units should measure 2½" × 4½".

B C B Make 4

Diagram 1

Step 2 Sew a D square to each side of the BC Unit, as shown in **Diagram 2**. Press toward D. Make two BCD Units.

❖ BCD Units should measure 2½" × 8½".

D D Make 2

Diagram 2

Step 3 Sew a BC Unit to each side of an A square, as shown in **Diagram 3**. Press toward A.

❖ Unit should measure 4½" × 8½".

A

Diagram 3

Step 4 Butt (page 69), pin, and sew a unit from Step 2 to the unit from Step 3, as shown in **Diagram 4**. Press as indicated by the arrows. Repeat Steps 1 through 4 with different bright fabrics to make a total of 36 Star blocks.

❖ Block should measure 8½" × 8½".

Diagram 4

Techniques used in the projects are referenced with their page number from the first half of the book.

All illustrations *include* seam allowances, so you know how it should look when you piece.

No-Fail
Rotary Cutting

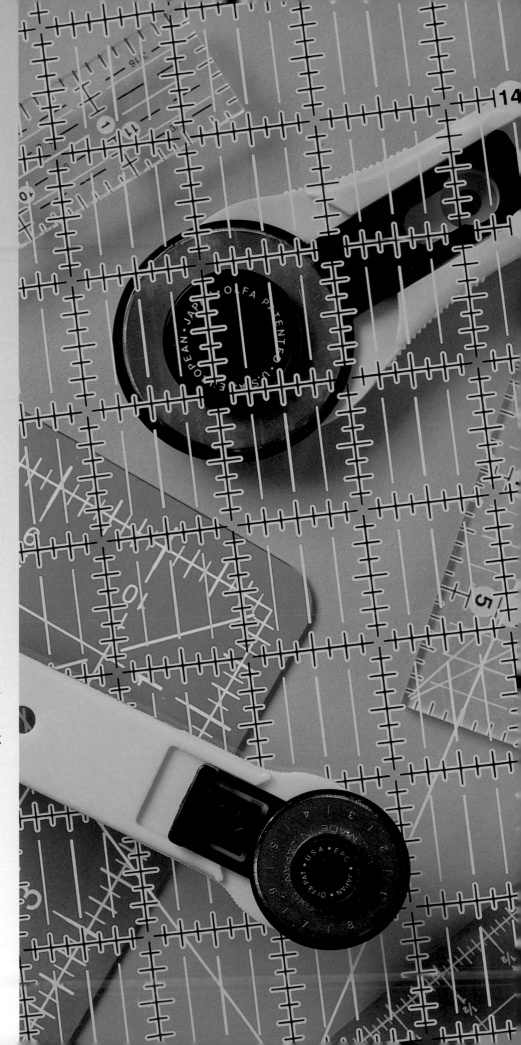

Selecting Your Rotary Cutting Equipment

You *must* have three pieces of equipment before beginning to rotary cut:

- a rotary cutter
- a cutting mat
- a ruler designed for rotary cutting

Read this section for descriptions of each of these necessities, as well as tips and techniques on using them most effectively. Then, check the comparison charts beginning on page 12 to find the rotary cutting equipment that's right for you.

Rotary Cutters

If rotary cutters hadn't been invented, I—and thousands of other quilters—wouldn't be quilting. I was introduced to a rotary cutter in 1984, and I remember thinking, "How am I going to cut fabric with a pizza cutter?" Now I wonder how I lived without one!

Rotary cutting is much more accurate for cutting quilt pieces than cutting with scissors. When you cut with scissors, you lift the fabric slightly off the table. Every time you cut, your scissors are ever so slightly misaligned with the previous cut. But when cutting with a rotary cutter, you don't disturb the fabric because the fabric isn't moving on the cutting mat. You don't have misaligned cuts because you are making a single long cut against a straightedge ruler.

There are numerous types of cutters on the market, and I recommend that you try as many as possible before buying one. Here are some things you should consider before making your purchase.

Handle

Does the cutter fit comfortably in your hand? If you cup your hand, the bottom of the cutter should fit in the crease in the center of your palm. When you extend your index finger up the edge of the cutter, it should fall comfortably on the ridged area. Wrap your hand around the handle; your fingers should *not* overlap your thumb—this stresses the carpal ligament. If the cutter feels too large or long or too small or short for your hand, try a different size or model.

What shape is the handle? There are straight handles, curved handles, and handles with finger grips. They all feel different when you grip them, so try them all. Some cutters are ergonomically designed to reduce hand and wrist stress, and you may find that a curved handle reduces your hand fatigue.

Nancy's Bag of Tricks

Reduce stress on your hand by using a large-handled rotary cutter. If you already own a rotary cutter, you can increase the diameter of its handle by wrapping and taping a layer of soft foam around it.

Blade Guard

The blade guard is there to protect your fingers from the razor-sharp blade. You open or close some guards with your finger or thumb; others are spring-loaded to automatically pull back and expose the blade when you press down on the cutter. The harder a blade guard is to open and close, the safer it is—especially if you have children around—but the safest ones can be more stressful on your hands.

Always close the cutter as soon as you're done cutting. Rotary cutter blades are *extremely* sharp, and they're just as dangerous at rest as they are in motion. You should get in the habit of closing the blade guard at the same time you're setting down the rotary cutter—even if it's "only for a second." You can easily get a severe cut just by brushing your hand against an open blade. And if you accidentally drop an open cutter, you'll certainly nick or damage the blade (not to mention what would happen if it fell on your foot).

Changing the Blade

Check for instructions on the package for changing the blade. (See page 6 for instructions if your cutter came without them or if you've misplaced them.) And while the relative ease or difficulty of changing the blade should not be your first priority when selecting a cutter, you should at least be familiar with how involved it will be.

Also, take a look at how many parts you will need to disassemble and reassemble each time. Again, this shouldn't be your deciding factor, but it may make a difference in your decision if you have limited mobility in your hands.

Adaptability

Can the rotary cutter be used by both right- and left-handed people? If you are ambidextrous enough to cut with either hand, can you use your cutter with either hand without reassembling it? Some cutters are made so that you can simply flip them over and cut with either hand; others must be reassembled to accommodate left-handed cutting. I strongly recommend that you do not try to cut left-handed with a cutter that has been assembled for a right-handed person, or vice versa.

Storage

Many rotary cutters have a hole in the handle for hanging the cutter. I always hang mine up high, well out of the reach of any curious little fingers. If you can't or don't want to hang your cutter, store it in a safe place where it won't get nicked (or nick anyone else). If you make the cutting table shown on page 29, store your cutter in the Rubbermaid box underneath.

Blade Sizes

There are two widely available rotary blade sizes: 28 mm and 45 mm. (These sizes refer to the diameter of the blade; usually, the handle diameter

Nancy's Bag of Tricks

Store your rotary cutter in an old eyeglass case—I prefer the kind that you slip your glasses (or cutter) into from the top. It protects the cutter and your fingers. It's also a handy way to take the cutter to classes or guild meetings. Just be sure to label the case so nobody gets a nasty surprise when searching for reading glasses!

increases with the blade size.) Olfa has also added a larger 60 mm cutter. I recommend using the largest cutter available in your preferred brand for a few reasons: A larger blade usually means a larger handle, and larger blades last longer and cut more quickly (as long as you're cutting straight).

I use a cutter with the smallest blade (28 mm) only for cutting around plastic templates, which I rarely do anymore. The small blade maneuvers more easily around curves. I keep a cutter with a medium blade (45 mm) near my sewing machine for nipping off dog ears (those little triangle tips that stick out when you sew a triangle to another shape). In general, I use a cutter with the largest blade (60 mm) whenever I am doing any cutting more involved than trimming dog ears.

My Favorite Things

After testing lots of rotary cutters, I found the largest size (60 mm) Olfa cutter works the best for me. It has the largest diameter handle, so it's more comfortable in my hand, and it causes less stress on my hand and wrist. Plus the large-diameter blade helps me cut more quickly and efficiently.

Uses

The fabric you work with will help you decide whether you need a large or small rotary cutter. If you use heavy woven fabrics like plaids or stripes, you will need a more hearty cutter with a larger blade to go through the coarser weave. Also, some fabrics are naturally stiffer and need a cutter with a larger, heftier blade. If you work mostly with lightweight, soft fabrics, a small cutter may work well for you.

Add-Ons

Some rotary cutters have guide arms available that you use to add seam allowances when cutting around templates or to cut strips of a certain width. I don't recommend using these—they are certainly not as precise as measuring and cutting against the solid edge of a rotary ruler.

There are also "creative" blades available for some cutters. These blades cut a pattern instead of just a straight line, and personally I think they are neato! They are mostly for craft and decorating projects, but I'm still working on ways to use them in my quilts.

Specialty Cutters

The combination cutter/straightedge, in my opinion, is mostly for crafts and paper. Quilters who make wearables where absolute accuracy isn't as important, such as woven wearables and garments with frayed strips, will also find these useful. For precise quiltmaking, though, I strongly recommend using an accurate rotary ruler and a separate cutter with a sharp, new blade.

Maintenance

The best rotary cutter won't do you any good unless you maintain it properly and treat it with care and respect. If you follow these simple suggestions, your cutter will last longer and cut straighter, and you'll be much happier with it.

Rotary Cutter Care

Always keep a sharp blade in your cutter. A dull blade causes inaccurate cutting and unnecessary hand fatigue. To minimize the expense of new blades, consider having your old blades resharpened. I sent a dozen blades that needed sharpening to L. P. Sharp (page 209) and was very pleased with the results. You may want to try sharpening your own blades. Look in your local quilt shop or in quilt supply catalogs for a tool you can purchase.

Take your cutter apart periodically (page 6) and clean it with a soft cloth (at least twice during cutting out a full-size quilt, or after each smaller quilt). You'll find that removing the lint buildup under the blade will keep the cutter rolling smoothly.

When handling the blade, pinch it between your thumb and fingertips, and never touch the edge! Fabric lint tends to build up under the blade—use a soft cloth to clean off the blade and the guard.

Each time you clean your rotary cutter, place one drop of sewing machine oil on the blade. This will allow the blade to turn more freely, helping with accuracy and reducing hand fatigue.

Rotary cut only on a mat designed specifically for rotary cutting (page 7). Any other surface will damage your cutter blade and will certainly not be "self-healing," as rotary mats are!

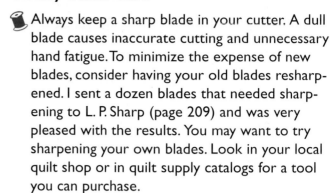

◉ Cut Smart

Here are some additional tips for using and reusing rotary cutter blades.

- **Mark the date** that you change the blade in your rotary cutter. This way, you'll always know exactly how long it's been since you changed it. I always use a permanent marker to mark the date right on my new blade.

- **Save your used blades** for other purposes instead of throwing them away! They're great for cutting wallpaper or light cardboard—and I love them for cutting nice, straight edges around my children's school pictures!

- **Safely store your used blades** in an empty plastic blade case on which you've written "Old Blades" with a permanent marker.

Changing Your Blade

The steps here are written specifically for the Olfa rotary cutter. Your cutter may vary slightly from the one that's pictured here. Refer to the directions or illustrations on your rotary cutter's package when you are ready to change the blade.

1. Close the blade guard. Place the rotary cutter on a work surface with the blade facing down. Unscrew the nut completely, remove the washer, and place them both on your work surface.

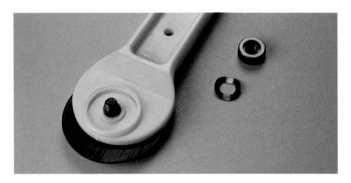

2. Lift the handle and the blade guard off the bolt, turn them over, and place them on the work surface. Clean them with a soft cloth, removing all lint and debris.

Lift the bolt by its shaft and carefully turn it over, dropping the blade onto your fingertips. Pinch the blade between your thumb and fingertips when handling it. *Never* hold the blade in your palm!

Note: If you can't remove the blade guard from the handle of your rotary cutter, don't worry. Some newer rotary cutters have nonremovable blade guards. Just follow the directions here for removing and replacing the blade, washer, and bolt.

3. Set the bolt back on your work surface and place the new blade on it. Invert the blade guard back onto the bolt shaft. Cover the blade completely with the guard (this photo shows a little of the blade sticking out for visual reference). Then invert the handle back on top of the guard.

4. Replace the washer so that it cups upward, then replace the nut with the notched side toward the blade.

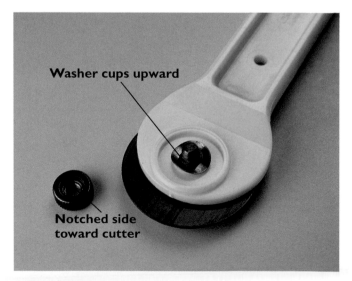

Washer cups upward

Notched side toward cutter

Mats

You will need to purchase a specially made rotary cutting mat to use with your rotary cutter. Quilters usually describe these mats as "self-healing." While this is not technically accurate, it describes how the cut in the plastic surface of the mat looks when it squeezes back together, leaving the cut still there but not quite visible. So, I like to think of them as "forgiving" mats. Keep in mind, though, that no mat really heals properly if you're cutting curves, as you would around some templates. For this reason, I recommend keeping a separate mat at your cutting table to use just for cutting curves.

Here are some things to consider when you're shopping for and purchasing a cutting mat. These tips will help you get the best quality mat you can for your money and the one that best suits your rotary cutting use.

Material

Most quilters don't pay as much attention as they should to the type of mat that they are using—mostly because they don't realize that there are things about the mats that they don't know! Rotary mats are made from plastic (hard, soft, or layered), and there are vast differences between mats. Each one has its advantages and drawbacks, of course.

I find that I tend to wear out the centers of some three-layer mats. This happens because I keep cutting in the same spot, and eventually the mat stops "forgiving" the cut areas. This isn't a reason not to use a layered mat; just be aware that when this happens to your mat, you can't cut accurately on it anymore—it must be replaced. Hard and soft plastic mats, on the other hand, can dull your blade more quickly than layered mats do, so be aware and change your blade more frequently when using them.

Colors

Some mats are reversible, with a light color on one side and a dark color on the other. These are useful because you can flip the mat from dark to light so that it contrasts with any fabric you are cutting. A reversible mat is like getting two mats for the price of one.

Some mats are translucent and let enough light through that they can be used on a light table. This is handy for tracing quilting motifs onto your quilt top because the textured surface of the mat helps hold the quilt top in place for more accurate marking.

My Favorite Things

I use an 18 × 24-inch Omnimat that is light gray on one side (for cutting dark fabrics) and green on the other side (for cutting light fabrics). I don't like gridded mats—the markings aren't necessarily accurate, and they can be quite distracting.

Markings

I usually buy mats without grids or markings. You should measure with an accurate rotary ruler, not the lines on the mat. The only use I would recommend for grid or angle lines on a mat is for cutting oversize pieces or approximate sizes and shapes, such as for foundation piecing or crazy quilting.

Some mats have designs printed on them, like scallops and arcs. These can be useful if you want to use them as quilting motifs—just place tracing paper over the designs to make templates, or use a light table to trace them onto your quilt top.

Storage

Always store your mat flat. Don't roll it or lean it against a wall, because it will develop a permanent warp or buckle that will prevent you from cutting accurately. And if you cut on a mat and then roll it, the cuts will open up, and your mat will crack. Some mats include holes for hanging. Just make sure that you never store your mat in direct sunlight because the plastic will warp and buckle.

When you're transporting your mat, whether it's from the shop where you bought it to home or to and from a quilt class, make sure to keep it flat. Also, avoid exposing your mat to extreme temperatures: Heat can warp the mat, and cold can make it very brittle. I have had students show up with mats that are missing a corner because it snapped off in the trunk of their car on the way to class!

Sizes

What size mat do you need? There are so many sizes of mats that it's hard to know which size to buy. I feel very strongly that an 18 × 24-inch mat is the best buy for your money, especially for a first mat. You'll only have to fold your fabric once to cut long strips, so your cutting will be more accurate. If you have a bigger mat you won't be able to rotate it when cutting, and you'll have to disturb the fabric with each cut.

Uses

I have a wide variety of mat sizes that I use constantly. I keep a 5 × 7-inch mat next to my sewing machine for nipping off dog ears or trimming down small pieces while sewing. I use my 18 × 24-inch mat for cutting long strips or very large pieces. I have an extra-large mat (40 × 60 inches) that covers the entire top of my cutting island (see the photo on page 63), and I use this for cutting borders or binding strips, squaring up large blocks, or when I'm working with medallions. I also keep an 8 × 10-inch mat handy on my cutting island. I place this mat on top of my other mats, and I use it only when I'm cutting curves.

Maintenance

Cutting mats are fairly expensive, so there are a few precautions you need to take and methods you need to use to ensure that your cutting mats last as long as possible.

Rotary Mat Care

- Vary the place on your mat where you cut. If you always cut down the right side of the mat, it will wear in that spot very quickly. By rotating the mat often and using it evenly, you will extend its life.

- If you need to clean your mat, rub it lightly with a small amount of Soft Scrub or diluted hand dishwashing liquid. I draft on my mat, and I sometimes need to remove pencil and pen marks.

- Some fabrics have dyes that can rub off onto your mat. You'll want to remove the dye as discussed above before cutting another piece of fabric.

Nancy's Bag of Tricks

Store your mats under a bed or couch when you're not using them. This keeps them flat and out of your way.

Rulers

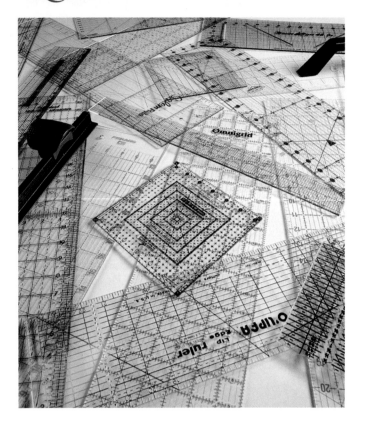

One of the reasons modern quilters have been so productive and made so many beautiful quilts is that special rulers made for rotary cutting have been introduced. Rotary rulers allow you to rotary cut accurate-size pieces—no more trying to draw shapes or tick marks on your fabric and then cutting the shape out with scissors! These rulers are made of clear acrylic, and they have numbers and lines printed horizontally and vertically for the various inch dimensions and fractions commonly used in quiltmaking. They also come in many different sizes.

Here are some important things to consider when shopping for rotary rulers. Keep in mind that *you* will be using the rulers that you buy, so you need to be happy with their features.

Markings

Do the markings on the ruler show up equally well on light and dark fabrics? Don't hesitate to grab a few different fabrics off the shelf at the quilt shop to test this out. How thick are the measuring lines on the ruler? If they're too thick, they make measuring and cutting less accurate because you have to position the fabric edge to the right or the left of a broad line. If they're too thin, they may not be visible on some fabrics.

Does the ruler have a grid (lines that go from edge to edge), or does it have tick marks (short lines only at the edge of the ruler)? Grids are easiest to work with, even if the lines of the grid are dashed or broken—you get more reference points across the ruler, and you can line up your fabric edge more accurately.

Is the ruler printed in ⅛-inch increments? This is a *must* for accurate measuring and cutting in quiltmaking. If there aren't ⅛-inch marks, choose another ruler.

Does the ruler have angle markings for both left- and right-handed quilters? You will use these extensively when rotary cutting special shapes. Some rulers have angle lines that go in only one direction (almost always for righties), and lefties have trouble figuring out how to position the ruler to make an angled cut. If you're a lefty or you cut left-handed, angle markings are extremely important.

Storage

Rulers, like mats, must be stored flat so they don't develop a "bow." Most rulers include a hole or slot for hanging. If you don't have wall space to hang your rulers, hang them on the back of a door or buy a clear plastic box big enough to store them flat.

Nancy's Bag of Tricks

To ensure cutting accuracy, always stay with the same brand ruler throughout your quilting project. Markings may vary slightly from ruler to ruler, but if you use the same brand consistently you eliminate most of the problems that this could cause during piecing.

My Favorite Things

Here are the four rulers I always keep near my cutting table:

- **6 × 24-inch Omnigrid** to cut long strips
- **6 × 12-inch Omnigrid** to easily subcut long strips into other shapes and sizes
- **6-inch square Omnigrid** for working on miniatures (because of the 3-inch grid marked in ⅛-inch increments and the single 45 degree line)
- **15-inch square Omnigrid** for squaring up blocks and cutting pieces wider than 6 inches

Sizes

If you are going out to buy your first rotary ruler, I recommend a 6 × 24 inch. This size is long enough to cut strips without folding your fabric more than once but still manageable enough that you can easily cut other shapes with it.

Uses

What type of quiltmaking will you be doing? If you are going to work on strip piecing and need to cut many long strips, you will definitely want to buy a 6 × 24-inch ruler. On the other hand, if you are going to concentrate on miniatures, you can buy a ruler ranging from 6 × 12 inches to 3 × 18 inches. Check the table on page 16 for the features of various sizes.

Special Features

Some square and rectangular rulers do more than just allow you to cut straight lines. Some have precut slots in them at various angles, which can be helpful if you're unsure about cutting angles.

If you sometimes have a hard time reading or manipulating your ruler because of eyesight or hand problems, precut slots can be very helpful because you don't have to change the ruler position or pick out printed lines on the ruler to cut angles. Slots can also be a great asset if you are teaching rotary cutting to children or older people, and you have worries about safety. The slots let you make the cut without endangering any fingertips.

Other special features of rulers include lip edges and T-square attachments that hook over the edge of the cutting mat to hold the ruler perfectly square to the mat. Also available are handles that attach to the rulers to make them easier to move around the cutting mat. In general, I prefer not to use these. I find that it's hard to carefully align my fabric with a lip or T-square, and the handles get in my way when I "hand walk" (page 31) while I'm cutting.

Ease of Use

Let's face it, rulers often tend to slip when you're making a long cut. To combat this problem, there are rulers that have raised markings on the underside. The markings grip the fabric while you are cutting. Other rulers come with self-sticking "dots" made of sandpaper or another gripping substance.

Nancy's Bag of Tricks

To prevent your ruler from slipping while rotary cutting, use SlipNots. This product is a 3-inch square of self-adhesive, nonslip, synthetic material for templates and rulers. It won't snag your fabric or scratch your tabletop. Punch out a few dots with a hole punch, then stick the dots to the underside of your ruler. Place the dots where they won't obscure the markings (directly under the numbers is usually a good place). Place your fingers directly on top of the dots for extra security when rotary cutting.

Another consideration, especially with specialty rulers and for beginners, is whether the ruler comes with any instructions for use. If not, ask at the quilt shop about demonstrations or classes that teach you how to make the most of your ruler.

Specialty Rulers

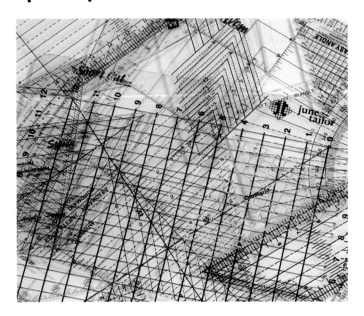

It sometimes seems that there are as many specialty rulers available as there are quilters. These rulers range from the commonsense to the obscure, but are all designed to make your quiltmaking easier and more enjoyable. Many are made specifically for working with one technique or cutting one shape, but some perform a wider range of uses. Because these specialty rulers come out so often—and just as often are taken off the market—I am not listing them here. Instead, here are some *types* of specialty rulers that you may want to purchase at some point.

Specialty Rulers

🧵 Triangles, for cutting equilateral, half-square, and quarter-square triangles.

🧵 45 degree rulers, with one end cut off at a 45 degree angle for mitering.

🧵 Special shapes, for cutting hexagons, octagons, trapezoids, diamonds, and other nonsquare shapes.

If you are looking for a specialty ruler for a very specific purpose, ask your quilting friends for recommendations, seek opinions from quilt shop owners, and above all, make sure that the ruler you select comes with excellent directions for use.

Maintenance

The surface of all rulers will eventually become scratched from use. Here are a few tips to lengthen the life of your ruler.

Rotary Ruler Care

🧵 Clean off any accidental glue or ink spills with isopropyl rubbing alcohol. Do *not* use nail polish remover or similar solvents—they can remove the markings on the ruler. Test the rubbing alcohol on a small part of the ruler before using it.

🧵 Avoid placing your ruler on top of rotary cutters, ink pens, paper clips, or other sharp objects that will scratch it.

My Favorite Things

O'Lipfa makes a 22-inch Safety Shield with an adhesive strip that will attach to any 24-inch ruler. When you stick this piece of acrylic plastic to your ruler, your fingers hold the ruler steady from behind a low acrylic "wall." This will keep your fingers safe from your razor-sharp rotary cutter.

Rotary Cutter Comparison Chart

(Based on rotary cutters supplied to the author for evaluation)

Brand	Handle Features	Blade Guard Features	Blade Changing Features
Dritz	Slightly curved. Soft plastic covering.	Locks in place when open. Operates with thumb pressure only. Separate plastic shield covers blade when not in use.	Diagram on package. Five parts to assemble.
Fiskars	Slightly curved. Looped design helps keep fingers away from blade. Handle thickness increases with blade size.	Locks in place when open. Push-button release easier for righties than for lefties. Protects fingers when blade is open or closed.	Instructions and diagram on package. Six parts to assemble.
Olfa	Straight. Handle thickness increases with blade size.	Locks in place when open. Slides open and closed.	Diagram on package. Five or six parts to assemble, depending on model.
Quilter's Rule	Curved. Has finger grips.	Locks in place when open. Push-and-slide open and close action.	Diagram on package. Six parts to assemble.
Specialty Cutter			
Fiskars Craft & Quilting Cutter	Curved, palm-shaped push handle attached to acrylic ruler.	Opens automatically when pressure applied to handle. Protects fingers when blade is open or closed.	Instructions and photographs on package. Two parts to assemble.

Cost Key	
$	Less expensive
$$	Moderately priced
$$$	More expensive

Adaptability	Storage	Blade Sizes	Cost	Add-Ons
Assembles only one way, for right-handed cutting.	Hang by hole provided for guide arm.	45 mm	$	Pinking and wave blades available. Free-arm guide available (for adding seam allowances when cutting around templates).
Assembles for either left- or right handed cutting.	Hang by looped handle.	28 mm	$	—
		45 mm	$$	Fiskars creative blades: pinking, tiara, squiggle, and scallop blades available for fabric. Scoring blade available for paper.
Assembles one way for either right- or left-handed cutting.	Hang by hole in handle.	28 mm	$	—
		45 mm	$$	Adjustable guide arm (for adding on seam allowances when cutting around templates).
		60 mm	$$$	Adjustable guide arm (for adding on seam allowances when cutting around templates).
Assembles for either right- or left-handed cutting.	Hang by hole in handle.	45 mm	$	—
Designed for righties but lefties can use easily. Cuts strips from 1¼ to 6½ inches wide only.	Hang by handle in ruler.	45 mm	$$$	Can use any Fiskars creative blade (see above).

Rotary Mat Comparison Chart

(Based on mats supplied to the author for evaluation)

Brand	Material	Colors
Cottage Tools	Soft plastic. Cut-absorbing. Gridded side textured; reverse side smooth. Can pin fabric to mat.	Translucent white.
Dritz	Soft plastic. Gridded side smooth; reverse side textured. Can pin fabric to mat.	Translucent white.
Fiskars	Three-layer compressed plastic. Self-healing.	Gridded side dark gray; reverse side light gray.
Olfa	Three-layer compressed plastic. Self-healing.	Green.
Omnimat	Three-layer compressed plastic. Self-healing.	Printed side green; reverse side gray. Some mats ungridded. Metric grids available.
Salem	Soft plastic.	Translucent. Printed side textured, reverse side smooth.
Sew/Fit	Soft plastic.	Translucent white. Printed side textured, reverse side smooth.
June Tailor Quilter's Cut 'n Press	Hard plastic on cutting side, muslin-covered foam on reverse (pressing) side. Carry to quilt classes as a portable cutting mat and pressing surface.	Dark gray.

Markings	Storage	Sizes (in inches)	Cost
Blue markings. ½" grid. ⅛" tick marks. 45° and 60° lines.	Store flat.	9 × 12	$
		12 × 18	$
		18 × 24	$$
		24 × 36	$$
Black markings. 1" grid. ⅛" tick marks. 45° lines, scallop designs, arcs.	Store flat.	18 × 24	$$
Orange markings. 1" grid. ⅛" tick marks. 45° lines.	Store flat or hang by hole.	12 × 18	$$
		18 × 24	$$
		24 × 36	$$$
Yellow markings. 1" grid. ⅛" tick marks. 45° lines.	Store flat.	12 × 18	$$
Yellow markings. 1" grid. ⅛" tick marks. 45° lines.	Store flat.	9 × 12	$
		12 × 18	$$
		18 × 24	$$
		24 × 36	$$$
Red markings. 1" grid. ⅛" tick marks. 45° and 60° lines.	Store flat.	18 × 24	$$
Blue markings. 1" grid. ⅛" tick marks on two sides. 1 cm tick marks on two sides. 45° lines.	Store flat.	40 × 36	$$$
White markings. 1" grid. ⅛" tick marks. ½ cm tick marks on two sides. 45° and 60° lines.	Store flat or hang by handle.	12 × 12	$$
		14 × 20	$$$

Rotary Ruler Comparison Chart

(Based on rulers supplied to the author for evaluation. Not all available sizes of all brands included.)

Brand	Markings	Storage	Sizes (in inches)
Cottage Tools	Pink and blue. ¼" lines in one direction. ⅛" tick marks throughout ruler.	Hang by hole.	3 × 15
			6 × 12, 6 × 24
			6 × 6
			12½ × 12½, 15 × 15
Dritz	Yellow and black alternating. ¼" lines in one direction. ⅛" tick marks throughout ruler.	Hang by hole/slot.	6 × 24
			12 × 12
EZ International—Draft 'n Cut 	Black. ⅛" grid throughout. ¹⁄₁₆" tick marks.	Store flat.	2 × 18
EZ International—Marti Michell Line	Black. ¼" grid throughout. ⅛" and ¹⁄₁₆" tick marks.	Hang by hole.	7½" Handi-Square, 10½" Is It Square
			3½ × 10½ The Second Cut
EZ International—Quickline (Nancy Crow)	Black. ⅛" tick marks.	Hang by hole.	3 × 24 Quickline
			3 × 12, 3 × 18, 3 × 24 Quickline
			6 × 24 Super Quickline
Fiskars 	Orange and black. ¼" grid. ⅛" tick marks.	Hang by hole.	6 × 12, 6 × 24
Holiday Designs	Black. ⅛" tick marks. ½" vertical lines; 1" horizontal lines.	Hang by hole (all but 6½" ruler).	6½ × 6½, 12½ × 12½, 16½ × 16½ Speedy
			6 × 12 Standard Jr., 6 × 24 Standard
Master Piece	Black. ⅛" grid throughout.	45 and 60 rulers include hole for hanging.	6 × 18 45 Jr., 8 × 24 45 6 × 18 60 Jr., 8 × 24 60
			6½ × 6½ 90, 12½ × 12½

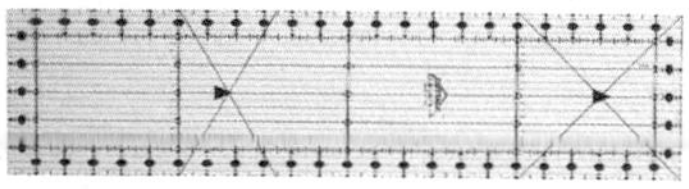

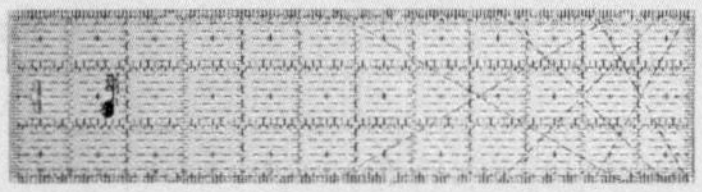

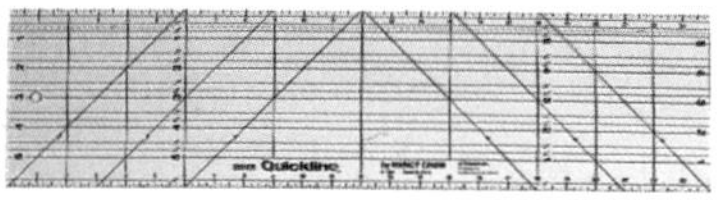

Cost	Uses	Special Features and Ease of Use
$	Cutting shapes from strips.	Removable acrylic T-guide lets you use it as T-square. 30°, 60°, and 45° lines for righties and lefties. Numbers read right from top or bottom of ruler. T-guide hooks over mat to keep ruler from slipping.
$ ($$ with T-guide)	Cutting short and long strips.	Removable acrylic T-guide hooks over edge of mat to keep ruler from slipping and acts as T-square. 60° and 45° lines for righties and lefties. 6" x 24" ruler has available locking T-square at 45°, 60°, or 90°. Numbers read right from top or bottom of ruler. Metric sizes available.
$	Miniatures.	⅛" grid. 45° and 60° lines. Instruction booklet included.
$$, $$	Squaring up blocks.	45° line. Right-angle lines.
$$	Cutting strips and constructing multiangle pieces.	30°, 45°, and 60° lines for both lefties and righties. Adhesives and paper dots available to prevent slipping. Suction cup handles available for easier handling.
$$	Squaring up blocks. Trimming seam allowances.	Adhesives and paper dots available to prevent slipping. Suction cup handles available for easier handling.
$	Cutting strips. Drafting accurate patterns.	1/16" marks useful for blocks set on point. Instructions included.
$, $$	Finding irregularities in blocks. Squaring up blocks. Trimming seam allowances.	22½°, 30°, 45°, 60°, and 90° lines. 7½" square has metric markings on one edge. Instructions included.
$	Cutting shapes from strips. Cutting strip sets. Miniatures.	15°, 22½°, 30°, 45°, 60°, 67½°, 75°, and 90° lines.
$$	Cutting strips.	Vertical lines for cutting different width strips. 45° lines.
$, $$, $$	Combination ruler and compass for marking arcs and their seam allowances.	30°, 45°, and 60° lines (12" has 45° only). ¼" vertical lines. ½" horizontal lines. ⅛" tick marks.
$$	Cutting long strips. Squaring up blocks. Mitering corners.	45° lines. Vertical lines for many strip widths. Horizontal ⅛" tick marks.
$, $$	Cutting shapes from strips. Cutting long strips.	30°, 45°, and 60° lines for both lefties and righties.
$, $$, $$	Squaring up blocks.	45° line. Slide & Grip strips available (included with 12½" ruler) keep ruler from sliding.
$, $$	Cutting strips and crosscutting into shapes.	³⁄₁₆" and ¼" seam lines.
$$$, $$$, $$$, $$$	Cutting 45° or 60° shapes. Cutting strips.	45°, 60°, and 90° slots are cut in the ruler for safe, accurate cutting of these angles. Instructions included, with directions for adding seam allowances and cutting 45° or 60° shapes. Instructional video.
$, $$$	Squaring up blocks.	Parallel slots in ruler allow safe, accurate cutting of squares. Includes gridded Static Stickers to stick on ruler as cutting guide. Instructional video.

(continued)

Rotary Ruler Comparison Chart–Continued

(Based on rulers supplied to the author for evaluation)

Brand	Markings	Storage	Sizes (in inches)
O'Lipfa 	Gold foil. ¼" lines in one direction. ⅛" tick marks throughout ruler.	Store flat.	6½ square, 12½ square
			5 × 18
			5 × 24 lip edge, 4 × 36 lip edge
			5 × 24 no-slip
Omnigrid 	Yellow and black. ⅛" markings throughout.	Hang by hole.	4 × 14, 6 × 12, 6 × 24
			6 × 6
			9½ × 9½, 12½ × 12½, 15½ × 15½
Precision Quilting Rule by June Tailor 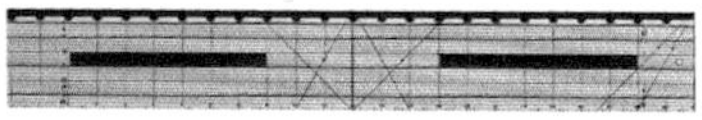 	Pink and black. ⅛" lines in one direction; ⅛" tick marks in the other direction.	Hang by hole.	3½ × 24
Quilter's Rule 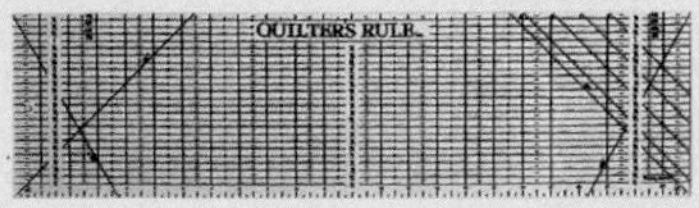 	Pink or black. ¼" lines in one direction; ⅛" tick marks in one direction.	Hang by hole.	6 × 24
Salem Rule 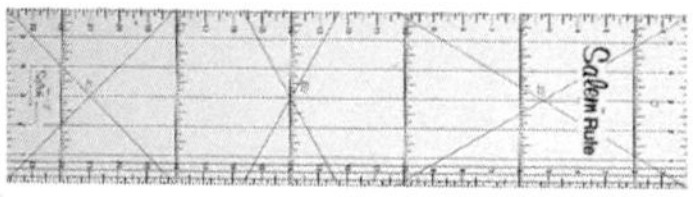 	Red and black. 1" lines in one direction; ⅛" tick marks in the other direction.	Hang by hole.	6½ × 24
Sew/Fit  	Yellow or black. Grid ranges from ¼" and ½" to 1".	Hang by hole.	5 × 24 5½ × 24

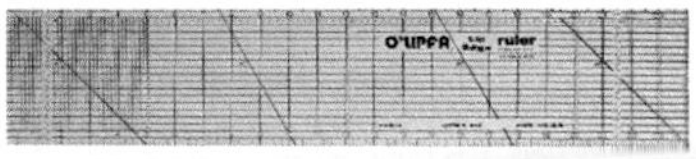

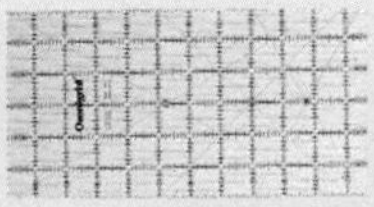

Cost	Uses	Special Features and Ease of Use
$, $$	Squaring up small and large blocks. Cutting angled pieces.	45° and 60° angle markings (one direction on 6½"). ⅛" markings for squaring up.
$	Cutting short and long strips.	Numbers run in both directions for left- and right-handed cutting. Large numbers for easy reading.
$$, $$	Cutting long strips.	First 5" is detailed mini-ruler. 45° and 60° angle markings in one direction. Lip edge hooks over cutting surface like T-square.
$$	Cutting long strips.	Special detachable no-slip handle holds fabric in place with small pins through the ruler and fabric into the mat.
$, $, $$	Cutting shapes from strips. Cutting angles.	30°, 45°, and 60° lines for left- and right-handed cutting. Metric rulers available. Fits inside most project totes. Numbers run left to right and right to left.
$	Small blocks and miniatures. Squaring small blocks. Checking half square triangles.	Two models available: ⅛" grid for smaller pieces and squaring up small blocks. Both available in metric size.
$$, $$, $$	Squaring up blocks. Cutting strips wider than 6".	Diagonal line and perpendicular grid for squaring up and checking size of larger blocks.
$$	Cutting long and short strips. Cutting shapes from strips.	45° and 60° angle lines. Inch lines are printed heavier than others for easier identification.
$$	Cutting long and short strips.	45° and 60° angle lines. Grid is on the bottom, as raised lines to help prevent slippage. Metric rulers available.
$$	Cutting long and short strips.	30°, 45°, and 60° angle lines. Suction handle available for ease of moving and lifting ruler. T-square attachment available to hook over mat or table edge.
$$$ $$$	Cutting long and short strips.	30° and 45° angle lines. Snap-on handle available for ease of moving and lifting ruler; also increases stability. T-square models available up to 48" long for cutting long borders.

Getting Your Fabric Ready

I'm constantly asked what type of fabric I use for quilt-making. The answer is easy: I *always* use 100 percent cotton fabric. I like the feel and the look of cotton, and it's traditional! To me, 100 percent cotton fabric is the common thread that ties my modern-day creations back to their quilting heritage. It's comforting to me to know that I'm using the same type of fabric that my great-grandmother did.

My First Quilt

I wasn't always sold on cotton. In 1972, when I made my first quilt, I was not at all knowledgeable about fabric. Not knowing any better, I used what fabric I had handy—wool, drapery fabric, poplin, terry cloth, whipped cream fabric, and lots of polyester knit. This hodgepodge of fabrics created what I meekly called my first masterpiece!

I cut all these fabrics into 6-inch squares, and I randomly pieced them together. I used a flannel sheet for the batting and a yellow bedsheet for the backing. Since I had never done any quilting, I tied the quilt with brown yarn. For the binding, I brought the excess backing over the quilt top edges, turned it under ⅜ inch for the seam allowance, and zigzagged that edge to finish the quilt.

I proudly gave this quilt to my mother as a gift, and she (supportive mother that she was and still is) encouraged me to continue. The final chapter of this saga: Thinking there was no sense in tinkering with success, I made a duplicate!

Fortunately, times have changed, my taste in fabrics has changed, and good cotton fabric is readily available from dozens of manufacturers these days. Now when I'm shopping for cottons, I have a quick checklist I go through when deciding what to buy.

Fabric Shopping Guide

- Read the label on the end of the bolt to make sure that the fabric you are considering is 100 percent cotton.

- Buy from a reputable quilt shop or fabric store. I'm not opposed to buying second-quality fabric for certain projects, but I want to know up front what I'm getting. Certain projects demand first- or top-quality fabrics, so shop at a store that truthfully labels their fabric for quality.

- Perform a fabric comparison test. Choose four to six swatches of cotton fabric from different manufacturers. After looking at and feeling your samples, you'll see a difference in the tightness of the weave. (The more threads that are woven together per inch, the tighter the weave.) Loosely woven fabrics tend to fray easily when handled, and they sometimes distort and start to unravel when pressed. If you have a choice, buy the more tightly woven fabric.

- Pull on the crosswise grain and then the lengthwise grain (page 24). Does either grain have a lot of stretch? I usually don't buy very stretchy fabric; it is just too hard to work with.

- Avoid fabric with a "silky" finish. I do, because its slippery surface can be hard to work with.

- Take along a "cheat card"—swatches of your stash glued to a large index card—if you're shopping to fill a gap in a color family.

Preparation

Once you've selected your fabrics and brought them home, you need to prepare them for your quilt. I usually try to prewash and press my fabrics as soon as I buy them so that when I'm ready to start creating I can use any of my stash at a moment's notice. (I just hate when I have to stop my creative process to drudge through washing and pressing.)

Prewashing

To prewash or not to prewash your newly purchased fabric is a personal decision. There are two reasons why quilters *don't* like to prewash their fabrics: First, once you wash your fabric, a certain amount of sheen is taken from the cloth. Second, washing takes away the sizing that gives the fabric "body" and its nice crisp look. On the other hand, prewashing your fabric will let you know immediately if the dye in the fabric is going to bleed or run. I always want to know this before I use the fabric in a quilt, so I almost always prewash my fabrics in warm, soapy water.

Every time I judge a quilt show, I see hundreds of quilts with wonderful design and perfect piecing. Too often, though, one or more of these quilts has an area where a fabric has bled into the background fabric, causing the quilt to lose a prize. Even if you aren't

Nancy's Bag of Tricks

To prevent your fabric from unraveling when prewashing, clip a small triangle off of each corner, as shown below. And *never* prewash loosely woven fabrics in the washing machine—they turn into a tangle of threads. Instead, fill a hand basin with warm, soapy water and swish them around by hand. Rinse them in a basin of cool water, then dry them on the delicate setting in your clothes dryer.

Wash and dry full loads of fabric. It's more economical, and you can group similar colors together in a load. Your fabric will have more wrinkles than if you wash smaller loads, but if you take it out slightly damp and use good pressing techniques (page 93), you shouldn't have a problem.

entering your quilt in a competition, don't risk having your work of art blemished by a fabric that bleeds.

From the washer, all my fabric goes into the dryer on a normal setting. I usually remove my fabric from the dryer while it's still slightly damp—this makes it a little easier to press. By doing this I also ensure that it is preshrunk, and I avoid any problems that could come up later when I wash a quilt that contains some (or all!) non-preshrunk fabrics. Since fabrics shrink at different rates, imagine the mess you'd have if a non-preshrunk fabric was the only one in your quilt that got smaller when you dried it!

Pressing

After washing and drying, I always press all of my fabric right away. To do this, I first fold the fabric once, selvage to selvage (page 24), with wrong sides together. (The cut edges of the folded fabric will not be even because of washing, drying, and the way it was cut at the store.) Also, I make sure that there are no wrinkles in the fabric along the inside of the fold. Take your time with this crucial step—getting your fabric folded correctly for pressing will affect your cut strips later! The straighter you fold now, the straighter your strips will be and the squarer your cut shapes will be.

I then lightly spray my folded fabric with a product called Magic Sizing, which I buy in the grocery store. It smoothes out the wrinkles, restores the "body" in the fabric, and also makes rotary cutting and sewing easier and more accurate because the fabric isn't limp. (I only spray one side of the fabric unless the fabric is very wrinkled.) I use a dry iron (steam is optional), pressing close to the fold, but never *on* the fold—this would form a fold line in the fabric, making it harder to align my rotary ruler with the fold when rotary cutting.

Thin or loosely woven fabric is usually harder to work with than regular cotton quilting fabric. If you are having trouble getting your fabric to behave during pressing, try this: Spray on a heavy application of Magic Sizing before you press. This will "firm up" the fabric, giving it more body and making cutting and sewing very easy.

When pressing many yards of fabric, this is the method that I prefer:

Pressing Large Pieces

1. Open your fabric completely.

2. Fold your fabric in half along its length, selvage to selvage.

3. Make sure there are no wrinkles along the fold of your fabric.

4. Measure halfway down the length of your fabric. Starting at this halfway point, press half of the fabric to the end.

5. Return to the halfway point and press the other half to the other end.

This method makes your large pieces of fabric much easier to handle when you're pressing them, and it helps keep the selvages aligned. When you're ready to fold your fabric for storage, you'll have a much easier time.

Storage

After washing and pressing, you need a good system of folding and storing your fabric for quick, easy access. My "smart folding" method is a great time saver. I pretend I'm wrapping the prewashed and pressed fabric back on an empty bolt.

1. Fold the bottom edge of your pressed fabric up by about 8 inches.

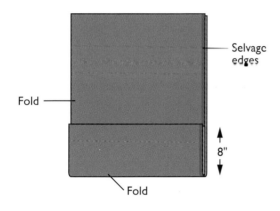

2. Wrap the fabric over itself, as if you were rolling it onto a bolt, until you reach the end.

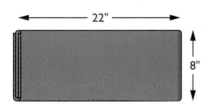

3. Fold the resulting 8 × 22-inch pile of fabric in half crosswise. It will now measure about 8 × 11 inches.

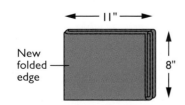

There are several things I like about this system of folding and storing fabric. First, all of my pieces of fabric end up the same size—no matter how big they were when I started—so when I pile one piece on top of another, my piles don't fall over. Second, if I'm making a scrap quilt and need only one strip of fabric from each piece, I only have to unfold 8 inches of fabric, not the whole piece, to cut my strip. Third, I am able to keep all the fabric on the cutting mat when rotary cutting. I don't have a cumbersome amount hanging over the edge of the table and pulling my fabric off the mat into a heap on the floor.

I like to store my fabrics according to color families on shelves in a closet (see the photo on page 63). This allows me to do a quick visual check for the fabric I'm looking for. It also allows me to see how different colors within the same color family interact with one another. I've found this to be one of the best ways to gain knowledge and judgment about color. I also keep a small, clear, plastic box with each color for my scraps.

My Favorite Things

I store all my small fabric pieces in clear plastic Rubbermaid boxes. I find that they stack together nicely, and I can see through them and instantly know what's inside. If you use cardboard boxes, attach a label for easy identification, and don't store the boxes on a concrete floor—the bottom of the box may absorb moisture.

If you store your fabric on shelves in an open room, cover the fabric when you're not looking at or using it. Remember that sunlight is harmful, and the fabric will fade from long exposure to outside light. This is especially true if you have skylights in your sewing room.

Grain

Before you begin to rotary cut your blocks, it's important to understand the different types of fabric grain that you will encounter. This way, you can plan where the different types of grain—crosswise, lengthwise, and bias—will be positioned on each piece in your quilt.

After working with fabric for many years, I have found that very few fabrics are woven so the grain lines formed by the threads run straight across (horizontally) or straight down (vertically) the run of the fabric. This is probably because of the manufacturing process. Therefore, when I'm cutting strips, I always try to cut as close to the straight grain (lengthwise or crosswise) as I can. If your cutting doesn't run quite true to the grain, just handle the fabric carefully during sewing and pressing, and you will be fine.

I create a grain line chart for every block in my quilt before I cut my shapes. This ensures that the most stable grain falls on the outside edges of each unit, block, and section of the quilt, as well as the outer edges of the quilt top. This keeps my blocks and quilts from becoming stretched out of shape.

For example, the **Grain Line Diagrams** for the Square within a Star block show that the large

Square within a Star Block

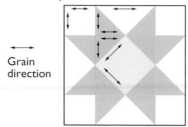

Grain direction

Straight grain is on outside edges of all units

Piecing Units

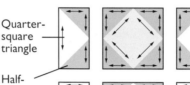

Quarter-square triangle

Half-square triangle

Grain Line Diagrams

Cut Smart

Know your grain! There are several different kinds of weave and grain in each piece of fabric. Use this handy diagram and the accompanying definitions to guide you as you plan your quilt. Also, refer to the "No-Fail Grain Line Guide" on pages 26–27.

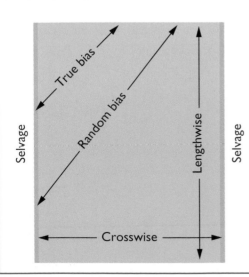

Lengthwise straight grain: The most visible threads that run along the length of the fabric. There is almost no stretch to the fabric on the lengthwise grain.

Crosswise straight grain: The most visible threads that run along the width of the fabric. Most fabric is 44 inches wide before washing and drying. There is a slight stretch to the fabric on the crosswise grain.

True bias grain: The line formed when the fabric is cut at a 45 degree angle. True bias has the most stretch of all the fabric grains.

Random bias grain: The line formed when the fabric is cut at an angle other than 45 degrees. Random bias has some stretch, but not as much as true bias.

Straight grain: Either lengthwise or crosswise grain.

Selvages: The tightly woven side edges of the fabric. The selvages run the length of the fabric, and usually the manufacturer's name is printed here.

triangles should be quarter-squares (page 39) and the small triangles should be half-squares (page 38). This ensures that straight grain will always be on the outside edge. If it were the other way around, you would have the stretchy bias edges all around the edges of this unit, making it hard to fit it to another part of a block or quilt. When I'm sewing a quilt top, I always treat each *piecing unit* of a block as if it were a separate quilt. This means that I want the least amount of bias on the edges every time I sew one piece to another.

Cutting Directional Fabrics

Some fabrics have an obvious direction to them, which makes them a bit more challenging to work with. I like to think of directional fabrics in two groups: plaids and stripes, and motif fabrics. By motif fabrics, I mean fabrics that have printed designs, pictures, or other patterns that I sometimes want to use whole, as in the center of a Log Cabin block. So sometimes I cut these out more carefully so that the motif stays intact in my cut shape.

Careful cutting of any directional fabric takes a little more time, but it brings good rewards. I guarantee that you'll be much happier with your results—straight, even lines in your plaids and stripes—once you've used these techniques.

When you're cutting directional fabrics, whether to use them in a block in your quilt or for a border or binding, there are a few tips to keep in mind.

Nancy's Bag of Tricks

The only time I *plan* to have bias grain on the outside edges of my block or quilt is when I am working with fabric that has a special motif. Sometimes I want the motif placed just so, and this causes the bias to fall on an outside edge. Then I'm very careful with the stretchy pieces; I try not to handle the bias edges at all, or at least as little as possible. When I'm ready to sew them to other pieces, I pin them using twice as many pins as usual.

Tips for Cutting Directional Fabrics

Cut through only *one* layer at a time.

Ignore the grain and align your ruler with the directional print in the fabric (an edge of a line on a plaid or stripe, for example).

Cut with the selvages to your right or left, not toward or away from your body. Many directional fabrics are woven so that the pattern is truer on the lengthwise grain, not on the crosswise grain as is usual.

Start cutting 1 to 2 inches from the selvage. The tightly, unevenly woven edges can often distort a directional pattern, so you won't want to try to cut from this section. (Save the scraps to use in miniatures, where the direction isn't as critical.)

Position the ¼-inch mark on your ruler slightly away from the edge of a stripe or plaid line. This way, if your sewing line is not perfectly straight, it won't show up as a "snakey" seam line as your print weaves in and out of your sewn seam.

If you are using directional fabric for a border or binding, here are a few tips to keep in mind.

Tips for Directional Borders and Binding

Borders cut on the *crosswise* grain will have the directional print moving from the center of the quilt toward the edges. The pattern of borders cut on the *lengthwise* grain moves around the perimeter of the quilt.

Binding cut on the crosswise grain (especially striped fabric) looks great as the binding "wraps" from the front to the back of the quilt. This binding is easy to cut, and it isn't complicated to attach.

To cut bias binding, align the 45 degree line on your ruler with a stripe on the fabric. This makes a very attractive binding (see Campbell House on page 134 and Square within a Square Miniature on page 172). Bias binding is a little harder to handle, but the outcome is well worth the effort.

I occasionally cut borders on the bias (usually only on miniatures). If you do this, be extremely careful while handling these very stretchy pieces.

No-Fail Grain Line Guide

I have included my "No-Fail Grain Line Guide" so you can quickly create your own chart when you're piecing. This chart is based on cutting straight strips of fabric on the *crosswise* grain, then cutting the strips into the desired shapes (pages 36–53).

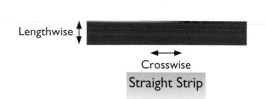
Straight Strip

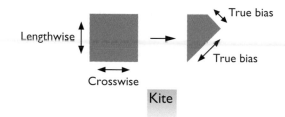
Kite

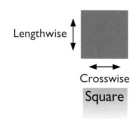
Square

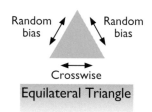
Equilateral Triangle

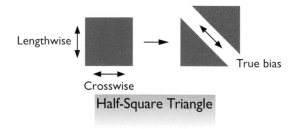
Half-Square Triangle

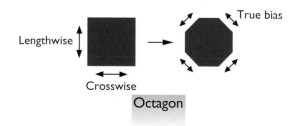
Octagon

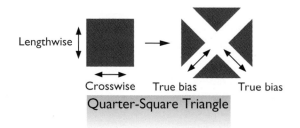
Quarter-Square Triangle

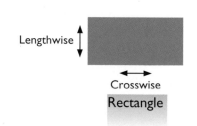
Rectangle

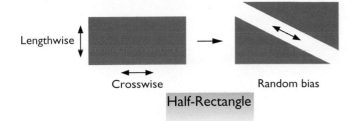

Half-Rectangle

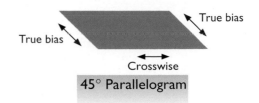

45° Parallelogram

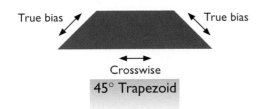

45° Trapezoid

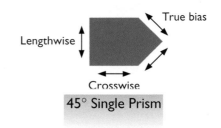

45° Single Prism

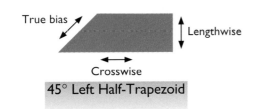

45° Left Half-Trapezoid

45° Double Prism

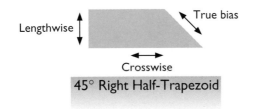

45° Right Half-Trapezoid

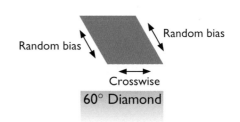

60° Diamond

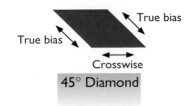

45° Diamond

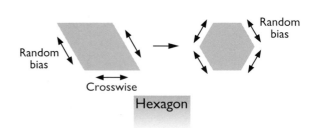

Hexagon

Rotary Cutting Basics Made Easy

This section presents the No-Fail methods I developed after many years of quiltmaking—and surgery on my wrists for carpal tunnel syndrome. The tips and techniques that follow will help make your rotary cutting safe and accurate, and they will also help prevent repetitive strain on your hands and wrists. Once you begin using the ergonomically correct techniques I describe here, you'll be able to cut just as accurately at the end of your cutting session as you do in the beginning!

Holding the Cutter

In 1988 I had wrist operations for carpal tunnel syndrome. After taking a few weeks off to recuperate, I was ready to start rotary cutting again. To my surprise, I couldn't hold the rotary cutter the same way that I did before the operation. I had been unknowingly stressing my hands when cutting, and now I had to find the best way to hold the cutter to produce minimum stress. The following method is what I now use, I recommend that you try it.

1. Drop your hands to your sides. Notice that your hands fall with the *back* of the hand facing outward. This simple exercise shows the natural position your hand assumes so it will put little or no stress on your shoulder, elbow, or wrist.

Hand faces outward   Extend first finger

2. Place the bottom of the rotary cutter in the palm of your hand, and place your first finger (I call this your driving finger) on the ridged area on the top of the cutter. The rotary cutter is now in direct alignment with your body. Let your hand fall down to your side. The back of your hand still faces outward, so there is little or no stress on your body.

This position works well for most people; if you aren't comfortable holding your cutter as shown here, try a different cutter, a different size handle, or as a last resort, a different hand position. Other hand positions include holding the cutter with your thumb and fingers wrapped around the handle while placing your thumb on the ridge, and wrapping your fingers around the handle. You're the best judge of what feels most comfortable for you. If you notice hand fatigue or pain while cutting, reexamine how you're holding your cutter. Try an alternate position. Don't do what I did, which was to cut my way into carpal tunnel syndrome and corrective surgery.

Nancy's Bag of Tricks

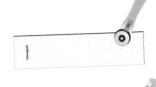

Make your own cutting table. It's fairly easy—and when you do, it's guaranteed to be the right height for you! Go to a home improvement center or contact a carpenter and buy a double sink cutout (the part of the countertop that is left over when you cut out the hole for the sink). Or, cover a 2 × 4-foot piece of ¾-inch plywood with heavy vinyl contact paper. Set your new cutting tabletop on several sturdy boxes on top of the table you'll be cutting on. Try different heights until you find the one that is the most comfortable and keeps your work close to your eyes. (I use an 8-inch-high, 17 × 23-inch plastic Rubbermaid box. It's also a great place to store my extra rulers and cutters.) If you want to get a little fancier and more permanent, use flanges to attach short table legs to the bottom of your tabletop.

Body Position

The blessing of the rotary cutter is that it lets us cut lots of shapes very quickly and accurately. The curse is that it can be a pain in the neck, back, and shoulders. Anyone who has rotary cut for a while knows how the aches and pains can set in. Here are a few things you can try to help prevent the discomfort.

Body-Smart Cutting Tips

Stand erect while you are rotary cutting (unless you have a physical disability). You won't have to reach so far to finish a long cut, and you'll have less shoulder and neck fatigue.

Place yourself so that you are able to look directly down onto your ruler and fabric while cutting. Your cutting will be more accurate, and you'll exert your back and shoulders less by cutting in a standing position, especially when you're cutting long strips.

Use a table that is the right height for you. You should stand erect, your shoulders should be relaxed, and your hands should fall naturally onto the mat. I'm most comfortable when my elbows are about 6 inches off the tabletop; you'll have to find the height that's most comfortable for you. Bending over a table that is too low will give you a backache.

If necessary, put blocks of wood or bricks under the legs of your cutting table to make it high enough to make cutting comfortable for you. Or make your own tabletop cutting table, as shown on page 29.

Cut Smart

Always cut *away* from your body when using a rotary cutter. That way, if you slip, there's no danger of an accidental appendectomy. You also have much more control over the cutter when cutting away from your body because you can see where you're going. This lets you steer more accurately and stay in better alignment with the ruler.

Hand Position

Once you're all set with your equipment and a place to cut, you're ready to start rotary cutting. This No-Fail method will ensure that your ruler doesn't slip while rotary cutting. I show this method for both left-handed and right-handed cutting below, so make sure you're referring to the correct photographs!

1. Place the ruler on the fabric. Firmly position your noncutting hand with the thumb on the bottom of the ruler, and place your four fingertips a comfortable distance up the ruler (you shouldn't stretch your fingers out too far or bunch them up too close to your thumb). Hold your cutter so the handle is at a 45 degree angle to the tabletop. (A 45 degree angle is halfway between lying flat on the cutting mat and standing straight up in the air.)

Left-Handed   Right-Handed

2. Cut *away* from your body, stopping when the blade is even with your fingertips. *Don't* lift the cutter from the fabric.

Left-Handed   Right-Handed

3. Move the thumb of your noncutting hand up to your fingertips. While your hand is "inch-worming" (or what I like to call "smart walking") its way up the ruler, your cutting hand remains still.

Left-Handed   Right-Handed

4. Move your four fingers up the ruler a comfortable distance. Continue alternately cutting and "smart walking" your hand up the ruler until you have cut to the end of the strip.

Left-Handed   Right-Handed

Cut Smart

Here are a few more tips for successful rotary cutting:

• **Rotary cut** only where your hand is stabilizing the ruler. If you try to cut outside of this area, the ruler is likely to slip.

• **Apply even pressure** on your fingertips.

• **Begin cutting** with your blade just off the fabric. This lets your cutter get rolling before it has to start cutting fabric.

• **Prevent hand pain** by holding the ruler with your fingertips only.

Avoiding the V

I will never forget the time I was making a Double Irish Chain quilt. This was going to be my first "real" quilt, so I wanted everything to be perfect. After squaring up my fabric for the first time, I went gung ho at cutting strips for the entire project. When I started sewing the strips together, I had a mess. For some reason, I couldn't sew a straight seam! My strip sets were warped, skewed, and misshapen. Then I realized what had happened: My strips had developed at their fold what quilters call a V.

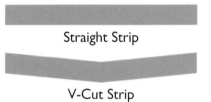

Straight Strip

V-Cut Strip

There are two problems that usually result in V-cuts. Here they are with their solutions.

First problem: During rotary cutting, your first few strips are usually fine, but each successive strip develops a slight V at the fold area, which is very apparent when you lay the strip against a ruler.

Solution: The fabric is only "in square" with the fold for the width of your ruler. Therefore, if you are using a 6-inch-wide ruler, you can cut up to 6 inches before you *must* resquare your fabric (page 32). Likewise, if your ruler is 4 inches wide, you can cut a maximum of 4 inches before resquaring.

Second problem: Sometimes you get multiple V-cuts, which result from folding the fabric twice and cutting through four layers. I try to avoid cutting through four layers of fabric, but sometimes it's unavoidable (as when I'm cutting long border strips).

Solution: Careful folding. First, fold the fabric selvage to selvage. Then fold the selvages over to meet the original fold, checking for wrinkles that may form on the inside layer. Check that you have folded evenly by laying your ruler on the fabric, aligning one of the inch lines with one fold. The measurement at the other edge of the fabric should be the same all the way across the width of your ruler. If it varies, you have not folded straight.

Squaring Up

Before you can cut strips or shapes from fabric, you have to square it up—create a straight edge that is perpendicular to an adjacent edge.

44-Inch-Wide Fabric

Fabric off the bolt is usually 44 or 45 inches wide, but only 40 to 43 inches wide after washing and drying.

Fold the fabric, aligning the selvages as best you can. Make sure the fold and fabric are smooth. Place the fabric on the mat with the fold away from you.

Align the top of the ruler with the fold. "Smart walk" (page 31) while rotary cutting the fabric. Continue until you have cut through the fold.

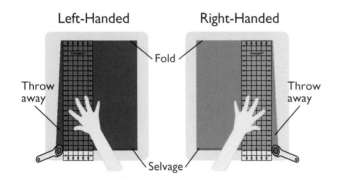

Left-Handed   Right-Handed

Fold

Throw away   Throw away

Selvage

Quilter's Quarter

A quilter's quarter (or fat quarter) results when a ½-yard piece of fabric is cut in half down the fold into two 18 × 22-inch pieces. Only one side has a selvage.

Align the selvage edge with the opposite raw edge. Make sure there are no wrinkles at the fold. Your fabric will now measure 11 × 18 inches. Square up the fabric as above.

Fold

Align the selvage and the raw edge

Strips

When you cut shapes to sew together into blocks for your quilt, you usually cut strips of fabric first. Before cutting these fabric strips into your desired shapes, you need to cut off the selvages or raw edges, and square up the ends of the strips.

Position the top edge of your ruler even with one long edge of your fabric strip. Using your rotary cutter, square up the short side of the strip by cutting off approximately ¼ inch from the selvage or raw edge.

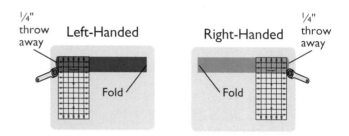

¼" throw away   Left-Handed   Right-Handed   ¼" throw away

Fold   Fold

Scraps

When working with scrap fabric that has no selvages, I find it best to work on the wrong side of the fabric. You can usually see the crosswise and lengthwise grain of the fabric better, and you can line up your ruler with the threads in the fabric to get straight cuts.

Align a line on the ruler with the crosswise or lengthwise grain as well as you can. Rotary cut into the desired shapes. Remember, if your rotary cutting, sewing, and pressing are accurate, it won't matter if you're slightly off grain.

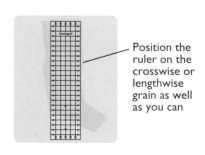

Position the ruler on the crosswise or lengthwise grain as well as you can

Cutting Borders

Wavy, puckered, or rippled borders are a heartbreak. After assembling a quilt, it hurts to see a case of "the waves" set in. Many things can give your quilts rippling edges: improperly placed grain line, inaccurately measured or cut borders, or the quilting on the edges. In this section, I will show you my method of cutting borders, which will help eliminate problems with grain line and fit. Before you cut your borders, measure accurately for them (page 103).

No-Fail Border Cutting

Position your cutting mat and fabric on a long table. After prewashing and pressing, your fabric will be folded selvage to selvage. Now, fold the bottom edge to the top edge. This gives you four layers of fabric. Keep the vertical folds aligned as well as you can, and don't worry if the selvages don't line up exactly.

First Cut

Position the fabric so the horizontal fold is near your body. Align the bottom of a 6 × 24-inch ruler with the horizontal fold. Holding the rotary cutter properly, "smart walk" (page 31) with your other hand to trim the selvages up to the end of the ruler.

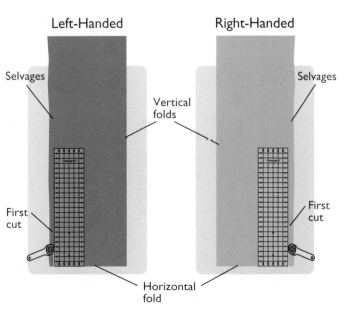

Left-Handed · Right-Handed · Selvages · Vertical folds · Selvages · First cut · First cut · Horizontal fold

Second Cut

Leave the ruler in place (for a 6-inch-wide border), or move it over (for a narrower border, line up your border width with the cut edge). Go to the other end of the mat and cut down the other side of the ruler.

Note: For a border wider than 6 inches, use a wider ruler for straight, accurate edges.

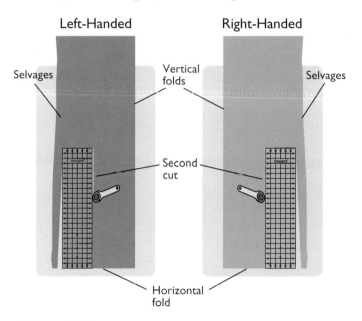

Left-Handed · Right-Handed · Selvages · Vertical folds · Selvages · Second cut · Horizontal fold

Third Cut

To continue cutting straight, move the ruler only 12 inches up the fabric, aligning the lower 12 inches of the ruler with the previous cuts. Continue cutting and moving the ruler up the fabric 12 inches at a time until you have cut the length of your fabric.

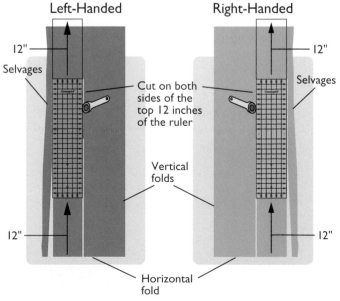

Left-Handed · Right-Handed · 12" · 12" · Selvages · Cut on both sides of the top 12 inches of the ruler · Selvages · Vertical folds · 12" · 12" · Horizontal fold

Guide to Rotary-Cut Shapes

Throw out those templates! Let your rotary cutter liberate you from the tedious chore of tracing around shapes and then laboriously cutting them out by hand. Nearly every shape commonly used in quiltmaking can be quickly and easily rotary cut if you know how. In this section I'll show you, step by step, the most accurate, most efficient way to cut any shape you need for a quilt—using just the markings and angle lines on your rotary ruler.

How to Use This Section

In this part of the book, I will show you how to cut almost any shape used in quiltmaking using only your rotary cutter and ruler. Each shape has the same basic instructions: First, you figure out your desired finished size, based on the measurements of your block. Then add the correct seam allowance, and cut out the shape. Here is a basic "road map" to each of the shapes.

Easy formulas help you figure out the exact size you need for any project.

The shape name. Used throughout the projects.

A block with the shape in it. The featured shape is highlighted in the same color throughout the page.

Finished size (height, length, width) means the size the patch will appear once it has been sewn into the quilt.

Cutting size (height, length, width) means the size you cut the patch. **This size includes ¼-inch seam allowances for all the shapes shown.**

At-a-glance add-on seam allowance formula for the shape.

Tips give you additional information that will help you cut the most accurate pieces.

The featured shape. This shape is repeated in the cutting charts for the projects that the shape is used in.

The cutting sequence, broken down into its basic steps so you can follow at a glance.

Cutting directions and illustrations are given for left-handed and right-handed quilters.

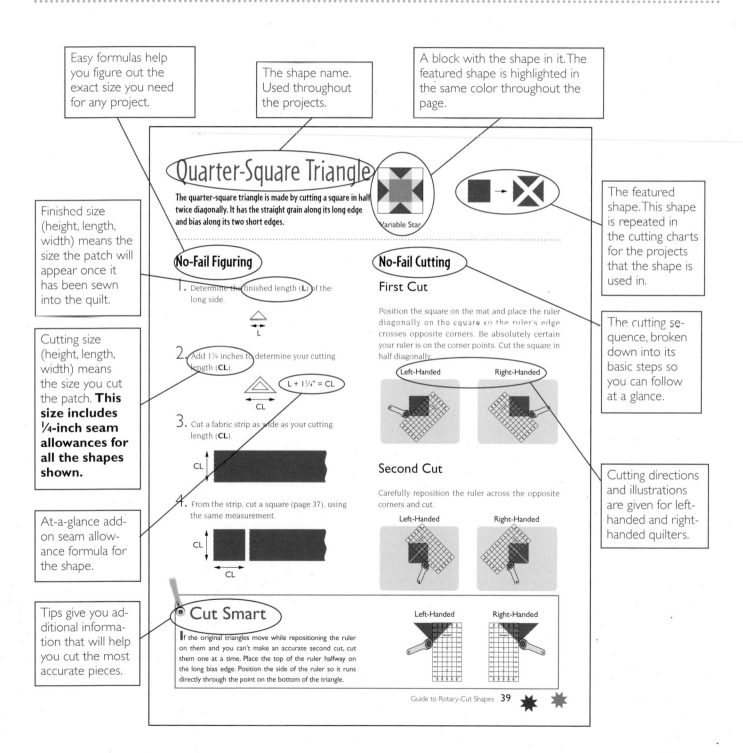

Quarter-Square Triangle

The quarter-square triangle is made by cutting a square in half twice diagonally. It has the straight grain along its long edge and bias along its two short edges.

Variable Star

No-Fail Figuring

1. Determine the finished length (**L**) of the long side.

L

2. Add 1¼ inches to determine your cutting length (**CL**).

$L + 1\frac{1}{4}" = CL$

CL

3. Cut a fabric strip as wide as your cutting length (**CL**).

CL

4. From the strip, cut a square (page 37), using the same measurement.

CL

CL

Cut Smart

If the original triangles move while repositioning the ruler on them and you can't make an accurate second cut, cut them one at a time. Place the top of the ruler halfway on the long bias edge. Position the side of the ruler so it runs directly through the point on the bottom of the triangle.

No-Fail Cutting

First Cut

Position the square on the mat and place the ruler diagonally on the square so the ruler's edge crosses opposite corners. Be absolutely certain your ruler is on the corner points. Cut the square in half diagonally.

Left-Handed   Right-Handed

Second Cut

Carefully reposition the ruler across the opposite corners and cut.

Left-Handed   Right-Handed

Left-Handed   Right-Handed

Guide to Rotary-Cut Shapes **39**

Straight Strips

When rotary cutting shapes that are commonly used in quiltmaking, you will almost always first cut a straight strip, then cut the strip into the desired shapes.

No-Fail Figuring

1. Determine the width of your strip. (You will get this information from the cutting height (**CH**) for the individual shapes on pages 37–53.)

Width of strip equals cutting height of shape

2. Square up your 44-inch-wide fabric (page 32).

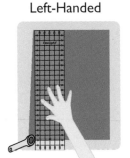 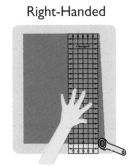

Left-Handed   Right-Handed

3. Rotate the mat 180 degrees. Do *not* move the fabric on the mat. The fold will be at the bottom of the mat.

Cut Smart

If you sometimes tend to accidentally nick or "round off" the corner of your ruler as you cut, here's a simple solution. When cutting long strips, place one of the inch lines—not the bottom edge of the ruler—on the fold. Now your cutter will stay safely away from the edge of the ruler, and that perfect corner will stay intact.

No-Fail Cutting

First Cut

Position one of the ruler's horizontal lines on the fold, and place the line corresponding to the width of your strip on the cut edge of the fabric. Using the "smart walking" method (page 31), rotary cut your strip.

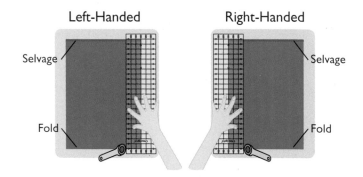

Left-Handed   Right-Handed

Selvage   Selvage

Fold   Fold

Second Cut

Turn the mat 90 degrees, and line up the edge of your ruler with the long edge of the strip. Cut about ¼ inch off the end to square up the strip.

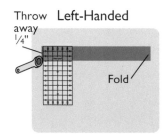 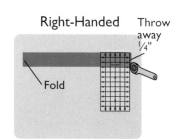

Throw away ¼"   Left-Handed   Right-Handed   Throw away ¼"

Fold   Fold

Square

Once you master cutting straight strips, it is simple to cut the strips into squares. I use a smaller ruler (6 × 12 inches) to cut the strips into smaller shapes.

Square within a Square

No-Fail Figuring

1. Determine the finished height (**H**) of one side.

2. Add ½ inch to determine your cutting height (**CH**).

$$H + \frac{1}{2}" = CH$$

3. Cut a fabric strip as wide as your cutting height (**CH**). Square up the short edge of your strip (page 32). Turn the mat 180 degrees.

No-Fail Cutting

Place the ruler on top of the fabric so that the inch mark corresponding to your cutting height (**CH**) lines up with the cut edge. Make sure the top of the ruler is even with the top of the strip. Cut the square.

Left-Handed	Right-Handed
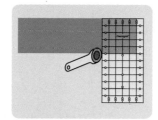	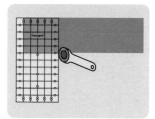

Cut Smart

Press your fabric before you rotary cut your shapes. If you use wrinkled fabric, your precut pieces will grow in size after you press the wrinkles out, and your pieces won't fit together perfectly.

Half-Square Triangle

The half-square triangle is probably the most frequently used shape in quiltmaking. It is made by cutting a square in half once diagonally.

Churn Dash

No-Fail Figuring

1. Determine the finished height (**H**) of one short side.

2. Add ⅞ inch to determine your cutting height (**CH**).

H + ⅞" = CH

3. Cut a fabric strip as wide as your cutting height (**CH**).

4. From the strip, cut a square (page 37), using the same measurement.

No-Fail Cutting

Position the square on the mat, and place the ruler diagonally on the square so the ruler's edge crosses opposite corners. Be absolutely certain your ruler is on the corner points. Cut the square in half diagonally.

Left-Handed 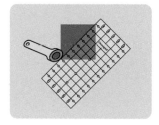 Right-Handed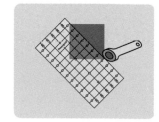

Cut Smart

When cutting a square in half diagonally, place one of your fingertips on the ruler directly over the corner of the square. This will prevent the fabric from moving.

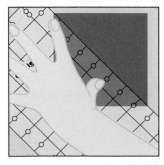

A half-square triangle has straight grain along its short edges and bias (stretchy) grain along its long edge. A quarter-square triangle has the exact reverse. When you construct a block, choose the triangle that will keep straight, stable grain along the outside edges to make the block less likely to stretch out of shape.

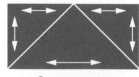

Half-square triangle

Quarter-square triangle

Quarter-Square Triangle

The quarter-square triangle is made by cutting a square in half twice diagonally. It has the straight grain along its long edge and bias along its two short edges.

Variable Star

No-Fail Figuring

1. Determine the finished length (**L**) of the long side.

2. Add 1¼ inches to determine your cutting length (**CL**).

 L + 1¼" = CL

3. Cut a fabric strip as wide as your cutting length (**CL**).

4. From the strip, cut a square (page 37), using the same measurement.

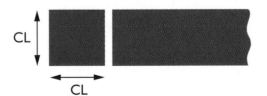

No-Fail Cutting

First Cut

Position the square on the mat and place the ruler diagonally on the square so the ruler's edge crosses opposite corners. Be absolutely certain your ruler is on the corner points. Cut the square in half diagonally.

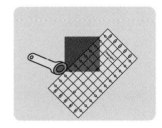

Left-Handed   Right-Handed

Second Cut

Carefully reposition the ruler across the opposite corners and cut.

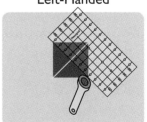
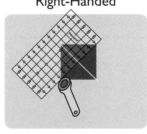

Left-Handed   Right-Handed

Cut Smart

If the original triangles move while repositioning the ruler on them and you can't make an accurate second cut, cut them one at a time. Place the top of the ruler halfway on the long bias edge. Position the side of the ruler so it runs directly through the point on the bottom of the triangle.

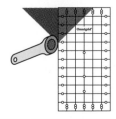
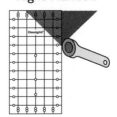

Left-Handed   Right-Handed

Kite

The kite shape is a half-square triangle with one tip cut off so it's symmetrical. The two short sides are equal in length, and the two long sides are equal in length.

Feathered Star

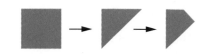

No-Fail Figuring

1. Determine the finished height (**H**) of one long side.

2. Add ⅞ inch to determine your cutting height (**CH**).

   H + ⅞" = CH

3. Cut a fabric strip as wide as your cutting height (**CH**).

4. From the strip, cut a half-square triangle (page 38).

No-Fail Cutting

Position the triangle so the long bias edge faces the top of the cutting mat. Align the top of the ruler with the top of the triangle. Find the line on your ruler that matches your cutting height (**CH**). Place your ruler on the triangle so the tip of the triangle is exactly at that CH line. Cut off and discard the small triangle.

Left-Handed   Right-Handed

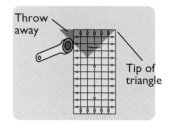
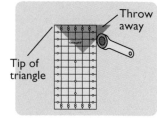

Cut Smart

Always use the *unfinished* size of the square (your cutting height) as the measurement for trimming the point off the triangle.

If you cut eight kites and sew them together along their long edges, you create a really exciting "pinwheel" octagon.

Equilateral Triangle

An equilateral triangle has three sides of equal length. The secret to cutting these is rotating the ruler between the two 60 degree lines.

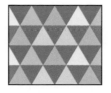

Thousand Pyramid

No-Fail Figuring

1. Determine the height (**H**) of your triangle.

2. Add ¾ inch to determine your cutting height (**CH**).

$$H + ¾" = CH$$

3. Cut a fabric strip as wide as your cutting height (**CH**).

Cut Smart

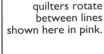

Here's a simple rule for cutting these triangles: *Left-handed quilters* will rotate between the two 60 degree lines located on the lower *left* edge of the ruler. *Right-handed quilters* will rotate between the two 60 degree lines located on the lower *right* edge of the ruler.

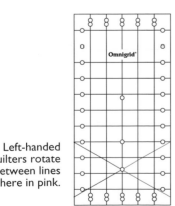

Left-handed quilters rotate between lines shown here in pink.

Right-handed quilters rotate between lines shown here in blue.

No-Fail Cutting

First Cut

Begin by cutting the strip at a 60 degree angle. *Right-handed quilters*: Align the 60 degree line on the lower *right* edge of the ruler with the bottom of the strip. *Left-handed quilters*: Align the 60 degree line on the lower *left* edge of the ruler with the bottom of the strip. Rotary cut and throw away the excess.

Left-Handed

Right-Handed

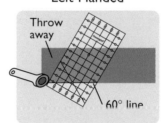

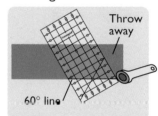

Second Cut

Right-handed quilters: Rotate the ruler so the other 60 degree line is on the bottom of the strip and the *right* edge of the ruler is lined up with the top edge of the first cut. *Left-handed quilters*: Rotate the ruler so the other 60 degree line is on the bottom of the strip and the *left* edge of the ruler is lined up with the top edge of the first cut. Rotary cut the triangle. To cut additional triangles, continue rotating the ruler between the two 60 degree lines.

Left-Handed

Right-Handed

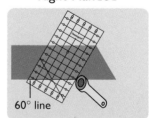

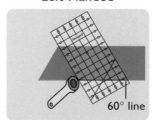

Octagon

An octagon is a square with its four corners cut off symmetrically. All eight sides of an octagon are equal in length.

Sunrise Star

No-Fail Figuring

1. Determine the finished height (**H**) of the octagon.

2. Add ½ inch to determine your cutting height (**CH**).

H + ½" = CH

3. Cut a fabric strip as wide as your cutting height (**CH**).

4. Cut a square (page 37), using the same measurement. On the wrong side of the fabric, lightly draw pencil lines diagonally in both directions.

No-Fail Cutting

First Cut

Place the square, wrong side up, diagonally on your cutting mat. Divide the cutting height (**CH**) of the square in half to determine your smart measurement (**SM**). (In this example, 6 ÷ 2 = 3.) Position the ruler so the line corresponding to your smart measurement (**SM**; here, the 3-inch line) is on top of the vertical pencil line. Cut off and discard the tip.

Left-Handed   Right-Handed

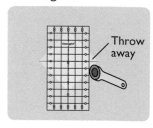

Second Cut

Rotate the mat 180 degrees. Position the ruler so the same line again covers the same vertical pencil line. Cut off and discard the tip.

Left-Handed   Right-Handed

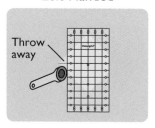

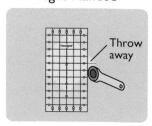

Octagon (continued)

Third Cut

Rotate the mat 90 degrees. Position the ruler so the smart measurement (**SM**) line runs over the second pencil line. Cut off and discard the tip.

Left-Handed | Right-Handed

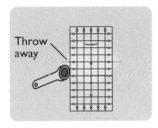
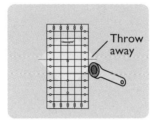

Fourth Cut

Rotate the mat 180 degrees. Position the ruler so the smart measurement (**SM**) line runs over the second pencil line. Cut off and discard the tip.

Left-Handed | Right-Handed

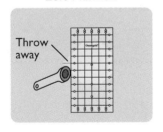
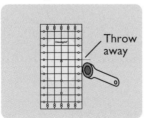

Cut Smart

Always cut the opposite sides of your octagon first, then the adjacent sides. This ensures that the size of your octagon will be accurate. A quick check that you have a perfect octagon is to measure from one straight edge to the opposite one. All four measurements should equal your original cutting height.

Same measurement in all directions

Rectangle

A true rectangle is twice as long as it is high. Both true and untrue rectangles are used in quilting. The add-on seam allowance is the same for both types of rectangles.

Cake Stand

No-Fail Figuring

1. Determine the finished height (**H**) of one short side and the finished length (**L**) of one long side.

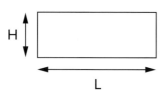

2. Add ½ inch to each measurement to determine your cutting height (**CH**) and cutting length (**CL**).

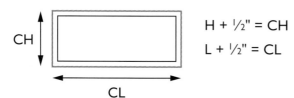

$$H + \tfrac{1}{2}" = CH$$
$$L + \tfrac{1}{2}" = CL$$

3. Cut a fabric strip as wide as your cutting height (**CH**). Square up one end (page 32).

No-Fail Cutting

Place the ruler on the strip so the line corresponding to the cutting length (**CL**) lines up with the short edge of the strip. Position the top of the ruler so it is even with the top of the strip. Rotary cut the rectangle.

Left-Handed · Right-Handed

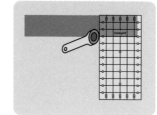 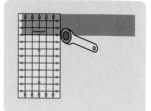

⊙ Cut Smart

If you are cutting rectangles that are more than 6 inches long, turn your ruler so that the length of the ruler runs in the same direction as the length of your strip.

Think of your lattice strips and borders as long rectangles when you're calculating their length and width. But remember to use my "smart walking" method (page 31) to help keep your ruler from slipping as you make these long cuts.

Half-Rectangle

Half-rectangles are made by cutting a rectangle in half diagonally. The add-on seam allowance noted below is for cutting a true half-rectangle (where the length is twice the width).

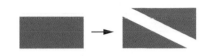

Sailboat

No-Fail Figuring

1. Determine the finished height (**H**) of the short side and the finished length (**L**) of the long side.

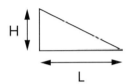

2. Add $\frac{11}{16}$ inch to the height (**H**) to determine your cutting height (**CH**) and $1\frac{5}{16}$ inch to the length (**L**) to determine your cutting length (**CL**).

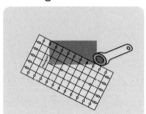

$$H + \tfrac{11}{16}" = CH$$
$$L + 1\tfrac{5}{16}" = CL$$

3. Cut a fabric strip as wide as your cutting height (**CH**). Square up one end (page 32).

4. From the strip, cut a rectangle (opposite page) as long as the cutting length (**CL**).

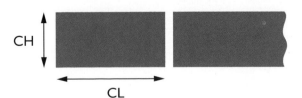

No-Fail Cutting

Position the rectangle on the mat and place the ruler diagonally on the rectangle so the ruler's edge crosses opposite corners. Rotary cut the rectangle in half.

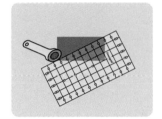

Left-Handed   Right-Handed

Cut Smart

Cutting $\frac{1}{16}$ inch can be a chore since most rulers do not have $\frac{1}{16}$-inch markings, but you can easily visualize where they would fall on the ruler. For example, $\frac{11}{16}$ inch is between $\frac{5}{8}$ inch and $\frac{3}{4}$ inch; $\frac{5}{16}$ inch is between $\frac{1}{4}$ inch and $\frac{3}{8}$ inch.

To create "mirror-image" half-rectangles, position two fabric rectangles with wrong sides together and rotary cut as shown above.

To determine the seam allowances for rectangles that are not true, draw the finished rectangle on graph paper. Draw a diagonal line and erase one of the half-rectangles. Draw $\frac{1}{4}$-inch seam allowances outside of all three sides of the half-rectangle. These are your *cutting* measurements for the *unfinished* size.

Trapezoid

A rectangle with both ends cut off at an angle is called a trapezoid. You can cut the ends off at any angle, but quilt-makers usually cut the ends off at 45 degrees.

Pinwheel Surrounded

No-Fail Figuring

1. Determine the finished height (**H**) and the finished length (**L**) of the trapezoid.

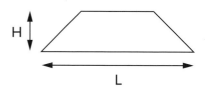

2. Add ½ inch to the height (**H**) to determine your cutting height (**CH**) and 1¼ inches to the length (**L**) to determine the cutting length (**CL**).

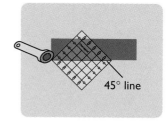

$$H + \frac{1}{2}" = CH$$
$$L + 1\frac{1}{4}" = CL$$

3. Cut a fabric strip as wide as the cutting height (**CH**). Square up one end (page 32).

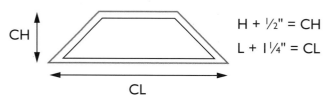

4. Cut a rectangle (page 44) as long as the cutting length (**CL**).

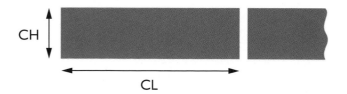

No-Fail Cutting

First Cut

Right-handed quilters: Place the ruler so its 45 degree line runs along the bottom of the strip and the tip of the ruler is exactly at the lower *right* corner of the rectangle. *Left-handed quilters:* Place the 45 degree line along the bottom of the strip and the tip of the ruler exactly at the lower *left* corner of the rectangle. Rotary cut the triangle off the end.

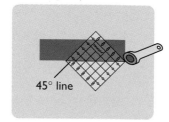

Left-Handed   Right-Handed

Second Cut

Rotate the mat 90 degrees. Keeping the 45 degree line along the bottom of the strip, slide the ruler to the other end of the rectangle. Rotary cut the triangle off the end.

Left-Handed   Right-Handed

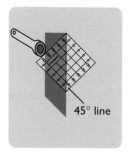
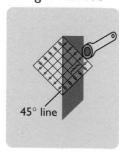

Half-Trapezoid

To make a half-trapezoid, you will cut off only one end of the rectangle at a 45 degree angle. To cut a 60 degree half-trapezoid, simply use the 60 degree line on your ruler.

Attic Window

Left
Half-Trapezoid

Right
Half-Trapezoid

No-Fail Figuring

1. Determine the finished height (**H**) and the finished length (**L**) of the half-trapezoid.

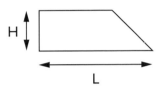

2. Add ½ inch to the height (**H**) to determine your cutting height (**CH**) and ⅞ inch to the length (**L**) to determine your cutting length (**CL**).

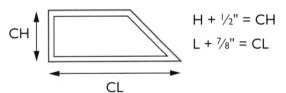

$$H + \frac{1}{2}" = CH$$
$$L + \frac{7}{8}" = CL$$

3. Cut a fabric strip as wide as the cutting height (**CH**). Square up one end (page 32).

4. Cut a rectangle (page 44) as long as the cutting length (**CL**).

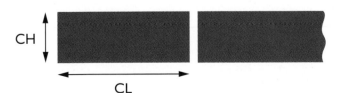

No-Fail Cutting

Pay attention to which side of the fabric should face you, as shown. *Right-handed quilters:* Place the ruler so its 45 degree line runs along the bottom of the strip, and the tip of the ruler is exactly at the lower *right* corner of the rectangle. *Left-handed quilters:* Place the 45 degree line along the bottom of the strip and the tip of the ruler exactly at the lower *left* corner of the rectangle. Rotary cut the triangle off the end.

Left-Handed   Right-Handed

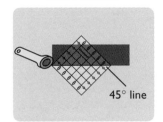
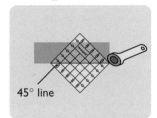

45° line   45° line

Left Half-Trapezoid:
Right side of the fabric
faces you

Left Half-Trapezoid:
Wrong side of the fabric
faces you

Left-Handed   Right-Handed

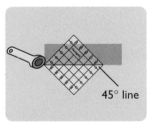
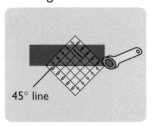

45° line   45° line

Right Half-Trapezoid:
Wrong side of the fabric
faces you

Right Half-Trapezoid:
Right side of the fabric
faces you

Cut Smart

To cut a left and right half-trapezoid at the same time, cut two rectangles placed with wrong sides together.

45 Degree Diamond

A key thing to remember when cutting a 45 degree diamond is that the height determines the width you cut the diamond.

Eight-Pointed Star

No-Fail Figuring

1. Determine the finished height (**H**).

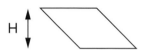

2. Add ½ inch to determine your cutting height (**CH**).

$H + \frac{1}{2}" = CH$

3. Cut a fabric strip as wide as your cutting height (**CH**).

Cut Smart

To check the accuracy of a 45 degree diamond, fold it in half, long point to long point. The sides of the long points should be equal in length.

When cutting 45 degree diamonds, right-handed quilters will always position the ruler on the strip diagonally, angled off to the left. Left-handed quilters will always position the ruler diagonally, angled off to the right.

No-Fail Cutting

First Cut

Begin by cutting the strip at a 45 degree angle. *Right-handed quilters:* Position the 45 degree line that is located on the lower *right* edge of the ruler on the bottom of the strip. *Left-handed quilters:* Position the 45 degree line that is located on the lower *left* edge of the ruler on the bottom of the strip. Rotary cut the triangle off the end.

Left-Handed   Right-Handed

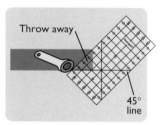
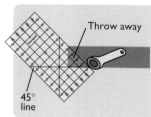

Second Cut

Find the line on your ruler that corresponds to your cutting height (**CH**). Place the ruler diagonally on the strip so this line is on the previously cut 45 degree edge. For added cutting accuracy, keep the 45 degree line along the bottom of the strip. Rotary cut the diamond. After cutting three diamonds, cut a new 45 degree edge.

Left-Handed   Right-Handed

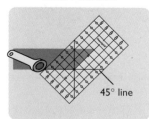
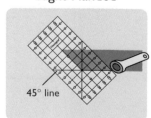

45 Degree Parallelogram

A 45 degree parallelogram looks like an elongated 45 degree diamond. It is easy to cut, but keep in mind that the width of the diagonal cut will never be the same as the height of the strip.

Schoolhouse

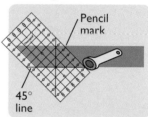

No-Fail Figuring

1. Determine the finished height (**H**) and the finished length (**L**).

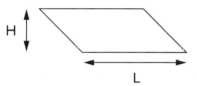

2. Add ½ inch to the height (**H**) to determine the cutting height (**CH**) and ¾ inch to the length (**L**) to determine the cutting length (**CL**).

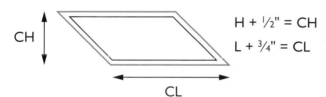

H + ½" = CH

L + ¾" = CL

3. Cut a fabric strip as wide as your cutting height (**CH**), and cut the end at a 45 degree angle (page 48).

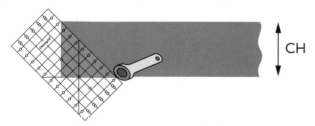

CH

4. Measure your cutting length (**CL**) across the top of the strip, and place a small pencil mark there.

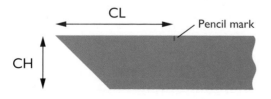

CL

Pencil mark

CH

No-Fail Cutting

To cut the parallelogram, place the ruler *diagonally* on the strip with the 45 degree line along the bottom of the strip and the side of the ruler aligned with the pencil mark. The number on the ruler that lines up with the 45 degree edge is the width of the diagonal cut. Rotary cut the parallelogram.

Left-Handed

Right-Handed

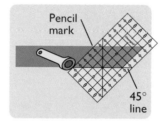

Pencil mark

45° line

Pencil mark

45° line

Cut Smart

If you are using a ruler that has only one 45 degree line on each end, *right-handed quilters* will use the 45 degree line located on the top part of the ruler, and *left-handed quilters* will use the 45 degree line located on the bottom part of the ruler.

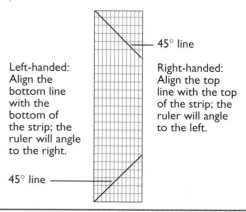

45° line

Left-handed: Align the bottom line with the bottom of the strip; the ruler will angle to the right.

Right-handed: Align the top line with the top of the strip; the ruler will angle to the left.

45° line

45 Degree Single Prism

A single prism is a rectangle with one end cut into a point made of 45 degree angles.

Bachelor's Puzzle

No-Fail Figuring

1. Determine the finished height (**H**) and the finished length (**L**).

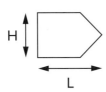

2. Add ½ inch to the height (**H**) to determine your cutting height (**CH**) and ⅝ inch to the length (**L**) to determine your cutting length (**CL**).

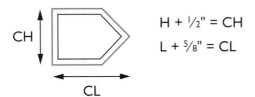

$$H + \frac{1}{2}" = CH$$
$$L + \frac{5}{8}" = CL$$

3. Cut a fabric strip as wide as your cutting height (**CH**). Square up one end.

4. Cut a rectangle as long as your cutting length (**CL**). Divide the cutting height (**CH**) in half and make small pencil marks in the middle of the short sides of the rectangle.

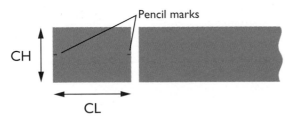

Pencil marks

No-Fail Cutting

First Cut

Place the rectangle on the mat as shown. Position a 6-inch square ruler diagonally on the rectangle with the 45 degree line running through both pencil marks and the tip of the ruler directly on top of one of the pencil marks. Rotary cut the triangle.

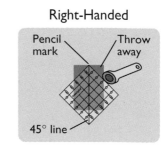

Second Cut

Rotate the mat 90 degrees, and cut off the other triangle.

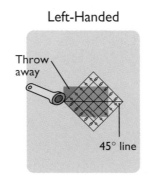
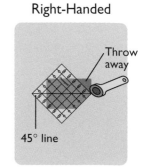

45 Degree Double Prism

Cutting a double prism with 45 degree angles is fast and fun if you use a 6-inch square ruler.

Nonesuch

No-Fail Figuring

1. Determine the finished height (**H**) and finished length (**L**).

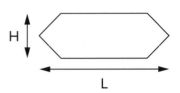

2. Add ½ inch to the height (**H**) to determine your cutting height (**CH**) and ¾ inch to the length (**L**) to determine your cutting length (**CL**).

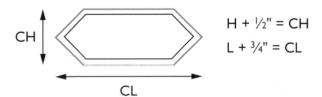

$$H + \tfrac{1}{2}" = CH$$
$$L + \tfrac{3}{4}" = CL$$

3. Cut a fabric strip as wide as your cutting height (**CH**). Square up one end (page 32).

4. Cut a rectangle as long as your cutting length (**CL**). Divide the cutting height (**CH**) in half and make small pencil marks in the middle of the short sides of the rectangle.

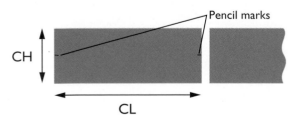

No-Fail Cutting

First Cut

Place the rectangle on the mat as shown. Position a 6-inch square ruler diagonally on the rectangle with the 45 degree line running through the top pencil mark and the tip of the ruler directly on top of the pencil mark. Rotary cut the excess triangle from both sides of the ruler, rotating the mat 90 degrees for the second triangle (see the opposite page).

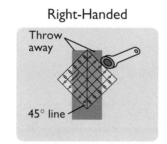

Second Cut

Rotate the mat so the opposite end of the rectangle is on top. Position the 6-inch square ruler diagonally on the rectangle with the 45 degree line and the tip of the ruler running directly through the pencil mark. Rotary cut the excess triangle from both sides of the ruler, rotating the mat 90 degrees for the second triangle.

60 Degree Diamond

A key thing to remember when cutting a 60 degree diamond is that the height determines the cutting width.

Tumbling Blocks

No-Fail Figuring

1. Determine the finished height (**H**).

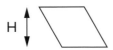

2. Add ½ inch to determine the cutting height (**CH**).

H + ½" = CH

3. Cut a fabric strip as wide as your cutting height (**CH**).

Cut Smart

To check the accuracy of the diamond, fold it in half, long point to long point. The long sides should be equal.

If your ruler has only one 60 degree line on each end, *left-handed* quilters will use the line located near the 1-inch line, and *right-handed* quilters will use the line located on the opposite end of the ruler.

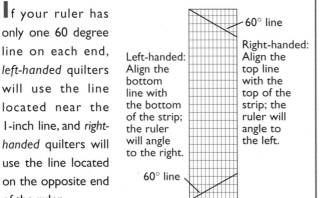

60° line

Left-handed: Align the bottom line with the bottom of the strip; the ruler will angle to the right.

Right-handed: Align the top line with the top of the strip; the ruler will angle to the left.

60° line

No-Fail Cutting

First Cut

Begin by cutting the strip at a 60 degree angle. *Right-handed quilters:* Align the 60 degree line on the lower *right* edge of the ruler with the bottom of the strip. The ruler will be angled to the *left*. *Left-handed quilters:* Align the 60 degree line on the lower *left* edge of the ruler with the bottom of the strip. The ruler will be angled to the *right*. Cut off the excess.

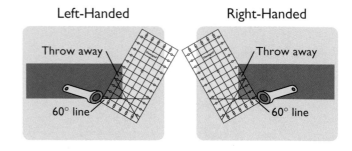

Left-Handed   Right-Handed

Throw away   Throw away

60° line   60° line

Second Cut

Find the line on your ruler that corresponds to the cutting height (**CH**). Place the ruler diagonally on the strip so that the line is on the cut 60 degree edge. For added accuracy, keep the 60 degree line along the bottom of the strip. Rotary cut the diamond. After cutting three diamonds, cut the edge at a 60 degree angle again.

Left-Handed   Right-Handed

60° line   60° line

Hexagon

A hexagon is actually a 60 degree diamond, minus two of its points. Once you see how easy it is to rotary cut a hexagon, you'll never go back to paper templates or patterns.

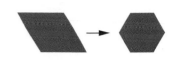

Grandmother's
Flower Garden

No-Fail Figuring

1. Determine the finished height (**H**).

2. Add ½ inch to determine the cutting height (**CH**).

$H + \frac{1}{2}" = CH$

3. Cut a strip as wide as your cutting height (**CH**).

4. Cut a 60 degree diamond (see the opposite page) using your cutting height (**CH**).

Cut Smart

Measure from one straight edge to another to quickly check that you have a perfect hexagon. The measurement in each direction should equal the original unfinished size of the 60 degree diamond!

Same measurement in all directions

No-Fail Cutting

First Cut

Place the diamond on the mat as shown. Divide the cutting height (**CH**) in half. *Right-handed quilters:* Position the ruler so the line corresponding to half your cutting height runs through the two short points and the 60 degree line is on the lower *right* edge of the diamond. *Left-handed quilters:* Position the ruler so the line corresponding to half your cutting height runs through the two short points, and the 60 degree line is on the lower *left* edge of the diamond. Rotary cut and discard the triangle tip.

Left-Handed

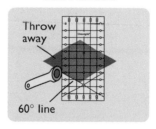

Right-Handed

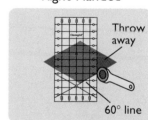

Second Cut

Rotate the mat 180 degrees. Position the ruler so the line corresponding to half your cutting height (**CH**) again runs through the two short points. For added cutting accuracy, keep the appropriate 60 degree line on the lower edge of the diamond.

Left-Handed

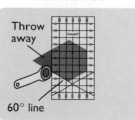

Right-Handed

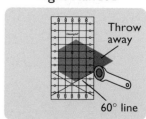

No-Fail Piecing

Selecting Your Sewing Equipment

Because I'm basically a skeptical person, I never use quiltmaking methods or tools simply because someone says they are good. I have tried out hundreds of products and pieces of equipment in my quiltmaking career, and I have become fond of a few essential tools that help me produce the highest-quality quilts possible. I share this information with you in this section, but remember: My preferences may not suit you exactly. Take the time to find the tools and equipment that fit your quiltmaking needs.

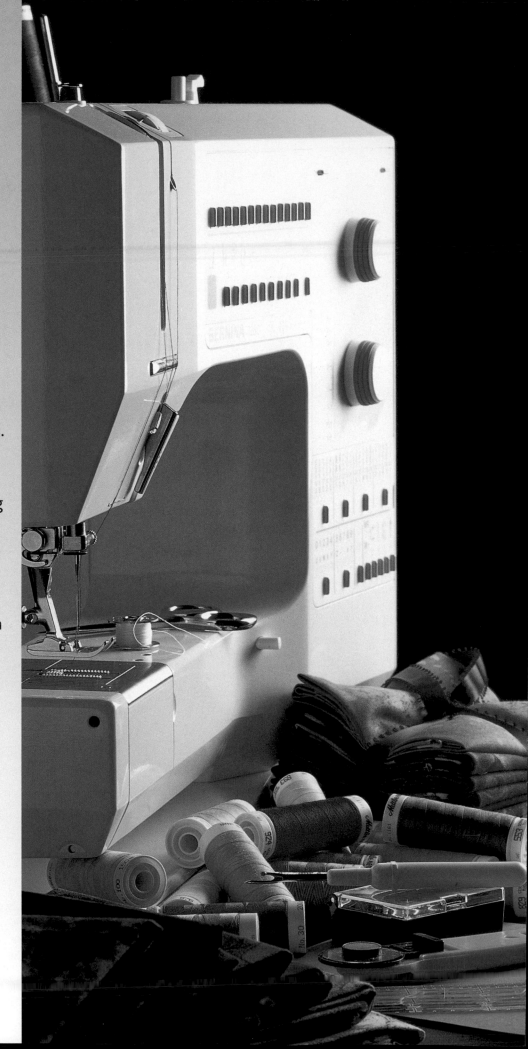

Sewing Machine

Quilters ask me all the time what type of sewing machine I use and what type they should buy. The more expensive the sewing machine, the better the quilts will be, right? Not necessarily. The most important consideration when buying a sewing machine is what *you* are going to use the machine for.

You have to be best friends with your machine. Once you've "bonded" and you understand how it works, you'll be able to tackle any technique. Do you want to machine piece and machine appliqué? If so, look for a model that either includes or can accommodate an open-toe or an appliqué foot—and the throatplate to use with it as well. Will you need the machine to zigzag or do machine thread embellishments? Make sure the machine you buy has these features. Do you want a real workhorse that will machine quilt contentedly for long periods at a time? Then you'll want to get one with a better motor and features especially suited to machine quilting.

For the past 25 years I have sewn primarily on a White sewing machine. I also sew on a Bernina 1260 and a Featherweight 221, and I like these, too. Each has advantages for certain projects, and I use them all, depending on what technique I'm doing. To find out which machine I'll sew on for a particular use, I try them out. You should, too, when you are shopping for your sewing machine.

Here are my general recommendations for you if you're ready to look for a sewing machine.

Buying a Sewing Machine

- If you have a very tight budget, scour yard sales and flea markets for an older model (30 years or more) that's an all-metal workhorse.

- If you have around $500, get a Featherweight 221 that will always guarantee you straight seams and an accurate ¼-inch seam allowance.

- If your budget is more flexible, buy a medium-priced middle-of-the-line model in any name-brand line (Bernina, Pfaff, or Viking).

- If you'll be doing a lot of machine embroidery or embellishments, invest in a computerized model.

I'm a great believer in knowing what you're looking for, so I created a Smart Shopper's Guide for Buying a Sewing Machine (page 58), which allows you to rate different machines on many different characteristics so you can make a wise choice. Here's what I recommend to anyone shopping for a new machine (and try all of these on each machine you are considering).

Road-Testing Sewing Machines

- Bring the type and size needles you normally use.

- Take along ¼-inch masking tape and do a sewing test (page 68) to see if it's capable of doing accurate straight-line sewing.

- See if the machine will slowly sew over your favorite straight pins.

- Sew a complete quilt block together. (Don't forget to take an iron.)

- Bring a small quilt sandwich (with fabric, batting, and backing) and try machine quilting it. (Don't forget to bring different needles and threads.)

- Carefully check out the availability (and cost) of different presser feet.

Exit quickly if the salesperson doesn't want you to test the machine or is only interested in showing you how the machine will sew over a leather belt or repair a sneaker! You are entitled to see how the machine will perform on the kinds of tasks you'll be doing at home.

Presser Foot

The presser foot you use for machine piecing is very important—almost as important as the sewing machine you use! I have found it's essential to be able to see exactly where my needle is sewing in relation to the fabric. Therefore, I use a foot that does *not* have a metal bar running across the two front legs, as shown in **Diagram 1A** on page 59. (Bars cover up the area where I am sewing, and I can't see exactly where my needle is.)

Sewing with an open-toe foot is critical to the

Smart Shopper's Guide for Buying a Sewing Machine

Photocopy and fill out this page before you leave your house, and make extra copies to fill out as you try out machines. Carefully consider each question, and rate how important it is to you that you buy a machine with that feature. Fill out a form for each machine as you try it, then compare the sheets to your original one at home to find the best machine for you.

Name of Machine/Model Number_____

Question	Answer	Comments
1. Is the sewing machine portable?		
2. Does the case or the sewing machine have a carrying handle?		
3. Can the machine be used both in and out of a cabinet?		
4. Does the machine have good lighting?		
5. Is there a large sewing surface surrounding the throatplate?		
6. Can the machine be turned into a free arm by removing the sewing tray?		
7. Does the machine have the option of a knee or foot control?		
8. Is the machine easy to thread?		
9. Is the bobbin easy to wind?		
10. Is the bobbin easy to get in and out of the machine?		
11. Are the top and bottom tensions easy to adjust?		
12. Does the machine stitch correctly if you use a different weight thread in the bobbin case than on top?		
13. Does the machine have a thread cutter?		
14. Does the machine have a "needle down" feature?		
15. Does the machine allow you to sew directly into reverse?		
16. Is the reverse button/lever easy to reach?		
17. Does the machine have stitch options?		
18. Will the machine zigzag?		
19. Does it have a zigzag throatplate and accompanying presser foot?		
20. Does it have a single-hole throatplate and accompanying presser foot?		
21. Do extra feet come with the machine?		
22. Does the machine come with an even-feed/walking foot?		
23. Do the feed dogs allow you to sew a straight seam?		
24. Can the feed dogs be dropped?		
25. Does the machine sew equally well on thin and heavy fabric?		

accuracy of set-in seams and mitered corners. The open area allows you to see where the needle is compared to the fabric and previously sewn seams. The underside of the foot should have either no grooved-out area or a small grooved-out area. Don't mistake this for an open-toe/appliqué foot, shown in **Diagram 1B,** which has too much space grooved out of its bottom and will not properly grip the fabric when you start to piece your quilt.

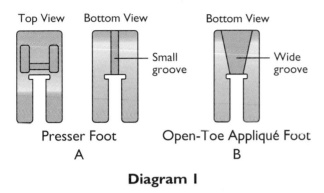

Top View   Bottom View   Bottom View

Small groove

Wide groove

Presser Foot
A

Open-Toe Appliqué Foot
B

Diagram 1

When I first realized that I needed a foot with an open toe, I tried to make one myself. I went into my husband's shop, put one of my presser feet in a vise, and took a saw to it. Needless to say, I destroyed a perfectly adequate foot. Then my husband took pity on me and used a sharp metal blade to saw off the little bars, and he filed down the rough spots.

To customize one of your existing presser feet for perfect piecing, choose a presser foot that looks like an appliqué foot but has a smooth bottom and two metal bars that run across the two front legs. Cut or file the two bars off with a hacksaw or a small metal file, as shown in **Diagram 2.** Be sure to file smooth any burrs or rough edges to prevent finger cuts and/or sewing problems. You will see this customized foot in the photographs throughout this book.

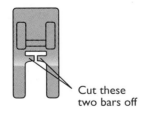

Cut these two bars off

Diagram 2

Notions

Even the fanciest, most accurate, straightest-sewing machine is only as good as the other equipment and supplies that you are working with. Here are some of my suggestions for notions to keep on hand when you're quiltmaking.

Thread

The thread you use depends on the fabric you are sewing on. Many people think that all 100 percent cotton thread is the same—not true! Some thread leaves a lot of lint buildup in your bobbin case. Other thread will unwind from the spool in only one direction without binding or tangling, so you can't put the spool on your spindle upside down.

There are several different weights of thread. I use a 50-weight cotton, which is about the middle weight of the commercially available threads. I like it because it's a little thinner and takes up a little less room in my seam allowance, but it's thick enough that I don't worry that my seams will come unsewn. Talk with your sewing machine dealer and quilt shop owner to see what will work best with your machine, and always try out new threads on scraps or samples before you sew a quilt.

I use only 100 percent cotton thread when sewing 100 percent cotton fabric. I learned this the hard way. I had previously used cotton-covered

My Favorite Things

I especially like Mettler cotton thread. It is 50-weight, my preferred weight to work with, and has a beautiful silk finish. There are over 100 colors to choose from.

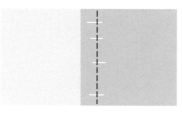
polyester for sewing garments, and I assumed it would be fine for quiltmaking. Several years ago I made an eight-pointed star. I hand quilted around the star using cotton-covered polyester thread. After about five years, I noticed that the quilting thread had cut that star shape into the background fabric. I examined all my quilts, and none that I had used cotton thread on had any damage. So from that moment on, I switched to 100 percent cotton thread, and I have not had any more problems.

Needles

Most quilters don't give needles enough thought or credit. Do you realize that without this long, slender piece of hardened steel, you wouldn't be able to use a sewing machine?

The simple assortment of needles I use regularly (see the opposite page) works very well for precision

Nancy's Bag of Tricks

To check your stitch length, sew two pieces of fabric together. Cut the thread off very close to the last stitch. If the last stitch comes unsewn, you have too *few* stitches to the inch. On the other hand, if you are having trouble ripping out seams, you have too *many* stitches to the inch. When sewing on 100 percent cotton fabric, I set my stitch length to between 10 and 12 stitches per inch.

If you're having tension troubles, try changing your needle before you adjust the top or bottom tension on your sewing machine! It may be that you need a different needle to sew best on the fabric you're working with.

piecing. They pierce the fabric cleanly instead of pushing the fibers apart. A size 12 or larger needle tends to mangle my pieces when I start to sew—this is most apparent when I sew diamonds together and the tips get pushed down into the throatplate.

Always keep a sharp needle in your machine! The most common problem with needles is that they become dull, and they aren't changed frequently enough. Remember that the needle is pushed through the fabric hundreds of times each hour, so change your needle after about 15 hours of sewing. The cost of a needle is insignificant compared to the cost of a damaged bobbin case or producing poor-quality work, which you may have to look at for years to come.

There are two symptoms of a dull needle. First, the sewing machine will start to make a dull "thud" sound while sewing. Second, you'll see little white pulls in the fabric along the seam allowance on the wrong side of your sewn unit, as shown in **Diagram 3.** This happens when the needle is so dull that it actually breaks the threads in the fabric.

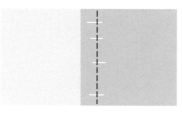

Diagram 3

Pins

I constantly marvel at how often during quiltmaking I use techniques I learned from my mother or grandmother. When my mother taught me to sew, she insisted that I pin frequently. At the time I didn't think it was necessary (who wanted to take the time to pin?), but I did it anyway. Years later, I'm glad I listened to her. This habit has helped me to precision-piece and make prize-winning quilts.

In 1987 I did extensive pin research. I was creating a "hump" when butting and pinning my pieces together, and my sewing machine wouldn't sew smoothly over it. The machine would either jam at the intersection or veer off. I wasn't getting the

My Favorite Things

Schmetz needles work best for me. They are readily available and come in lots of sizes. I do all my machine piecing with one of the following needles:

- **Universal, size 11/75** for normal machine piecing.
- **Denim/Jeans or Microtex Sharp, size 10/70** for loosely woven fabric or fabric with a silky finish. These needles are slightly sharper, so they go through difficult fabrics more easily.

I use only #5004 IBC Fine Silk Pins by Clotilde. I can successfully sew over them without breaking a needle, and they don't create a "hump" when pinning. They are long and thin, have a small head, and are very sharp. If you need a pin with a larger head, try the #5003 IBC Fine Silk Pins by Clotilde. These pins are the same diameter and length, and they have the smallest glass head that I've been able to find.

professional results I wanted. After some thought, I realized that the problem was my straight pins. Conventional pins were too large in diameter, creating a hump, and the large head on the pin didn't allow the fabric to rest flat on the throatplate of the machine. The fabric was being fed through the machine at a slight angle, causing inaccurate sewing.

Armed with this information, I collected 24 different types of straight pins. For a while, the straight pins that came with JCPenney shirts were high on my comparison chart. The only problem was that I couldn't keep buying my husband dress shirts! After a lot of searching, I found pins I liked (see above).

Seam Ripper vs. Scissors

After having carpal tunnel surgery on my wrists some years ago, I found that the pressure of a seam ripper in the palm of my hand was very stressful—compounded by the jerking motion of ripping out stitches.

A friend gave me a small pair of surgical scissors. I immediately saw the benefits of using these rather than a seam ripper. They exert no pressure on the palm; the finger holes in the handle are large, so you can easily and quickly get your fingers in and out; and your fabric distorts less while snipping stitches.

Surgical scissors can be found at medical supply stores and are very inexpensive. I've also found them at quilting shows and even flea markets! To successfully rip out stitches with surgical scissors, use the following technique:

1. Clip the stitches along the length of the seam at approximately 1-inch intervals.

2. Turn the fabric over.

3. Gently pull out the bobbin thread with your fingernails.

This method is much gentler on your fabric than ripping with a seam ripper. Also, you won't have tons of little pieces of thread to pick off!

Masking Tape and Strapping Tape

I use these two types of tape to locate the ¼-inch seam allowance on my sewing machine (page 68). Be sure to purchase masking tape that is truly ¼ inch. (I usually take a small rotary ruler to the store to check and make sure.)

Strapping tape is also known as packing or filament tape. It has nylon threads that run along its length, and it is super-strong. It can't be ripped; it must be cut with scissors or a rotary cutter. (Another reason to save your old rotary blades!)

Nancy's Bag of Tricks

Recycle those large-headed pins! I stuck mine into a small bulletin board at a slight angle (see the photo on page 63), and I store my spools of thread on them. My thread is always at hand, and I can see all the colors at a glance.

Setting Up Your Workspace

For many years I sewed on our kitchen table. I would haul out my heavy sewing machine, my cutting equipment, and my ironing setup, spread all my fabric out on the table, and start working. At four o'clock I would pack up and put everything back into a closet to get ready for dinner. Poof! My sewing room would change back into a kitchen. Needless to say, I wasn't thrilled with this arrangement. When I was finally able to move everything into a separate room just for sewing, I was delirious with joy! Since I've worked in both kinds of spaces, I have tips to share on making the most of your workspace, wherever it is.

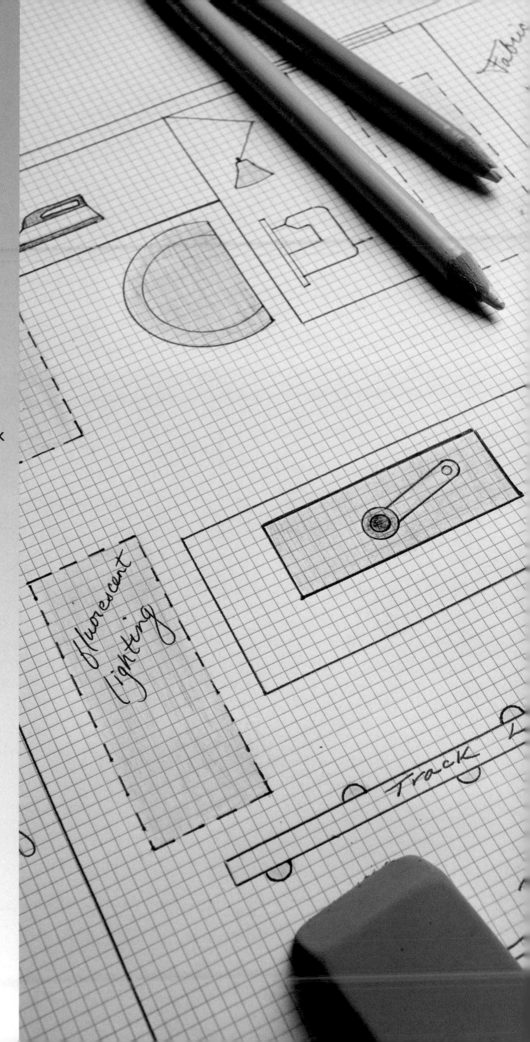

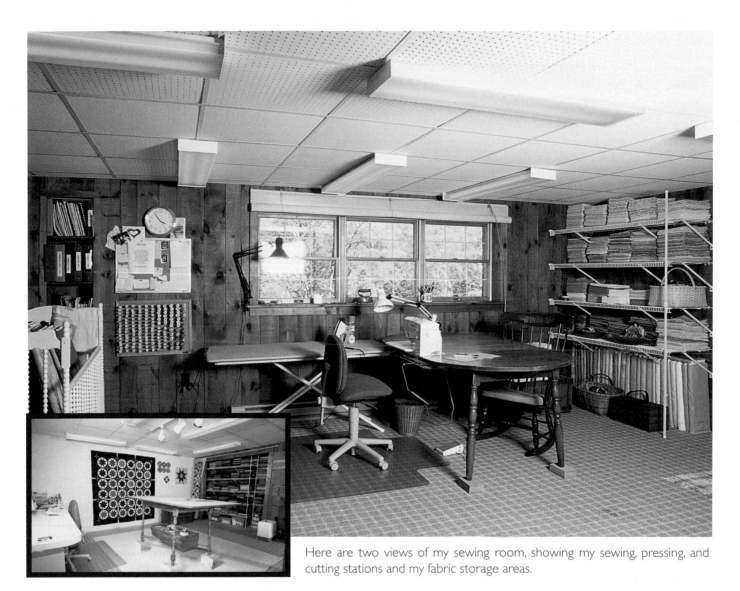

Here are two views of my sewing room, showing my sewing, pressing, and cutting stations and my fabric storage areas.

Lighting

My sewing room has four types of lighting: natural lighting, fluorescent overhead lighting, my sewing machine light, and a swing-arm lamp attached to my sewing table. Natural lighting is important because it is the best light for being able to accurately see color and the action happening underneath your needle. If at all possible, try to position your sewing machine next to a window. Not only will you be able to take full advantage of the natural light, you'll also be able to look outside every so often to relax your eyes, neck, and shoulders.

Overhead lighting is also a must. I prefer fluorescent overhead lights because they light up a bigger area and cascade into a bigger space than regular lightbulbs do. Your sewing machine light is

a given—never, ever buy a sewing machine that doesn't have a light that shines directly down on your sewing area.

A swing-arm lamp is important because it intensifies the brightness of your work area so you can always see exactly what's happening where you're sewing. Also, if you are doing other close work—like accurate pinning, nipping off dog ears, or cutting apart chain-pieced patches—you can reposition the swing-arm lamp to illuminate other areas of your workspace.

The combination of these four light sources eliminates shadows and adds to my depth perception when I'm working with different fabric patterns and weaves. Of the four lights, I think the swing-arm lamp and the sewing machine light are the most important. Here is how I have the lighting in my sewing room set up.

Lighting Setup

- I like the natural light to cascade onto the throat-plate of my machine because that's the most important area of my workspace. I position my sewing machine near the window in my sewing room with the needle end toward the window to take advantage of this natural light.

- Overhead fluorescent lighting should provide plenty of overall general-purpose lighting, so I have lights positioned in my ceiling that reflect onto either side of my machine.

- My swing-arm lamp is adjusted so that it shines onto the throatplate, directly onto the fabric that is being fed through the machine. This ensures that I can see where my needle is in relation to the fabric.

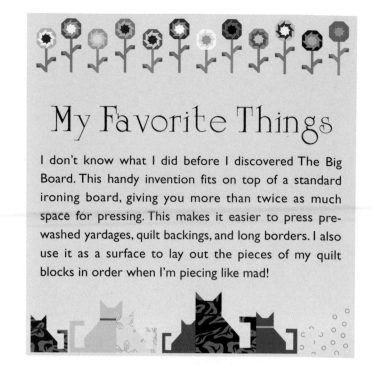

My Favorite Things

I don't know what I did before I discovered The Big Board. This handy invention fits on top of a standard ironing board, giving you more than twice as much space for pressing. This makes it easier to press pre-washed yardages, quilt backings, and long borders. I also use it as a surface to lay out the pieces of my quilt blocks in order when I'm piecing like mad!

Sewing Table

I like to have my sewing machine fit *into* a table because I find it awkward and hard on my arms if I sew with the machine sitting *on* a table. When my machine sat on top of a table, I always had aches in my shoulders and neck from reaching up too high to sew. I had to stop frequently when I was sewing to stretch my weary neck and shoulders.

I had my husband cut a section out of a wooden table so the bed of my sewing machine would be flush with the tabletop. He attached two iron supports beneath the tabletop to hold the weight of the machine. This gives me plenty of work space and keeps my machine at a comfortable height while I sew. This, in turn, lets me work for longer periods without discomfort, so I think about piecing accurately, not about getting a pain in my back or neck!

I have an L-shaped arrangement, with an ironing board (see "My Favorite Things," this page) at my side that I can use for pressing, laying out shapes to be pieced, or supporting the weight of a quilt or quilt top when attaching borders. I adjusted the height of the ironing board so that my left elbow can rest on it while I'm sewing. This reduces arm strain and helps keep my arm from getting tired as quickly as it otherwise would.

Chair

One of the most important items to invest in is a secretarial swivel chair that has an adjustable back and height. Secretarial chairs are ergonomically designed for long hours of sitting. Arms are optional (I find they get in my way), but make sure that you purchase a chair with *five* legs and wheels, not just four. Five-wheel models are much more stable, and they tend to be sturdier, too.

I also recommend investing in a plastic rug-guard. These mats serve two purposes: They let you move around easier, especially on carpeted surfaces, and they save your carpet from being ruined by a chair with wheels. And as an added bonus, if you spill your pins, they're easy to find and pick up off the plastic mat!

Spend time adjusting the height and tilt of your chair. Match the height of your chair to the height of your sewing machine, not the table. Make sure that your feet rest comfortably on the ground and that you don't have to reach up to sew. Your shoulders should be relaxed, and you should bend only your neck to sew at your machine. If you're having trouble finding a chair position that lets you sew comfortably, you may need a lower sewing table.

Ironing Board

Unless you want the aerobic exercise of sprinting from your sewing machine to the ironing board, it's a smart idea to set up your ironing board and iron next to your sewing machine. You will cut down on wasted steps, and it's really a time saver. Since it will be much more convenient, you will also be more inclined to press *each* seam as you sew.

When pressing sewn pieces, I have found that I get better results if the foam pad on my ironing board is a *maximum* of ¼ inch thick. If you use a thicker pad, the pieced units will sink into the foam, and you won't get a good, crisp seam. I use a thick foam pad only when pressing appliquéd blocks.

Iron

After having carpal tunnel surgery on my wrists, I realized how harmful a heavy iron can be. I now use a lightweight iron. Most people don't understand that it's the *heat* of the iron that does the pressing, not the weight. For more details, see page 95.

If you're like I am and you knock your iron over frequently, eventually the thermostat never really allows the iron to turn the heat all the way off. For this reason, always unplug the iron (turning it off just isn't enough) when you're not using it.

My Favorite Things

I use a Black & Decker Light & Easy iron. It's light enough for me to lift without hurting my wrists, and it presses like a dream. As an added bonus, they now make models that come with an extra-long power cord!

Design Wall

A design wall is a way for you to look at your work in progress from a distance and get a better idea of how your quilt is coming together and what it will look like when it's assembled.

I didn't have a design wall when I first started quiltmaking, so I would lay out my work on a full-size bed and stand on a chair to get an overhead view. (This didn't work too well.) Then I graduated to placing the pieces of my quilt on the living room sofa—I could see the pieces on the back fine, but I couldn't see the pieces on the seat as well. With both of these methods, it took a great deal of imagination to visualize what the quilt was going to look like! Fortunately there are easy, inexpensive ways to make your own design wall.

Most types of fabric will stick to flannel or cotton batting without pins, so a flannel sheet or cotton batt pushpinned to a wall is a great idea. I hung a full-size white flannel sheet on one wall after I moved into my own sewing room. I used this as my design wall for several years, and it worked very well. But I really went to town when I moved into an even larger sewing room (25 × 25 feet), and I covered one whole wall with Warm and Natural batting—and I love it. I just stuck pushpins through the batting and into the wall every 6 inches along the ceiling and floor. The cotton batting doesn't sag as the flannel sheet did, and I have a whole wall—one entire end of my sewing room—to use for laying out quilts.

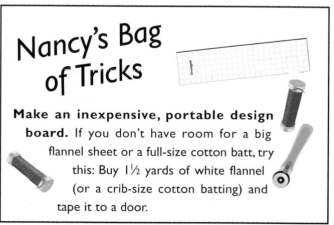

Nancy's Bag of Tricks

Make an inexpensive, portable design board. If you don't have room for a big flannel sheet or a full-size cotton batt, try this: Buy 1½ yards of white flannel (or a crib-size cotton batting) and tape it to a door.

Piecing Basics Made Easy

Of all the piecing techniques that I use and teach, there are a handful that I just can't live without. These are techniques that I use every day, on every quilt that I make, and they are essential to accurate quiltmaking. I developed these techniques through trial and error—and lots of it!—to be understandable, easy, and accurate. No matter what class I'm teaching, if we're going to be piecing a project, I make sure everyone has these six basic techniques under their belts before we start.

Accurate ¼-Inch Seam Allowance

Getting an accurate ¼-inch seam allowance is probably both the most important and the most challenging task facing quiltmakers. It's important because a ¼-inch seam allowance is the industry standard—which means that virtually all quilt patterns available are based on being able to sew an accurate ¼-inch seam.

Here's an example of why a ¼-inch seam is so important. If you're a little off on your ¼ inch and you sew two 1½-inch squares together with a slightly larger seam allowance, they will measure slightly less than 2½ inches long. When you try to fit them precisely to an adjacent 2½-inch rectangle, they just won't fit! Just two seams into your quilt, and already you're having accuracy problems.

I say that the ¼-inch seam allowance is challenging because it takes time, practice, and a little determination to find—and then you have to train yourself to use it accurately all the time. But if you just take the time up front to get yourself set in the pattern of a truly accurate ¼ inch, you'll be much happier with the results you get when you're piecing your blocks together into a quilt top.

There are two things you need to be aware of before you try to locate the ¼-inch seam allowance on your sewing machine. First, the thickness (diameter) of your sewing thread will affect the accuracy of your ¼ inch. Thinner thread takes up less space than thicker thread. There's not much of a difference, but the more seam allowances you sew, the bigger the difference. Just think: If one seam is off by $\frac{1}{32}$ inch, by the time you get all the way across a 9-inch pieced block you could be off by as much as

⅛ inch. And that's just one block in an entire quilt! When you try to sew a block like that to a lattice strip or to another block, your compounded errors will certainly come back to haunt you.

But don't give up—just remember to allow for the variation in the thickness of your thread. Find your ¼-inch seam allowance each time you change thread types (page 59), and test it (page 68) before beginning to piece a quilt.

The second factor to keep in mind when you're finding your ¼ inch is that when you press your seam allowance to one side, it forms a small "hump" or ridge on the front of the piece. One layer of fabric must fold 180 degrees over the thread when you press your seam allowance to one side, so the finished size of that piece will be *slightly* smaller than desired. But don't let this discourage you—just remember to account for it, and use good pressing habits (page 92).

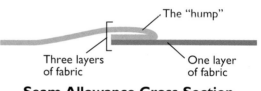

The "hump"

Three layers of fabric

One layer of fabric

Seam Allowance Cross-Section

Because of the combination of the thread thickness and the hump, you lose a tiny amount of fabric during piecing. To compensate for this loss, you should sew with a *scant* (slightly undersize) ¼-inch seam allowance. (That's what I show you how to set up here and what you test for when you follow the steps in "Piece Smart" on page 68.) Follow this simple, No-Fail method for getting an accurate ¼-inch seam allowance, and you will always have blocks that are the right size. And accurate blocks make assembling your quilt top a breeze!

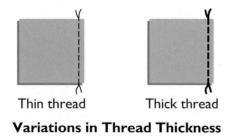

Thin thread   Thick thread
Variations in Thread Thickness

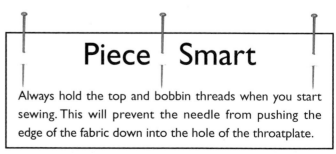

Piece Smart

Always hold the top and bobbin threads when you start sewing. This will prevent the needle from pushing the edge of the fabric down into the hole of the throatplate.

Setting Up Your Seam Allowance

1. Position the needle so that the point is ready to enter the hole in the throatplate. Place a long piece of ¼-inch masking tape on the throatplate so the needle just barely touches the left edge of the tape.

2. Butt another piece of tape to the right of the first piece. Run the tape just up to the front edge of the feed dogs. (If you cover the feed dogs, the fabric won't feed through the machine properly.) Remove the first piece of tape.

Nancy's Bag of Tricks

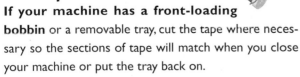

If your machine has a front-loading bobbin or a removable tray, cut the tape where necessary so the sections of tape will match when you close your machine or put the tray back on.

Piece Smart

Perform this simple sewing test to be sure you are sewing an accurate ¼-inch seam allowance. I always have students do this before beginning their class project.

1. **Cut** a 2⅞-inch fabric square (page 37).
2. **Cut** it in half diagonally to make two triangles (page 38). Place the triangles right sides together.
3. **Butt** the fabric edges against your tape guide, and sew the two triangles together along the long bias edge to make a square.
4. **Press** the triangle square open.
5. **Place** a ruler on top of the square and measure it.

If you have used a perfect ¼-inch seam allowance, your new pieced square will measure 2½ × 2½ inches. If your test square measures too *small*, move your tape guide *toward* the needle. If your square is too *big*, move the tape *away from* the needle. Sew another test square until you have a perfect ¼ inch.

3. Stack six to eight layers of strapping tape on top of the masking tape, exactly lining up the edge nearest to the needle. This creates a ridge to butt fabric against so it won't ride over the top of the tape.

Butting Seams

Matching seams when sewing units of a block together is something that every quilter I know struggles with. I think that it's the first thing people look at in a quilt: "Oh! Look how well you matched your seams!" But it shouldn't be a struggle to get compliments on your matching seams. This simple method for butting seams makes it quite easy to match seams. All you do is press opposing seam allowances in opposite directions, and carefully match up sewn seams when sewing units together.

Notice that the seam allowance on the top unit in **Diagram 1A** is pressed to the left, and the seam allowance on the bottom unit is pressed to the right. When you butt these seams together to join them (into a Four Patch, in this case), the bulk of the seam allowances gets evenly distributed on the back of the block, as shown in **1B.** Half of the bulk lies to the left, and half lies to the right. This gives you a nice, flat block. This is one of my secrets to creating professional-quality work.

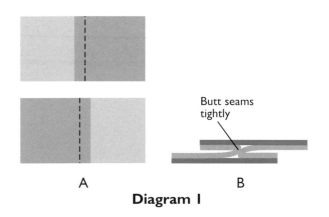

Butt seams tightly

A   B

Diagram 1

I draft each block before I sew a single seam in any quilt. I take this opportunity to make a grain line chart (page 24), and at the same time I analyze the block and decide which way to press each seam.

This sounds much more complicated than it is. Simply make sure that seams that will butt are pressed in opposite directions. Why take the time? Because you will avoid pressing and re-pressing your blocks, which can make them stretch, be misshapen, and not fit together as precisely as they should. Practice analyzing your blocks by drafting

different blocks and then making samples from your sketches. After a few times, you'll know which way to press so seams will butt.

Pinning

If you're from the "hold-and-sew" school (if you hold your unpinned patches together as they feed into the sewing machine), I'd guess that you very often have trouble matching your seams. And the same goes for all you quiltmakers who "stick" your patches together by pressing them one on top of another with a hot iron. To all of you I say this: Nothing beats pinning.

This is a lesson my mother and grandmother drilled into me over and over. At the time I shrugged them off, but I did what they told me just to humor them. And then one day I realized my sewing and seams were accurate every time! It's important to understand how critical pinning—and the exact placement of your straight pin—is, especially in relation to where the seam is butted.

Pinning holds your seams exactly in place, preventing the machine's tendencies to pull the top and bottom pieces at slightly different rates. To ensure a perfect seam, place a pin a hair (about $1/16$ inch) ahead of your butted seams, *not* exactly in the seams, as shown in **Diagram 2.** This placement prevents the seams from separating (which often happens when you pin right through the seam), and the centers of your blocks will match.

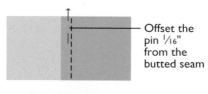

Offset the pin $1/16$" from the butted seam

Diagram 2

Accurate ¼-Inch Stop

In quiltmaking, the term *setting in* means sewing a precut shape into a matching angled opening. I can't tell you how many times quilters have told me they avoid any patterns with set-in seams. This is a shame because these folks will never know the joy of making wonderful blocks like Lone Star or Tumbling Blocks. After troubleshooting this vexing problem, I realized that the first sticking point for most quilters is knowing where to stop sewing a seam to get it ready for a set-in piece. So I developed a simple No-Fail method for a perfect ¼-inch stop that I always share with students.

A ¼-inch stop means that when you're sewing along a seam you stop exactly where that seam will meet the next seam. Once you master a perfect ¼-inch stop and use it when you're joining seams, you'll end up with a perfectly flat block with no gap or ridge where the seams come together. If you use this in conjunction with my No-Fail method for setting in pieces (page 72), you'll have perfectly accurate set-in seams every time. Here is an example using 45 degree diamonds (page 48).

1. Position two diamonds with right sides together. Gently butt the diamonds against your ¼-inch tape guide (page 68). Start sewing at the top of the diamonds.

2. Sew until you come to what you think is ¼ inch from the bottom edge of the diamonds. Stop sewing with the needle only one-quarter of the way into the fabric. (Don't go so far that you engage the bobbin; you don't want to create a stitch.)

3. Lift the presser foot up and turn the diamonds counterclockwise to see if they butt against your tape guide. If the diamonds butt against the tape, you have a perfect ¼-inch stop; proceed to Step 5. If they don't, as shown below, follow Step 4.

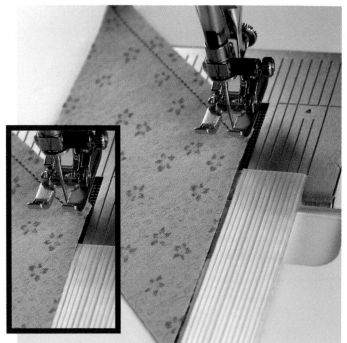

4. Turn the handwheel away from you until the needle comes out of the fabric. Carefully move the diamonds over until they butt to the tape.

5. Turn the handwheel toward you until three-quarters of the needle is in the fabric. (This time you want to engage the bobbin thread so you will create a stitch.)

6. Rotate the diamonds back to their original position. Lower the presser foot and backtack three stitches to create a perfect ¼-inch stop. And you know that the seam allowance will match when you set in squares and triangles because you will use the same tape guide.

◀ Backtack three stitches.

Nancy's Bag of Tricks

When you're sewing seams that require a perfect ¼-inch stop, such as when you're setting in pieces or mitering corners, never use a thread that matches your fabric color exactly. I use off-white thread on everything but navy and black fabrics (page 60). This way, your stitches will stand out from the fabric when you need to use the end of a sewn seam as a visual reference. This makes it much easier to see your previously sewn stitches!

Setting In Seams

If you have mastered the ¼-inch stop (page 70), you're ready to set in some pieces. My students tell me that even after they have mastered the ¼-inch stop, they still have problems with setting in. Usually the problems can be divided into two categories, and they both have to do with when you stop sewing the set-in seam.

 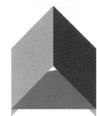

Problem 1   Problem 2

First Problem: A tiny pucker or pleat forms because you have sewn past the ¼-inch stop intersection.

Second Problem: A small hole forms because you have stopped sewing before you are close enough to the ¼-inch stop intersection.

Solution: When setting a shape in, stop sewing a "hair" (about 1⁄16 inch) from the ¼-inch stop in the previously sewn seam.

The proper technique is shown in the photo sequences on pages 72–75.

Always set triangles in before squares. Since the triangle and the diamond are cut at the same angle, their tips line up exactly. If you try to set a square in first, the tip of the diamond overhangs the edge of the square and it's harder to line up.

My No-Fail method for set-in seams will save you countless hours of frustration and ripping out—and who doesn't want to avoid that? For the example that follows, I will use an Eight-Pointed Star that was sewn together using my perfect ¼-inch stop technique (page 70).

Note: The presser foot shown in these photos is not commercially available. I altered an existing foot (Bernina's #0 foot) to make one that is more accurate for piecing (page 57). If you don't have an open-toe foot, follow the instructions in "Nancy's Bag of Tricks" on page 75.

Setting In Triangles

1. Number the wrong sides of the star and the triangles, as shown. It is very important that you have the correct piece facing you when you sew set-in seams.

2. Pin diamond side 1 to the corresponding triangle side 1, with right sides together. (The white triangle is hidden beneath the diamond, but ¼ inch extends past the bottom of the diamond.)

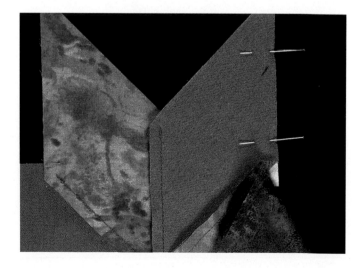

3. Butt the pieces against your tape guide (page 68), with the diamond on top, and sew from the outside tip toward the ¼-inch stop. Move the seam allowance out of the way as you sew toward the intersection. **Stop sewing ¹⁄₁₆ inch from the ¼-inch stop,** as shown in the inset photo, and backtack.

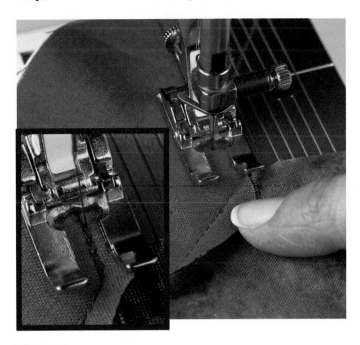

4. Pin triangle side 2 to diamond side 2, with right sides together and the wrong side of the diamond up.

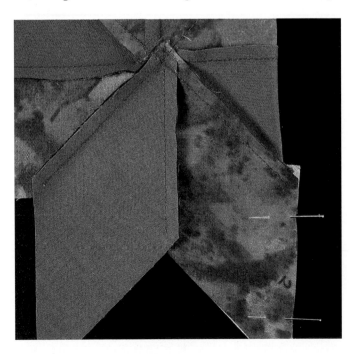

5. Butt the pieces against your tape guide and gently move the diamond seam allowance out of the way. Start sewing ¹⁄₁₆ inch from the ¼-inch stop. Take one stitch, backtack one stitch, then stitch to the end of the seam. (See "Nancy's Bag of Tricks" on page 75 for an alternate method if you don't have an open-toe foot.)

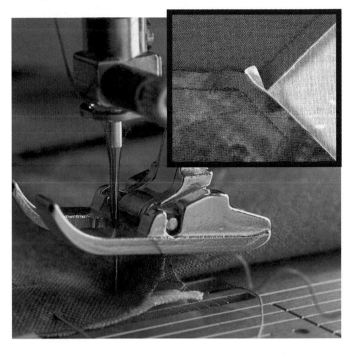

6. Press toward the triangle and nip off the dog ears with a small pair of scissors (page 77).

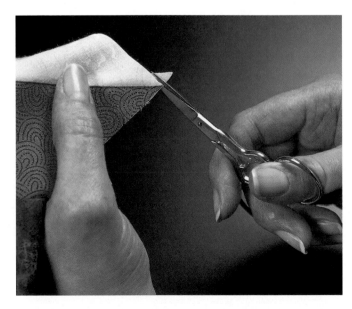

Setting In Squares

1. Number
the wrong sides of the star diamonds and squares, as shown. It is very important that you have the correct piece facing you when you sew set-in seams.

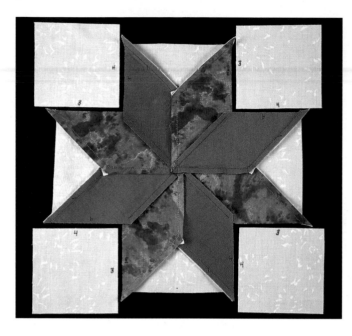

2. Pin
diamond side 3 to the corresponding square side 3, with right sides together. (The white square aligns with the outside edge of the triangle, and ¼ inch extends past the bottom of the diamond.)

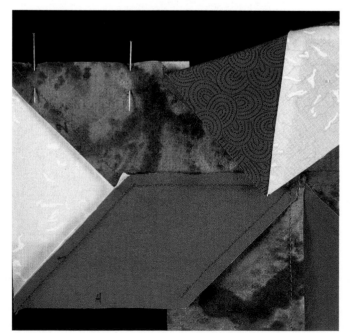

3. Butt
the pieces against your tape guide (page 68), with the diamond on top, and sew from the outside tip toward the ¼-inch stop on your pair of diamonds. Gently move the diamond seam out of the way as you sew toward it, as shown in the inset photo. **Stop sewing ¹⁄₁₆ inch from the ¼-inch stop, and backtack**.

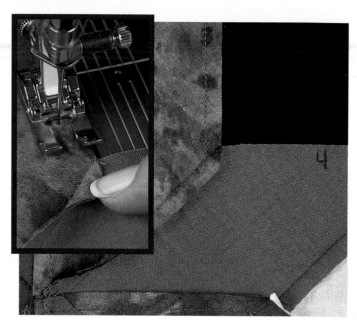

4. Pin
diamond side 4 to square side 4, with wrong sides together and the wrong side of the diamond facing you. (See "Nancy's Bag of Tricks" on the opposite page for an alternate method if you don't have an open-toe foot.)

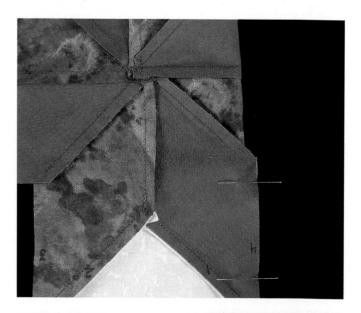

5. Butt the pieces against the tape guide and gently move the diamond seam out of the way. Start sewing 1/16 inch from the 1/4-inch stop, as shown: Take one stitch, backtack one stitch, then stitch to the end of the seam. Press.

If you have carefully followed my instructions for setting in triangles and squares, this is what your finished eight-pointed star will look like.

6. Press your seam allowances toward the triangles and squares so the stitching lines form an X at the outside points of the diamond. Then, when you join the blocks to each other or to lattice strips, stitch just to the outside of the X. No more cut-off diamond points!

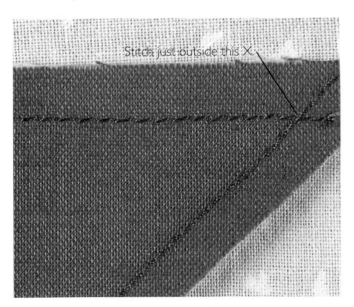

Stitch just outside this X.

Nancy's Bag of Tricks

If you don't have an open-toe presser foot (page 57), you won't be able to sew from the inside out in Step 5, as I do. Instead, sew with the triangle on top, and start at the outside of the seam. Stop sewing 1/16 inch from the 1/4-inch stop.

Chain Piecing

Chain piecing describes sewing two or more pairs of fabric patches together without cutting the thread or lifting the presser foot between pairs. With this technique you can sew sets of squares, half-square triangles, or any other shape one after another without removing them from the machine. This saves on time and thread and is very efficient—in fact, it's sometimes called assembly-line piecing!

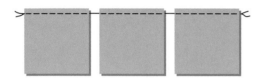

Cut threads to separate

After sewing a series of pieces, you will end up with a "chain" that has the individual units just barely joined together with connecting threads. To separate the units, simply snip the threads.

I chain piece whenever I can. The only time I don't is when I'm piecing seams that require a ¼-inch stop. Chain piecing doesn't offer the same advantages with those pieces because I can't butt the pieces one after another.

When I was piecing my full-size miniature feathered star quilt (shown on page 63), I had 36 blocks to piece. Each block had 48 feathers (half-square triangle pairs) to sew together. I chain pieced those 1,728 half-square triangles in one big, long chain. It wrapped around my sewing room several times, and I had to keep getting up to move it so the chain wouldn't get tangled. But it was worth it: I knew I had 1,728 accurately pieced squares when I was done!

Half-Square Triangles

Chain piecing half-square triangles can be a bit tricky if you own a temperamental sewing machine. A common problem occurs when you are nearing the end of your seam. The tip of the triangle tapers to a point, commonly known as a dog ear, and there is nothing on the left side of the feed dog for you to hold onto and steer with while sewing. Consequently, the beginning of the seam allowance is correct, but the seam allowance near the end can become either too small or too large as the tip wanders under the presser foot.

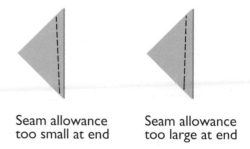

Seam allowance too small at end

Seam allowance too large at end

There are two tricks I combine to prevent my triangle pairs from veering off course: steering with a pin and overlapping tips. This combination works well because your machine is always sewing on fabric, so both sides of the feed dogs are grabbing fabric, and your triangles tend to stay straighter.

1. Pin a pair of triangles together where your seam will end. Start sewing the triangles together. Hold on to the pin head and "steer" the triangle when you get near the end to maintain a ¼-inch seam allowance.

2. Stop a hair (about ⅟₁₆ inch) from the edge of the piece with the needle down. Raise the presser foot and insert your next triangle, overlapping the dog ears as shown. Lower the presser foot and resume sewing. To separate, snip the threads that connect the triangles. (Don't worry if you snip into the fabric a hair—you'll be trimming off the dog ears eventually anyway.)

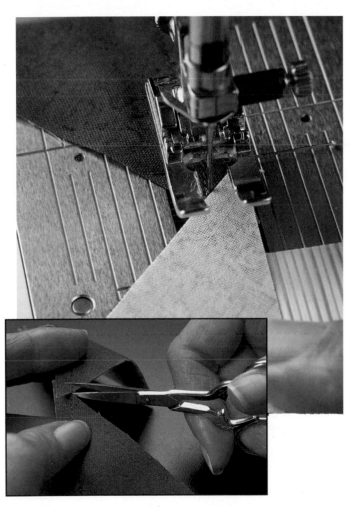

Piece ┊ Smart

When you cut your chain-pieced shapes apart, stack them carefully, all facing in the same direction. This way, you won't have to handle and manipulate them as much, and you'll avoid stretching them out of shape. And pieces that aren't stretched out of shape make square blocks!

Trimming Dog Ears

A dog ear is the excess fabric that hangs past the ends of the seam allowance when you sew a triangle to any other shape. The most common dog ear is formed when you sew two half-square triangles together along the long bias edge, and then press the seam allowance to one side. Each of the resulting dog ears has one bias edge, which can cause your squares to become elongated when you press. So cut the dog ears off *before* pressing to ensure perfectly square triangle pairs. When sewing triangles to other shapes, I press first, then trim the dog ears.

There are two methods for trimming dog ears. I prefer to trim my dog ears off with a pair of small, sharp embroidery scissors. I hold the sewn patches in my left hand. I place one straight edge of the triangle toward my body and the other one to my left, then I snip off the first dog ear as if I were cutting the third side of a square. Then I snip the second dog ear as if I were cutting the fourth side of a square. The important thing here is to make the snips perpendicular to the straight edges of the triangle.

Snipping Dog Ears

The second method produces the same result but is more precise, takes longer, and is slightly more stressful on your hands. Place your triangle on a cutting mat. Line up the top and side of a small ruler with the points where your seam lines end. Rotary cut the dog ears off.

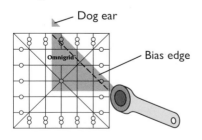

Cutting Dog Ears

Special Piecing Techniques

I'm always looking for piecing techniques that take the frustration out of quilt-making. I also love to find ways to save time. There are a handful of methods I have developed that give you the best of both worlds — timesavers that increase your personal satisfaction with the quilts you make. These tricks allow you to go that extra "yard" and make everything just a little more accurate, or make a block in an easier yet more precise way. I use all these techniques every day in my own quiltmaking and I teach them in my classes. I guarantee that you'll be much happier with your finished quilts if you take the time to learn to do them properly.

Mitering Corners

A mitered corner is one that forms an angle out from the corner of the quilt (when you're mitering a border) or quilt block (when you're mitering lattice). Many people think mitered border corners are more visually pleasing than straight borders, which is one reason why they're popular. While mitering corners is more difficult than adding straight borders or lattice, it can be a snap if you follow these simple steps for No-Fail results. This method is based upon an accurate ¼-inch seam allowance (page 68) and a perfect ¼-inch stop (page 70), so make sure you have your ¼-inch tape guide ready to go. This example shows a quilt top and borders, but the steps are the same if you're adding lattice strips to a block.

1. Align the border with the quilt top, right sides together, leaving enough border hanging over each edge of the quilt to complete the miter (this should be at *least* the width of the border strip). Pin the border to the quilt top every 1½ inches. On the wrong side of the quilt, place a small pencil mark on *one* corner, ¼ inch in from the edge.

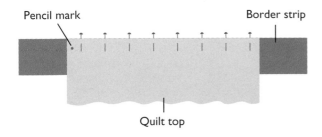

Pencil mark · Border strip · Quilt top

2. Sew the border to the quilt top, beginning at the pencil mark. Sew *one* stitch forward, backtack one stitch, then continue sewing the seam.

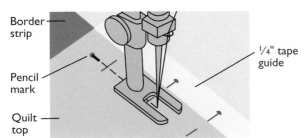

Border strip · Pencil mark · Quilt top · ¼" tape guide

3. Stop ¼ inch from the edge of the quilt top (page 70), with the needle just about to begin a new stitch. Turn the handwheel on your sewing machine toward you just enough to lower the tip of the needle into the fabric (but not so much that you take a stitch). Lift the presser foot.

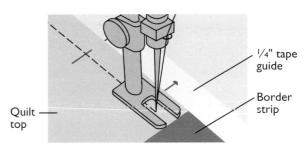

Quilt top · ¼" tape guide · Border strip

4. Rotate the quilt counterclockwise to see if the adjacent quilt edge butts against your ¼-inch tape guide. If not, turn the handwheel away from you until the needle comes out of the fabric. Gently move the quilt over until it butts against the tape guide.

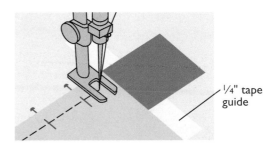

¼" tape guide

5. Turn the handwheel toward you so that the whole needle is in the fabric. Rotate the quilt back to its original position and lower the presser foot. Backtack three stitches. You now have a perfect ¼-inch stop! Press the seam allowance away from the quilt.

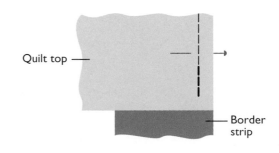

Quilt top · Border strip

6. Repeat

Steps 1 through 5 for each remaining border strip, adding the next strip beginning where you just finished sewing the previous one. Begin your sewing just a hair (1/16 inch) away from the 1/4-inch stop on the previous border so that the stitching doesn't overlap. When you have sewn all four borders on, lay the quilt out on a flat surface.

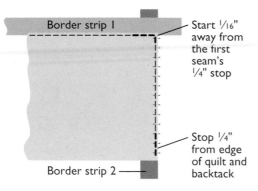

Border strip 1

Start 1/16" away from the first seam's 1/4" stop

Stop 1/4" from edge of quilt and backtack

Border strip 2

7. Fold

the top (horizontal) border up and align it with the side (vertical) border. Press the resulting 45 degree line that starts at the 1/4-inch stop and runs to the outside edge of the border.

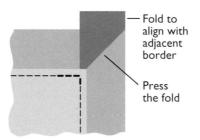

Fold to align with adjacent border

Press the fold

8. Repeat

Step 7 for the side border, carefully bringing the strip out from beneath the top border and folding it to align with the top border. Press it to create a 45 degree line. Repeat this process for each corner.

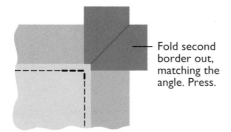

Fold second border out, matching the angle. Press.

9. Align

the horizontal and vertical borders in one corner by folding the quilt diagonally.

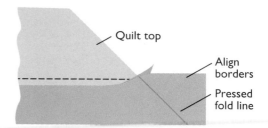

Quilt top

Align borders

Pressed fold line

10. Stitch

the miter. Sew on the pressed 45 degree line that you formed by folding the border strips. Align the creases you've pressed in both of the strips. Place the needle just a hair (1/16 inch) away from the 1/4-inch stop, take one stitch, backtack one stitch, then continue to the end of the seam. Backtack three stitches.

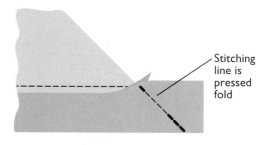

Stitching line is pressed fold

11. Trim

the excess of the border strips 1/4 inch from your sewing line. Repeat Steps 9 through 11 for each remaining corner.

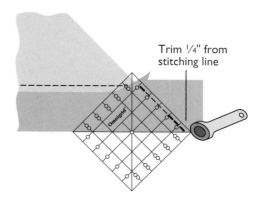

Trim 1/4" from stitching line

Strip Piecing

Errors in piecing can make your block get ever-so-slightly out of whack. Strip piecing is a good way to eliminate a lot of those errors. It's done by cutting strips of fabric on the straight grain, sewing them together, and then cutting the sewn strip sets into shapes. I like strip piecing because it saves time and is more accurate than cutting out individual shapes and sewing them together separately. Strip piecing increases accuracy because it requires less starting and stopping while you're sewing—you just sew long seams and cut the strip sets into units.

A Four Patch made from four squares and a 45 degree diamond made from four smaller diamonds are good examples of patterns that are ideal for strip piecing—they are made of small shapes that join to form a larger unit of the same shape. Once you know how to recognize where strip-cutting shortcuts will work, you can apply this technique to projects without relying on directions to tell you what to do. And I've even included easy ways to figure out the math for the five most common geometric shapes where quilters frequently combine rotary cutting and strip piecing.

Four Patch

A Four Patch is made from two different fabric strips sewn together, cut into segments, and then sewn back together.

Four Patch

No-Fail Figuring

1. Determine the height (**H**) of one square.

2. Add ½ inch to determine your cutting height (**CH**).

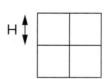   H + ½" = CH

No-Fail Strip Piecing

1. Cut strips (page 36) as wide as your cutting height (**CH**) from two different fabrics.

2. Sew the strips together along their long edges. Press toward the darker fabric (page 99).

3. Cut segments as wide as your cutting height (**CH**).

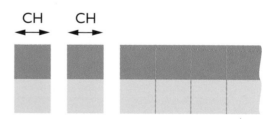

4. Rotate one segment, butt the seams (page 69), pin, and sew the segments together into a Four Patch.

Nine Patch

A Nine Patch is made from three fabric strips that are sewn together into two different strip sets, cut into segments, then sewn back together.

Nine Patch

No-Fail Figuring

1. Determine the height (**H**) of one square.

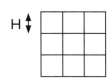

2. Add ½ inch to determine your cutting height (**CH**).

$$H + \tfrac{1}{2}" = CH$$

No-Fail Strip Piecing

1. Cut strips (page 36) as wide as your cutting height (**CH**) from two different fabrics.

2. Sew the strips together along their long edges. Make two strip sets, as shown. Press toward the darker fabric after adding each strip (page 99).

Strip Set 1

Strip Set 2

3. Cut segments as wide as your cutting height (**CH**) from each strip set.

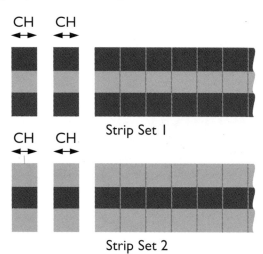

Strip Set 1

Strip Set 2

4. Position the segments as shown, butt the seams (page 69), pin, and sew the units together into Nine Patches.

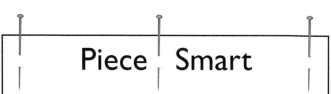

Piece Smart

Resquare the strip set by cutting a new straight edge after every third cut.

Press after each strip is added, not just after the set is complete. This way, you only have to manage one seam at a time, and your pressing will be accurate. This helps ensure that your seams will butt and your Nine Patch will be pieced perfectly.

Square and Rectangle Combination

A block made of squares and rectangles can easily be strip pieced, even though it is made of two different shapes.

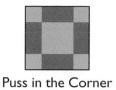

Puss in the Corner

No-Fail Figuring

1. Determine the height (**SH**) of one square.

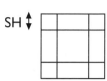

2. Add ½ inch to determine your square cutting height (**SCH**).

SH + ½" = SCH

3. Determine the height (**RH**) of the rectangle.

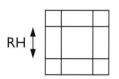

4. Add ½ inch to determine your rectangle cutting height (**RCH**).

RH + ½" = RCH

No-Fail Strip Piecing

1. Cut strips (page 36) as wide as your square cutting height (**SCH**) and your rectangle cutting height (**RCH**) from two different fabrics.

2. Sew the strips together into two sets, each with the narrower strips on the outside. Press toward the darker fabric (page 99).

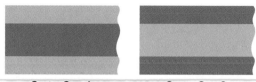

Strip Set 1   Strip Set 2

3. Cut Strip Set 1 into segments as wide as your square cutting height (**SCH**). Cut Strip Set 2 into segments as wide as your rectangle cutting height (**RCH**).

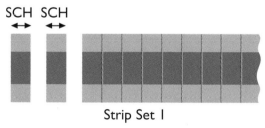

Strip Set 1

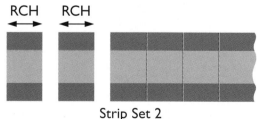

Strip Set 2

4. Position the segments as shown, butt the seams (page 69), and sew the units together.

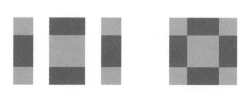

60 Degree Diamond

This six-pointed star block has six large diamonds, each made of four smaller diamonds in three different fabrics. Strip piecing diamonds eliminates the need to sew the small diamonds together along their stretchy bias edges.

Six-Pointed Star

No-Fail Figuring

1. Determine the finished height (**H**) of one diamond.

2. Add ½ inch to determine your cutting height (**CH**).

$$H + \frac{1}{2}" = CH$$

No-Fail Strip Piecing

1. Cut strips the same width as your cutting height (**CH**) from three different fabrics.

Piece Smart

Cut the strip set at a new 60 degree edge after every third cut.

Handle the edges of your pieced diamonds carefully and as little as possible so you don't stretch the bias edges out of shape.

---

2. Sew the strips together into strip sets, offsetting the strips at the end by the amount of your cutting height (**CH**). Press toward the darker fabric (page 99).

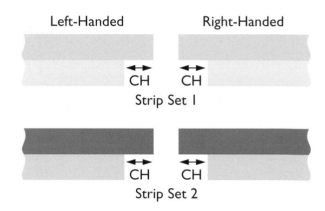

Left-Handed   Right-Handed

Strip Set 1

Strip Set 2

3. Cut the strip at a 60 degree angle (page 52). Cut segments as wide as your cutting height (**CH**).

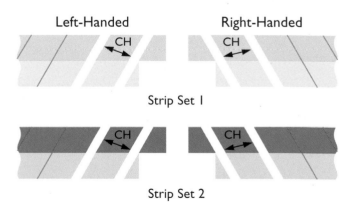

Left-Handed   Right-Handed

Strip Set 1

Strip Set 2

4. Position the segments as shown and sew the segments together.

Left-Handed   Right-Handed

45 Degree Diamond

The strip-pieced Lone Star block is one of the most popular star patterns for quilt-makers. Each of the eight large diamonds is made of four smaller diamonds in three different fabrics. Strip piecing these diamonds is especially helpful because these small diamonds have edges on the true bias, the stretchiest bias of all.

Lone Star

No-Fail Figuring

1. Determine the finished height (**H**) of one diamond.

2. Add ½ inch to determine your cutting height (**CH**).

 H + ½" = CH

No-Fail Strip Piecing

1. Cut strips the same width as your cutting height (**CH**) from three different fabrics.

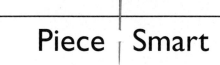

Piece Smart

Cut the strip set at a new 45 degree edge after every third cut.

Cut only as many diamonds as you will sew together at that time. Leaving the diamonds lying around with their bias edges exposed increases the chance that they'll stretch. The more you handle your pieces, the more chance of stretching them out of shape.

2. Sew the strips together into strip sets, offsetting the strips at the end by the amount of your cutting height (**CH**). Press toward the darker fabric (page 99).

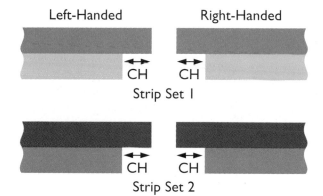

Left-Handed   Right-Handed

Strip Set 1

Strip Set 2

3. Cut your strip set at a 45 degree angle (page 48). Cut segments as wide as your cutting height (**CH**).

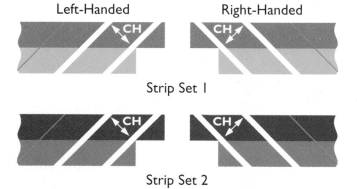

Left-Handed   Right-Handed

Strip Set 1

Strip Set 2

4. Position the segments as shown and sew the segments together.

Left-Handed   Right-Handed

Sewing Partial Seams

A partial seam is when you sew only part of a seam instead of sewing from one end all the way to the other. You finish sewing the seam closed after sewing other pieces or sections to the block. This method is sometimes used to avoid setting in pieces or to accommodate an "added-on" fabric shape.

The first time I ran into a partial seam, I was making a Feathered Star block. The pattern stated that I should sew only part of the seam, but it never indicated when I should finish sewing the seam. Needless to say, I was very confused and it took me a whole evening to figure out the proper way to make the block. I'm sure you've run into similar problems with patterns. So to help you out, here is my method for sewing partial seams, using a Feathered Star block as an example. You can put this technique to work in the Floating Stars quilt on page 118.

1. Sew the seam, ending at the pencil mark (this is the partial seam).

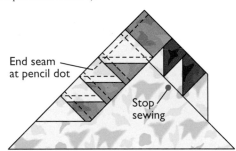

End seam at pencil dot

Stop sewing

2. Fold the triangle point out of the way, then sew the side unit onto your middle unit. The triangle point is still unsewn.

Fold triangle points up when sewing the side units on

3. Finish sewing your partial seam.

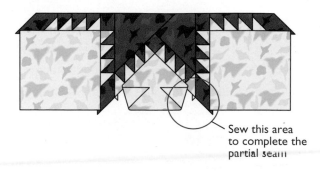

Sew this area to complete the partial seam

Nancy's Bag of Tricks

I never backtack when I'm sewing a partial seam. Occasionally I find I've sewn too far, and I need to re-move a couple of stitches. That's easier when there's no backtacking. Besides, you overlap your stitches when you finish the seam, so there's no danger of its coming unsewn.

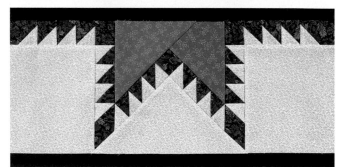

Here is a sample of what this section of a Feathered Star will look like after you have sewn your partial seams closed. The top photo shows the wrong side, with the partial seams all pressed toward the large light triangles.

Sewing 4 Triangles to a Square

The Square within a Square block (page 172) is made by sewing four half-square triangles around the perimeter of a square. This is a fun and easy pattern to make if you know the proper way to align the pieces. The trick here is to get the triangles in the proper position, and to accomplish this, you have to do two things.

First, use half-square triangles (page 38) around the square so that you avoid having stretchy bias grain on the outside edges of the block. (Bias on the outside of a block makes it very difficult to join one block to another accurately.) The second thing you have to remember is to align the triangle edge with the edge of the square properly. This can be a little tricky because the long bias edge of the triangle will always be longer than the edge of the square. With my method, there's no guesswork and you get perfectly centered triangles every time!

1. Fold the square in half in both directions.
Pinch a small crease mark at the midpoint on each side of the square. Similarly, fold each triangle in half along the long (bias) edge and pinch a fold mark.

2. Match the fold mark on a triangle with a fold mark on one side of the square, with the wrong side of the square facing you. This will place the triangle

correctly on the side of the square, with dog ears hanging equally off the two edges of the square. Pin and sew the seam. Repeat with the opposite side of the square.

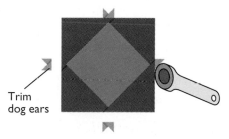

3. Press the seam allowances toward the triangles. You should have dog ears of equal size on each end of the triangles.

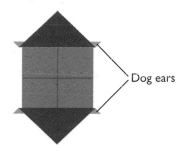

Dog ears

4. Align the fold marks on the remaining two triangles with the fold marks on the edges of the square. Pin, sew, and press. Trim off all the dog ears (page 77).

Trim dog ears

Note: This method is also good for sewing four triangles to an octagon, as in a Snowball block.

Nancy's Bag of Tricks

If you have an unexciting block, try turning it on point and placing triangles around it like a Square within a Square block. Often this is just enough to add visual excitement to what was otherwise a ho-hum block.

Piecing 45 Degree Shapes

Pinwheel

The Pinwheel block is one of the many blocks that have eight 45 degree points that must come together perfectly in the center. The secret to getting perfect center seams and sharp points is in the pressing and pinning of each unit—always press your seam allowances toward the *darker* triangle, and master the butting and pinning technique (page 69) before beginning this block.

1. Pin the two halves of the pinwheel together at each end to ensure that the outside edges of the block will stay even.

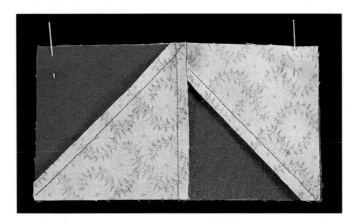

2. Fold the top unit down by ½ inch. If you pressed correctly when making the halves, the light points are slightly recessed, and the dark points are slightly raised. Align the units so the raised dark points fall into the recessed light points.

3. "Walk" the top unit closed with your fingers, rolling your fingers and thumbs toward each other. Make sure the four points all come together in the center.

4. Pin the units a hair (about ¹⁄₁₆ inch) ahead of the butted seams, *not* directly in the butted intersection (page 69).

5. Sew the seam, stitching a hair above the middle of the X formed by the stitching. (If you sew directly through the middle of the X, you will cut a small amount of the point off on the front of the piece.)

Making Flying Geese

Flying Geese

Sewing two half-square triangles to a quarter-square triangle produces a unit known as Flying Geese. This is such a versatile unit that there are hundreds of ways you can use it. You can combine Flying Geese units to make a block, or you can make other distinctive-looking blocks using one Flying Geese unit with other shapes. There are a few tricky parts to making this pieced unit. First, you have to work with all the bias edges of the triangles. Second, you need to align the triangles correctly to sew them together. Remember that you should always try to keep the straight grain on the outside of all your piecing units (page 24) so that they are less likely to stretch out of shape and will join to other piecing units accurately. By using both half-square and quarter-square triangles in this unit, you can position them so the stable straight grain is always on the outside.

1. Position half-square triangles and quarter-square triangles as shown to keep the straight grain on the outside edges of the Flying Geese unit. This will prevent the block from stretching out of shape. (Keep in mind that half-square triangles have only one bias edge, while quarter-square triangles have two bias edges.)

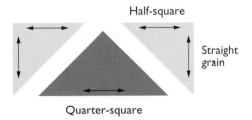
Half-square

Straight grain

Quarter-square

2. Align the bottom outer corner of the half-square triangle with the bottom outer corner of the quarter-square triangle, as shown. Notice that the

bias edges are in alignment, and one dog ear hangs over the top edge. Stitch along the bias edges.

Dog ear

Align bias edges and bottom corners

3. Press the seam allowances (page 98) toward the half-square triangle.

4. Repeat to align, sew, and press the second half-square triangle in the same way.

Align bias edges and bottom corners

5. Trim the dog ears (page 77). You will have a ¼-inch seam allowance between the top of the quarter-square triangle and the top of the block.

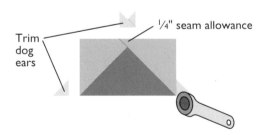
Trim dog ears

¼" seam allowance

Piece | Smart

Press your seam allowances toward the half-square triangles so the stitching lines form an X. Then, when you join the blocks to each other or to lattice strips, stitch just to the outside of the X. No more cut-off points!

Squaring Up Blocks

No matter how accurate you are in cutting, sewing, and pressing, your quilt blocks will not come out to be absolutely, perfectly square. This all-too-common problem is very frustrating to quilters, but I have accepted this fact and encourage you to do the same. I always say that the only time you *will* have a perfectly square block is when you draft its image on graph paper! Does this ruin your quilt? Not necessarily. Just follow these simple steps for squaring up, and you will have blocks that you know will fit together to make a square quilt.

Trimming Large Blocks

Use a 15-inch square ruler with ¼-inch markings that run vertically, turn the corner at 90 degrees, and then run horizontally. Place the ruler on top of your block so the outside *finished* edges (where you will sew your seam to attach the block to another block or a border) on the top and right side of the block are touching the first ¼-inch line on the ruler. (Left-handed quilters: Align the *top* and *left* side of the ruler with the finished edge.) Blocks with angled seams forming points at the outside edge provide a handy reference point for trimming. In **Diagram 1,** the star points are your guide for aligning the ¼-inch line.

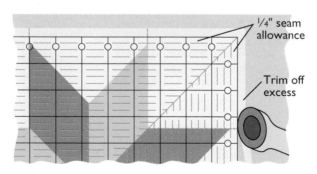

Diagram 1

If you're using a block with seams that are perpendicular or parallel to the outside edges, such as a Nine Patch, line up one of the sewn seams inside the block with the appropriate line on the ruler and measure out, as shown in **Diagram 2.** As you can see, for blocks like this one without points at the

edge to guide your trimming, you may have to do a little math. But don't panic! Just start with the finished size of your outermost piece, add ¼ inch for the seam allowance, and measure out that amount from the seam. Each small square in this block has a finished size of 1 inch, so I place the 1¼-inch line on my ruler on top of the sewn seam (1 + ¼ = 1¼).

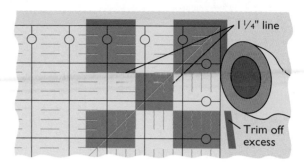

Diagram 2

Once you've placed your ruler correctly, trim any excess fabric beyond the edge of the ruler. Rotate the mat 180 degrees and repeat the process for the remaining edges. You now have a perfect ¼-inch seam allowance around the block perimeter.

Undersize Seam Allowances

It's easy to trim down a large block, but what if the block's outside seam allowance is *smaller* than ¼ inch? First, assess whether it is *too* narrow to use the block in your quilt. If after squaring up you have smaller than an ⅛-inch outside seam allowance in any section, I recommend remaking the block. That's not enough fabric to hold your quilt together.

Wherever the seam allowance along the outside edge is just *slightly* less than ¼ inch, place a pin along the edge. When you get ready to sew the block to the lattice strip or border, the pin will remind you that block edge is slightly irregular and you're not working with a full ¼ inch at that point.

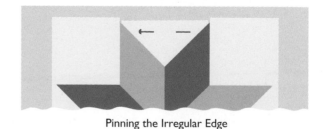

Pinning the Irregular Edge

Attaching Lattice Strips and Borders

My friends comment that it takes me longer to sew lattice strips and borders onto my quilts than it does for me to make all the quilt blocks! This is true, and it's because I get chills when lattice strips and borders are not horizontally and vertically straight. I'll explain how I sew lattice strips onto a block here, but the procedure is the same whether you're sewing blocks together or adding borders to a quilt top.

No-Fail Figuring

1. Measure opposite sides of the block.

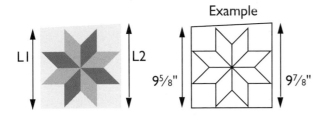

Example

2. Subtract the smaller number from the larger one. (Note: If the difference is more than $\frac{1}{8}$ inch, you may want to consider remaking the block, since it's difficult to hide more than that with lattice.)

$$L2 - L1 = DIFF \qquad 9\frac{7}{8}" - 9\frac{5}{8}" = \frac{1}{4}"$$

3. Divide the difference in half.

$$DIFF \div 2 = N \qquad \frac{1}{4}" \div 2 = \frac{1}{8}"$$

4. Add the result to the smaller measurement from Step 1 to get your cutting length (**CL**).

$$L1 + N = CL \qquad 9\frac{5}{8}" + \frac{1}{8}" = 9\frac{3}{4}"$$

No-Fail Lattice

1. Cut lattice strips as long as your cutting length (**CL**). Cut the strips $\frac{1}{8}$ inch wider than the pattern states. (This includes my patterns and other commercial patterns.)

CL

2. Place the lattice strip right side up, and the block right side down on top. The block edge should line up with the lattice edge, except for sections you marked with a pin as irregular (opposite page). Carefully pin the block to the lattice strip.

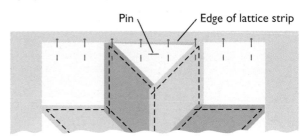

Pin — Edge of lattice strip

3. Sew the strips to the block, using the edge of the *lattice*, not the block, as your guide. If necessary, slightly ease or stretch the block (not the lattice) to fit. Press toward the lattice (page 99).

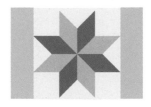

4. Trim the lattice strip to the correct width. Use your rotary ruler to measure out the finished width of the strip *plus* a $\frac{1}{4}$-inch seam allowance.

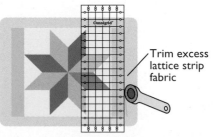

Trim excess lattice strip fabric

No-Fail Pressing

Selecting Your Pressing Equipment

Pressing is the most misunderstood and least-talked-about process in quiltmaking. It's the third critical step to good quilts (after accurate cutting and piecing), yet pressing techniques and supplies often get overlooked when quilters are shopping for equipment. The right ironing surface can be just as important as your rotary mat, and your choice of iron can affect the quality of your quilt just as your sewing machine can. If you stop to think about it, you press your quilt just as much as you cut or piece it—first the yardage, then the seams, then the blocks. So follow my tips, and you'll get crisp, flat, straight seams every time you press.

Ironing Board

I never thought about my pressing surface until I purchased a new foam pad and cover for my ironing board. The pad was very thick, and my quilt pieces sank into the foam when I pressed them. I wasn't getting the precise pressing results that I wanted. I replaced the thick pad with my old thin pad and immediately saw my crisp, flat, even seams reappear. The moral of the story: If you have more than ¼ inch of foam under your cover, buy a thinner pad.

Here are my favorite features to look for in an ironing board and some tips for using it.

Ironing Board Tips

🧵 Buy an ironing board with four separate legs for more stability.

🧵 Look for a solid top, not one with holes in it. This provides you with an even surface for more even pressing.

🧵 Cover your board with a light, solid-color cover. A cover with a strong pattern and many colors will make small pieces of fabric hard to spot.

🧵 Pin a piece of muslin or flannel on top of the part of the ironing board where you do the most pressing. When it gets dirty or torn, throw it away.

Iron

The adage "bigger is better" is not true when it comes to irons. It is the *heat* of the iron that does the pressing, not the iron's weight. A heavy iron just puts a lot of stress on your wrist; it doesn't necessarily guarantee a better pressing job. In the course of making a quilt, you will lift your iron hundreds of times. Give your wrists a break — use a lightweight iron. (See page 65 for more on irons.)

I like a *really* hot iron. Heat is the only way to get crisp seams. I find irons with a Teflon bottom don't get hot enough. When my iron isn't getting hot enough to press well, or I find that I'm pushing down on the iron to get a crisp, flat seam, I replace the iron.

Press Smart

If you can't find a thin foam pad for your ironing board, make your own pad. Buy a piece of Warm and Natural cotton batting and cut it to fit your ironing board, plus an extra inch or so to wrap around the edges.

Steam

I don't use steam when quiltmaking, and I've never understood why some quiltmakers say, "Give it a good shot of steam." I find that steam tends to stretch blocks if I'm not *really* careful. Also, it can make the areas where seams butt look shiny. And if you over-steam, you have to press longer to get rid of the excess moisture, which can compress the fibers in that area and make the fabric discolor, shrink, or pucker.

Sizing

I've already talked about Magic Sizing (page 22). I use it only before rotary cutting to restore the body that was washed out of fabric, and this makes my cutting and sewing much easier. For the times when I need extra body added to my fabric, such as when I'm working with very thin or loosely woven fabrics, I use spray starch. This helps keep them from stretching out of shape. I never use sizing on sewn blocks—there is too much of a tendency to stretch them.

Nancy's Bag of Tricks

To make a lightweight, portable workspace for class, take a 10 × 12-inch piece of paneling and glue one or two layers of cotton batting (cut to fit the paneling) on the front side for an ironing surface. Cover the batting with a piece of flannel that is at least 16 × 18 inches, wrap the edges of the flannel around to the back, and glue the edges down. Then add a cutting surface by gluing an 8 × 10-inch cutting mat on top of the flannel edges on the back side.

Special Pressing Techniques

When quilters talk about pressing, they frequently joke that you *iron* shirts but you *press* quilt blocks. When ironing, you slide the iron back and forth and side to side. When pressing, you very gently use the heat of the iron, not the motion, to get superb results. I believe that good pressing makes the difference between an amateur and a professional-looking quilt block. Here I share how to make sure that your quilts are pressed for the best possible results.

Pressing Personalities

I am always amazed at the personality change that comes over a quilter when she gets a hot iron in her hand! Here are some of the personalities I have observed while teaching quiltmaking across the country (and while looking in the mirror once in a while..).

The Aggressor attacks the sewn pieces with a vengeance and keeps the iron in constant exaggerated motion over the block, strip set, or quilt top. Her seams tend to meander, and her pieces are stretched out of shape.

The Steamer loves to spray the block with water and then steam it to death. Her blocks often are out of square because the steam makes the fabric distort more easily.

The Big Tipper's favorite part of the iron is the tip or point. She pushes and pokes the tip into the seam allowances on the front of the block until she can see little dots of thread peeking through the seam allowances.

The Side Swiper is a person who loves the side of the iron. She glides the iron onto the block and then presses down firmly to push the iron over the seam allowance "hump." Her seam allowances are often wavy and distorted.

I must admit that I have been all of these personalities! Through trial and a lot of error, I have finally developed good pressing methods, which I'm happy to share with you. If you suffer from arthritis or carpal tunnel syndrome, these methods are especially easy on your hands, as well as your fabric.

Nancy's Bag of Tricks

To avoid re-pressing blocks and stretching them out of shape, store them flat in an out-of-the-way place. I store my finished blocks in a clear plastic container with a lid. This way, they're less likely to be handled, they stay pressed, and they're less likely to stretch out of shape before I can sew them into a quilt top.

Pressing Don'ts

Bad habits are hard to break, but they are relatively easy to prevent. If you find yourself engaging in any of these behaviors, stop immediately! And if you don't do these things, avoid picking up on them.

Pressing Pitfalls

- If you discover that a seam is pressed in the wrong direction, don't simply flop the seam allowance to the other side to re-press it. This causes the appearance of crooked seams on the front of the block. Just set the seam again (page 98), then press it in the direction you want it to lie.

- Never spray starch or sizing after piecing a block. Both these products contain moisture, and when you place your hot iron on them, you steam your block. The steam makes the block easier to distort and pull out of shape when you're pressing. Use starch or sizing *before* you cut your shapes, and make sure your iron is hot enough to do a good job of pressing.

- Don't push the iron along the grain (either lengthwise or crosswise). Move your iron in different directions as you press your seam so you're not stretching the fibers along the grain.

- Don't let your quilt top hang over the edge of your ironing board when you're pressing seams between rows. This creates a lot of drag on the quilt top and stretches it unnecessarily. Instead, fold over the edges you're not working on to keep them on top of the ironing surface.

Pressing Seams

Once you've started piecing with a perfectly accurate seam allowance, you'll want to maintain the accuracy in your quiltmaking when you start pressing. I have found a few simple techniques that I always use when I'm pressing, and I get results that I'm happy with every time.

After sewing each seam, always "set" it by pressing it as sewn (without opening up the pieces). By doing this, you ease in any puffiness in the seam caused by the tension on your sewing machine, and you prevent the seam line from distorting. Then, when you open up the pieces to press the seam allowance to one side, all you have to concentrate on is pressing the seam open correctly, as described here in "Short Seams." Please note that the only time I ever recommend pressing on the wrong side of the quilt is when you're setting your seam. Otherwise, press on the front of your quilt or quilt block.

Place your pieces on the ironing board with the seam allowance toward your body and the darker piece on top. This way, you don't have to turn your pieces over after you set the seam. (If you're pressing toward the lighter fabric, place it on top.)

I finger-press my seams before I press them with the iron, and it's really one of the important parts of my technique. It involves using the balls of your fingers (not the tips or nails) to gently press the fabric in place. Make sure that you finger-press gently—don't stretch the fabric out of shape at the seam.

Nancy's Bag of Tricks

Sewn pieces tend to get out of square on the ends, not in the middle of the sewn seam. To prevent this when finger pressing, I crowd as many of my fingertips onto the seam as I can fit—I even have them running off the ends of the seams. This helps ensure that my seam will be pressed straight, even at the ends.

Short Seams

1. Place the sewn piece on the ironing board with the seam allowance *toward* your body, and set the iron on the seam allowance area. If you're pressing your seam allowances toward your darker fabric, position your piece so the darker patch is on the top.

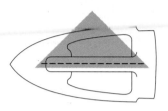

2. Fold the top layer of fabric back and finger-press the seam open with the balls of your fingers. Use as many of your fingers as you can fit across the seam; this will help to hold the fabric in place until you can place the iron on the seam. (I use the fingers on both hands for this.) Do not run your thumb or fingernails along the seam allowance—you will stretch the pieces!

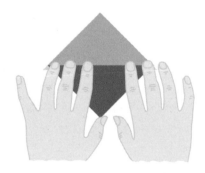

3. Set the iron gently on the seam, removing your fingers only at the last second, when the iron is at the seam. Do not move the iron from side to side.

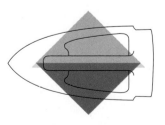

Long Seams

"Bowing" and stretching of long seams is a common problem. Once you stretch a seam out of shape, you cannot press it straight again. When pressing long seams, as you do when sewing long strips or rows of blocks together, remember that you want to move the iron *opposite* to the length of the strips: If your strips are positioned east-west, your iron should move in a slight north-south direction. Otherwise you will be working with the stretchy part of the fabric, and the strips can easily become bowed. My method for pressing strip sets lets you press the seams fully without any distortion.

1. Position the sewn strip set on the ironing board with the seam allowance *toward* your body. This helps you press more accurately since you will be pressing toward your body, and your hands have a natural tendency to work and fall toward you.

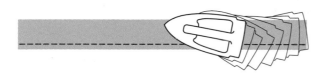

2. Set the seam by setting the iron on one end of the strip set, then moving it in a slight zigzag (north to south) direction along the length of the seam. This keeps the iron off the actual lengthwise grain, and it helps keep the fabric from stretching.

3. Pull the top layer of fabric back gently, beginning in the center of the strip set. Grasp the top layer with your nonironing hand. Keep your fingers on top and your thumb underneath the fabric.

4. Position the iron just behind your fingers. As in Step 2, zigzag the iron down the strip toward your nonironing hand, continuing to finger press ahead of the iron. Use your thumb to hold the seam allowance in place. Press all the way to the end of the strip.

5. Move to the unpressed end of the strip. Beginning 3 inches in from the end of the strip, press toward the center, as you did in Step 4.

6. Finger-press the 3-inch unpressed area, then set the iron on this section. Do not move the iron around. Now you have a perfectly pressed straight strip!

Press Smart

When you're strip piecing, always press the seam after attaching *each* strip. If you sew all the strips together and then press all those long seams afterward, you will "bow" the strips. So, to keep your strip sets even along their whole length, and to get segments that fit together into square blocks, press after each strip.

No-Fail
Finishing

Keeping Your Quilt Square

I have made more than 200 quilts and over 1,000 miniatures, and I still *always* have to square up my quilts—so rest assured that you're normal (or at least as normal as I am) when your next quilt top isn't quite square. But I have a few tricks I developed when I realized my quilts weren't finishing as I wanted them to, and I share those with you here. Hopefully, you'll find these tips easy to use, and they'll help you get your quilts as square as possible.

Cutting Accurate Borders

Borders are what make your quilt square. The edges of a quilt are seldom the same length as the center of the quilt, so you must allow for that to avoid wavy or rippled borders. You *must* measure your quilt top correctly when you're figuring border lengths and then cut your border strips to that exact length just before you are ready to sew them to the quilt.

No-Fail Figuring

1. Measure the height of the quilt on both edges and in the middle.

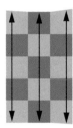 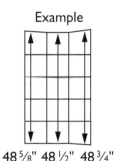

Example

HI   H3   H2   48⅝" 48½" 48¾"

2. Subtract the smallest measurement from the largest measurement.

H2 − H3 = DIFF   48¾" − 48½" = ¼"

3. Divide the difference in half.

DIFF ÷ 2 = N   ¼" ÷ 2 = ⅛"

4. Add the result to the smallest measurement from Step 1 to get your cutting length (**CL**).

H3 + N = CL   48½" + ⅛" = 48⅝"

No-Fail Borders

1. Cut two border strips as long as your cutting length (**CL**).

CL

2. Fold the border strips in half and mark the center of each with a pin.

3. Pin the borders to the sides of the quilt top, matching centers and ends. Then pin about every 1½ inches along each border.

4. Sew the borders to the quilt top, slightly easing or stretching the *top* (not the border) to fit. Press toward the borders (page 99). Repeat all these steps for the top and bottom borders.

Nancy's Bag of Tricks

Once your borders are cut to size, always ease the quilt top to fit the borders, not the other way around. This assures that you'll have a square quilt.

Squaring-Up Borders

Sometimes the squarest borders can end up wavy after you finish quilting. Quilting stitches draw the layers of a quilt together, and each stitch makes the quilt ever-so-slightly smaller in size. The more quilting there is, the more the quilt gets "drawn up" in the quilted areas. If there is more quilting in the center of the quilt than in the borders, the edges of the quilt will be wavy and rippled. This is very common, and I have grown to expect it from the quilts I make, so I always square up my quilted quilt before I sew on the binding. Here is the method I use.

1. Trim the corners of the quilt to the correct width. Use a 15-inch ruler (turned upside down) to measure out the desired width of your border plus ¼ inch (for the binding seam allowance). Cut off the excess batting and backing on each side of the ruler.

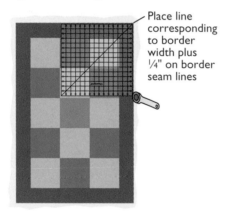

Place line corresponding to border width plus ¼" on border seam lines

2. Finish squaring up the sides of the borders with a 6 × 24-inch ruler.

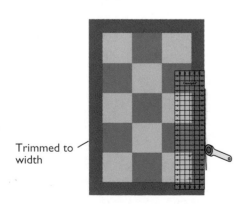

Trimmed to width

Preventing Wavy Edges

I occasionally find that despite being very careful with my sewing, cutting, pressing, and squaring up, sometimes a quilt still won't hang correctly. This is often due to the unevenness of the quilting in the body of the quilt, which causes a very slight but perceptible wave or ripple on the edge. I once worked for many weeks trying to find a way around this problem, and I finally remembered an old trick for setting in dress sleeves that my mother taught me when I was a young girl—shirring!

Shirring the edge of your quilt will ease in that tiny bit of extra fabric without causing pleats along the edges of the quilt. Shirring stabilizes the three layers of fabric by *slightly* gathering the edge. This technique will work every time, as long as the quilt has only slight waves or ripples. I use this method on all of my miniatures, wallhangings, and quilts.

1. Position your quilt in the sewing machine, ready to sew down one side. Begin stitching 2 inches in from the corner. (This will prevent the corner of the quilt from flipping up.) Adjust your stitch length to one slightly longer than you normally use for piecing. Place the fingers of your left hand behind the presser foot and on top of the corner of the quilt.

2. Hold your fingers in place, and sew a row of stitches just inside the ¼-inch seam allowance (approximately ³⁄₁₆ inch from the edge of the quilt). Your fingers behind the presser foot will fight the tendency of the quilt to move away from you as it is sewn, causing the quilt to bunch up. The more fabric you let bunch up, the less shirring effect there will be; the less you bunch up, the more shirring there will be.

3. Stop sewing after 2 to 3 inches and let go of the bunched-up fabric. Replace your fingers behind the presser foot, and repeat Step 2 until you have completed the seam along one edge of the quilt. Stop about 2 inches from the edge of the quilt.

4. Clip your threads and take the quilt out of your machine. This is what the edges will look like after you have shirred them. Repeat the shirring process on each of the four edges of your quilt, remembering to leave the corners free by stopping and starting 2 inches away from each one.

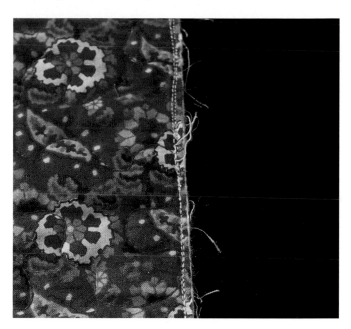

5. Hang the quilt. If it bunches up or gathers too much in one section, gently pull on the edge to relax the shirring in that area. If it gaps or ripples in one section, shirr just that section again. In any areas that you reshirr, stitch just a hair inside your previous row of stitches, and use a shorter stitch length, as shown in the inset photo.

Rippled area to be reshirred

Binding and Mitering

Once your quilt is square and flat, it's time to finish it off. Binding is the last touch that you'll put on your quilt, the last chance you have to make a statement, and it can either make or break your beautiful work. When I teach, students always have the same questions about binding—whether to use bias or straight grain, how wide to cut the strips, how to miter the corners, and how to start and end the binding. In this section, I'll give you tips and advice for binding your quilt so that it stays square and flat and has perfectly mitered corners.

Making Perfect Binding

Many years ago, people were saying that quilts without bias binding would never win awards. I'm happy to report that they didn't know what they were talking about. My quilts won over a dozen national awards in a two-year period, and I rarely cut bias strips for my binding. Surprised? Don't be. I use bias binding only when I'm working with striped or plaid fabrics, and I want a special effect (see the photos of Campbell House on page 134 and Square within a Square Miniature on page 172). Otherwise, I cut binding strips on the crosswise or lengthwise grain of the fabric. I find that bias binding is stretchy and hard to work with, so why tangle with it when you don't have to?

Finish Smart

There are two common types of binding: single-fold and double-fold.
Single-fold binding has one layer of fabric covering the edge of your quilt, and double-fold has two layers. I use double-fold binding because it's stronger and wears better—and it's easier to work with because there are no long edges to press under, as with single-fold binding. (But I always use single-fold on my miniatures.) I cut the strips for double-fold binding 2 inches wide so I have the same width of binding on the back and the front of the quilt.

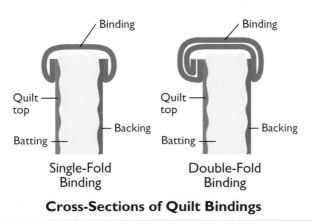

Cross-Sections of Quilt Bindings

Single-Fold Binding   Double-Fold Binding

Sewing the Strips Together

I always sew my binding strips together with a 45 degree angle seam. If you just put your strips right sides together and sew straight across the width, you get a big lump in your binding. This is hard to sew over accurately, and it stands out much more obviously than an angled seam.

Here's my technique for sewing angled seams. I find that by cutting the ends of the strips at 45 degrees and trimming the dog ear *before* I sew the strips together, I always get perfectly aligned binding strips.

1. Cut both ends of your binding strips at 45 degrees, as you would for a parallelogram (page 49). Make sure you cut parallel edges, as shown.

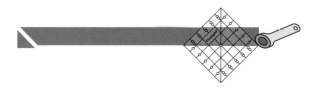

2. Measure in ⅜ inch from each sharp point, aligning your ruler with the long edge of the strip. Cut the tip off.

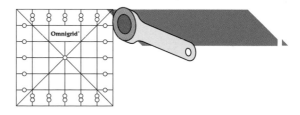

3. Align and sew the binding strips together. Press in either direction. For double-fold binding, press the binding in half lengthwise, wrong sides together, and you're ready to attach it!

Attaching the Binding

I've been a judge at many national quilt shows, and you would be surprised at how much importance is placed on binding—many great quilts don't win because of binding problems. When the judging gets tough, one of the tie-breakers is always how well the corners of the binding are finished. Even if you aren't entering your quilt in a show, your binding should be pleasing to look at. And once you see how easy my method of mitering binding corners is, you'll never look back.

Sewing the Binding to the Quilt

I think of a mitered binding corner as a set-in seam. Therefore, I use many of the same sewing techniques that I use for that technique (page 72). Here are the steps for my No-Fail binding method.

1. Align the raw edges of the binding and the raw edges of the quilt top. Beginning in the center of the side, pin the binding to the quilt top every 1½ inches. Leave the first 12 inches of the binding unpinned.

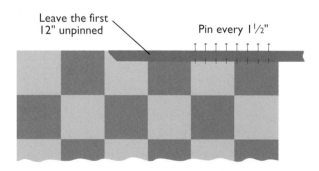

Leave the first 12" unpinned

Pin every 1½"

2. Sew the binding to the quilt top, beginning at the first pin and using an accurate ¼-inch seam allowance (page 68). Sew *one* stitch forward, backtack one stitch, then sew the seam, stopping where you

think is ¼ inch from the edge of the quilt (page 70). Leave the needle one-quarter of the way in the quilt so you don't create a stitch. Lift the presser foot.

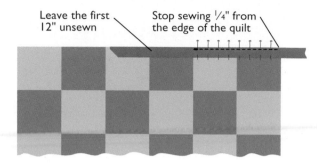

Leave the first 12" unsewn

Stop sewing ¼" from the edge of the quilt

3. Rotate the quilt counterclockwise to see if the adjacent edge butts against your ¼-inch tape guide. If not, turn the handwheel away from you until the needle comes out of the fabric, and gently move the quilt over until it butts against the tape guide. Turn the handwheel toward you so that the whole needle is in the fabric, and rotate the quilt back to its original position. Lower the presser foot and backtack three stitches. You now have a perfect ¼-inch stop! Remove the quilt from the machine and lay it out on a flat surface.

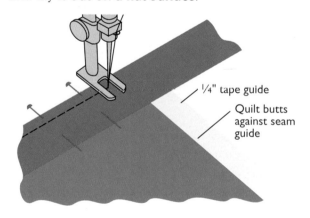

¼" tape guide

Quilt butts against seam guide

4. Fold the binding up and away from the quilt to form a 45 degree fold.

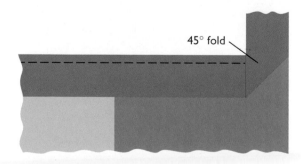

45° fold

5. Fold again, bringing the binding down toward the quilt and aligning it with the top and right side of the quilt. Keep the edges on all three sides even. Take your time—the binding edges must be perfectly in line with the edges of the quilt or the mitered corner will not turn correctly.

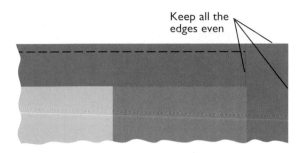

Keep all the edges even

6. Pin the binding to the adjacent side of the quilt. Place the first three pins on the back of the quilt and the remaining pins on the front side.

Pin every 1½"

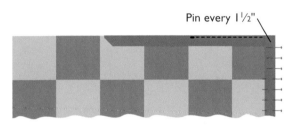

7. Flip the quilt so the back is facing you. Start sewing 3 to 4 inches from the corner you just pinned, and sew toward the corner, stopping a hair (¹/₁₆ inch) ahead of the ¼-inch stop. Backtack three stitches.

Back of the quilt

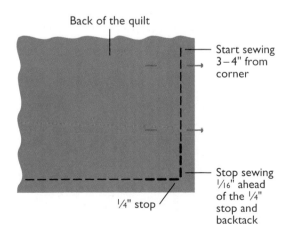

Start sewing 3–4" from corner

Stop sewing ¹/₁₆" ahead of the ¼" stop and backtack

¼" stop

8. Flip again so the front is facing you. Overlap your stitches with the last inch or so of those you took in Step 7, and sew until you have a perfect ¼-inch stop on the other end.

No stitching

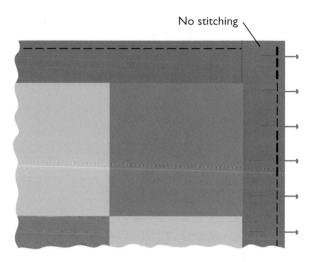

9. Repeat Steps 2 through 8 for each corner. After sewing the fourth corner, stop sewing about 12 inches from your original starting point.

12" unsewn space

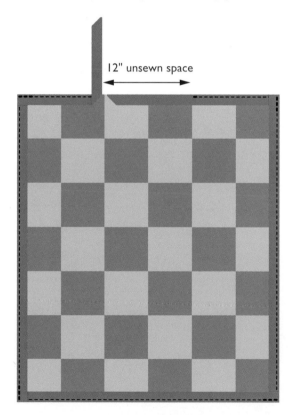

Connecting the Binding Ends

Once your binding is sewn on, you need to finish it off professionally by joining the beginning binding strip to the ending binding strip. With my method, it's almost impossible for anyone to tell where I started sewing the binding on.

1. Trim the ending binding strip (you'll need to unfold it first) at a 45 degree angle so that it overlaps the beginning binding strip by about 5 inches.

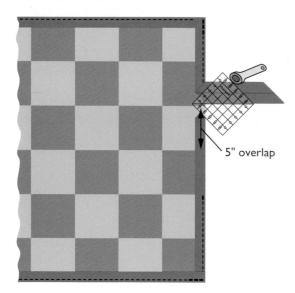

5" overlap

2. Unfold both strips and lay them flat with the beginning strip on the bottom. Pin them as shown to hold them in place. Use a pencil to mark lightly on the beginning (bottom) strip where the mitered (top) strip ends.

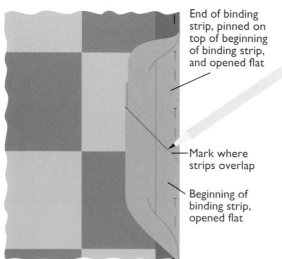

End of binding strip, pinned on top of beginning of binding strip, and opened flat

Mark where strips overlap

Beginning of binding strip, opened flat

3. Unpin the strips and place the bottom strip on a cutting mat. Using a 6 × 6-inch ruler, line up the 45 degree line with the strip's edge, and cut it **½ inch longer** than where you marked in Step 2 (for the seam allowance when you sew the strips together).

Cut strip ½" past pencil mark

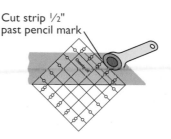

4. Sew the beginning and ending strips together, following Steps 2 and 3 on page 107. Fold the quilt out of the way to sew the strips on your machine.

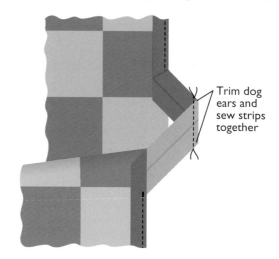

Trim dog ears and sew strips together

5. Pin this section of the binding to the quilt top. Sew, overlapping the previously sewn stitches by ½ inch on each end.

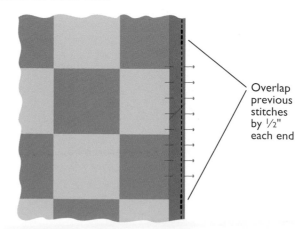

Overlap previous stitches by ½" each end

Finishing the Binding

If you're lucky, you have a mom like mine, and at this point you put your quilt in a box and send it off to her to finish the binding process. If your mom doesn't perform this vital function for you, follow the steps below to finish off your binding.

Start pinning your binding to the quilt back in the middle of a side, then work out toward each corner. This prevents you from pulling the binding to one side as you work your way down a long stretch of binding, and it helps prevent ripples or puckers in the binding.

1. Fold the binding to the back of the quilt and pin it in place every inch. Whipstitch the binding to the back of the quilt, stopping about ½ inch away from each corner.

Fold binding to back of quilt and pin

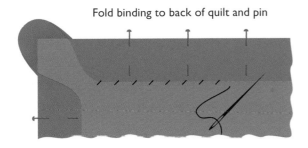

2. Fold one corner of the binding down and hold it with your thumb.

3. Fold the other side to complete the miter. Check the miter on the front to make sure it is smooth. If it's not, refold the miter on the back until it is.

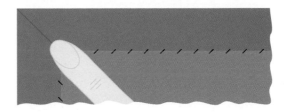

4. Stitch your miters closed on the front and back of the quilt using tiny, invisible stitches.

Stitch miter closed · Stitch miter closed

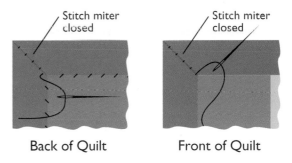

Back of Quilt · Front of Quilt

Nancy's Bag of Tricks

Make excellent miters every time! To get your miters flat on both the front and back of your quilt, try this trick. When you're folding the binding into a miter, fold one side down, then the other (see Steps 2 and 3 on this page). Check the miters on the front and back to see if they lie flat, then unfold the binding and fold it down again in the opposite order. One way will give you a much better, flatter miter on both the front and back of your quilt—and that's the way you should fold and stitch!

No-Fail Problem-Solving Guide

In this chart, you'll find some of the most common problems and complaints that I run into when I'm teaching—and when I'm quilting. Take a look through these pages for the situation that has been troubling you, and you'll see how to fix it, as well as how to prevent it in the future. You may even find a few things that you wouldn't have thought to prevent—and now you can!

Problem	Cause	How to Prevent	How to Fix
Body Related			
Hand gets tired while cutting.	Holding rotary cutter improperly.	Select the most comfortable cutter for you.	Hold your cutter properly (page 29).
	Lint build-up on blade or axle causes blade to bind.	Clean the cutter frequently and put a small drop of sewing machine oil on the blade when assembling.	Clean and lubricate your cutter (pages 4–6).
	Dull blade.	Install a new blade frequently.	Replace the dull blade (page 6).
Wrist gets tired when pressing.	Pressing too hard on iron.	Let the heat of the iron, not the weight, do the work.	Purchase a lighter iron.
	Iron is too heavy.	Don't press down hard on the iron.	Purchase a lighter iron.
	Older irons often won't become as hot after extended use.	Set iron on hottest setting.	Purchase a new iron if yours won't heat up enough.
Shoulders and neck get achy while quiltmaking.	Stooping over while cutting.	Maintain proper body position while cutting (page 30).	Stand erect.
	Reaching up too high while sewing.	Position your sewing machine at the proper height for you (page 64).	Try fitting your sewing machine *into* your table instead of setting it on top.
	Chair is at incorrect height.	Adjust your chair so you are comfortable while sewing.	Invest in a chair that is height-adjustable.
Equipment Related			
Rotary cutter skips a thread while cutting.	Blade has a nick or burr.	Keep the cutter closed when not in use. Examine cutter blade if you drop it. Do not cut over pins.	Replace the old blade (page 6).
	Mat is not on a completely flat surface.	Always cut on a perfectly flat surface, such as a tabletop.	Move your mat from its current location to a flat space.
Blade dulls quickly.	Improper cutting mat.	Cut only on a mat designed for rotary cutting.	Purchase a mat that is designed for rotary cutting (page 7).
	Cutting through very stiff or woven fabrics.	Install a new blade frequently when cutting through "tough" fabrics.	Keep one blade set aside for cutting "tough" or heavy fabrics.

Problem	Cause	How to Prevent	How to Fix
Equipment Related — Continued			
Safety guard or screw catches on ruler while cutting.	Improper assembly of the cutter.	Always assemble your cutter according to the instructions on the package.	Disassemble and reassemble your cutter (page 6).
	The back of the cutter is against the ruler.	Cut with the blade, not the back side of the cutter, against the ruler.	Hold the rotary cutter correctly (page 29).
Cutting mat doesn't lie flat.	The mat is warped or bent.	Store your cutting mat flat, out of direct sunlight.	Buy a new mat.
Grid lines on mat don't line up with ruler markings.	Either the ruler or the mat grid is inaccurate.	Don't use the grids on the mat.	Use your ruler for all measuring, and stay with the same brand of ruler throughout your project.
Mat has an odor.	Chemical solvent from manufacturing process.	Check the mat before buying.	Odor will sometimes fade away after use.
Mat damaged by cleaning.	Harsh cleaning technique and/or cleaning solvent.	To clean, rub lightly with a small amount of Soft Scrub or diluted dishwashing liquid.	Buy a new mat.
Mat has small cuts that don't "heal" properly.	Improper angle of rotary cutter while cutting.	Cut with the handle at a 45 degree angle to the table and the blade straight up and down.	Buy a new mat.
Can't measure in $\frac{1}{8}$" increments.	No $\frac{1}{8}$" markings on the ruler.	Buy a ruler that has $\frac{1}{8}$" markings.	Buy a new ruler with $\frac{1}{8}$" markings.
Ruler damaged by cleaning.	Harsh cleaning technique and/or cleaning solvent.	Clean with rubbing alcohol. Do not use fingernail polish remover.	Buy a new ruler.
Ruler doesn't have markings for left-handed people.	Manufacturer's design.	Be a wise shopper. Don't buy a ruler that isn't designed for you.	Purchase the correct ruler for you!
Ruler slips when cutting.	Not enough pressure on the area of the ruler that you're cutting against.	"Smart-walk" while cutting (page 31).	Cut new pieces if the ruler slips while you're cutting.
	Not enough friction between the ruler and the fabric.	Use SlipNots on the bottom of your ruler (page 10).	Cut new pieces if the ruler slips while you're cutting.

(continued)

No-Fail Problem-Solving Guide – Continued

Problem	Cause	How to Prevent	How to Fix
Cutting Related			
Rotary cutter drags across the fabric.	Improper blade tension.	Maintain proper blade tension, as specified in the manufacturer's directions.	Loosen or tighten the nut to adjust to your personal cutting techniques.
	Dull blade.	Install a new blade frequently.	Replace the dull blade.
	Hand pressure too light.	Develop a "feel" for using uniform hand pressure on the cutter.	Hold the cutter tightly and press firmly as you cut.
	Too many fabric layers.	Cut through only two layers of fabric at a time.	Reduce number of layers of fabric.
	Blade angle misalignment.	Always hold the handle at a 45° angle to the fabric.	Increase or decrease angle to make it 45°.
The cutter "runs away" from the ruler when cutting long strips.	Improperly holding the rotary cutter.	Hold your cutter properly (page 29).	Keep your "driving finger" on the etched ridge located on the top of the cutter.
Dark fabric is hard to see on a dark mat.	Insufficient contrast.	Buy a mat that is reversible. One side will be light and the other side will be dark.	Switch mats.
Cannot see markings on the ruler when working with dark fabric.	Insufficient contrast.	Buy a ruler with contrasting color values. This is a must for accurate cutting.	Switch to a new ruler better suited for dark fabric.
Ruler slips while cutting.	Unstable ruler.	Use the "smart walking" method (page 31).	Keep even pressure on the ruler, especially over the fabric you are cutting.
	Ruler is too slippery.	Place SlipNots (page 10) or small pieces of fine sandpaper on the bottom of the ruler.	Cut new pieces if the ruler slips while you're cutting.
Piecing Related			
Strips are not straight after cutting; there is a slight "V" at the fold.	Failure to resquare often.	Always resquare the edge of fabric with the fold every 6", or the width of your ruler.	Cut new strips.
	Fabric misalignment.	Rotate the mat, not the fabric, when cutting.	Cut new strips.
Strip sets are wavy and irregular.	Improper pressing.	Press after sewing each strip on, not after joining all the strips in a strip set (page 99).	Make new strip sets.
	Inaccurately cut strips.	Follow proper cutting habits to ensure straight strips (page 31).	Cut new strips and make new strip sets.
	Strips stretched out of shape.	Cut stretchy fabric (loosely woven plaids or stripes) on the lengthwise grain.	Cut new strips.

Problem	Cause	How to Prevent	How to Fix
Piecing Related — Continued			
Block doesn't fit together properly.	Rotary cut pieces are not the correct size.	Printing is inaccurate on the ruler.	Buy a new ruler with accurately printed lines.
	Fabric was not pressed before cutting and cut pieces are too large.	Always press the fabric flat before cutting any strips or shapes.	Recut the shape from properly pressed fabric.
	Pieces are misshapen from stretching and being handled.	Handle your cut pieces as little as possible after cutting them.	Cut new shapes.
	Inaccurate seam allowance.	Sew with a perfect ¼" seam allowance (page 67). Do a sewing test (page 68) before sewing all your blocks.	Remake the block.
	Half-square triangles are distorted.	Trim dog ears before pressing (page 77) and "steer" the pairs through the sewing machine with a pin (page 76).	Remake the triangle squares.
Seams don't match up properly.	Improper pinning when sewing.	Always butt the seams tightly, pin properly (page 69), then sew.	Remake the block.
	Inaccurate seam allowance.	Sew with a perfect ¼" seam allowance (page 67). Do a sewing test (page 68) before sewing all your blocks.	Remake the block.
	Pieces are the wrong size.	Cut accurately with a reliable ruler (page 9), on properly pressed fabric (page 22).	Cut new pieces and remake the block.
Puckers and/or holes appear where miters join.	Improper setting in or mitering of corners.	Use a perfect ¼" stop (page 67).	Take out the stitching and redo the seams.
	View of needle position is blocked by presser foot.	Sew with an open-toe foot (page 57).	Purchase or make an open-toe presser foot and remake the block.
Borders are wavy or ripply.	Quilting in the border draws up the fabric, often unevenly.	Cut your border strips ⅛" to ¼" wider than the pattern states to allow for the drawing up.	Square off your border after quilting and before binding the quilt.
Pressed seams don't lie flat.	Iron is not hot enough.	Set iron on hottest setting.	Purchase a new iron if yours won't heat up enough.
	Foam pad on ironing board is too thick.	Purchase an ironing board with a foam pad no thicker than ¼".	Replace your thicker pad with a thinner one (¼" or less).
	Seam pressed in wrong direction.	Press away from the side that has multiple seam allowances within the seam allowance you are pressing.	Set seam and re-press the seam allowance in the opposite direction (page 98).

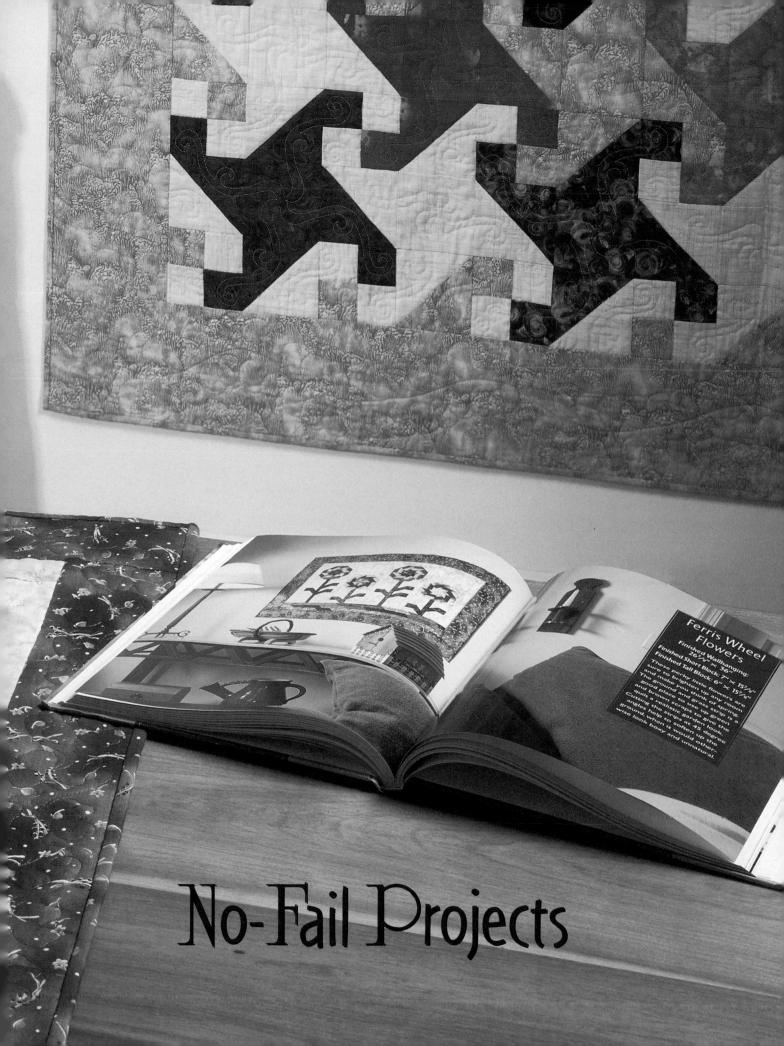

Ferris Wheel Flowers

Finished Wallhanging:
26⅞" × 36"
Finished Short Block: 7" × 15⅛"
Finished Tall Block: 6" × 15⅛"

These perky little flowers are sure to brighten up any room and make you think of spring. The ground and grass strip is a good place to use up green and brown scraps to give the quilt a realistic garden look. Cutting the strips at 45 degree angles help to soften up the ground when it would otherwise look boxy and unnatural.

No-Fail Projects

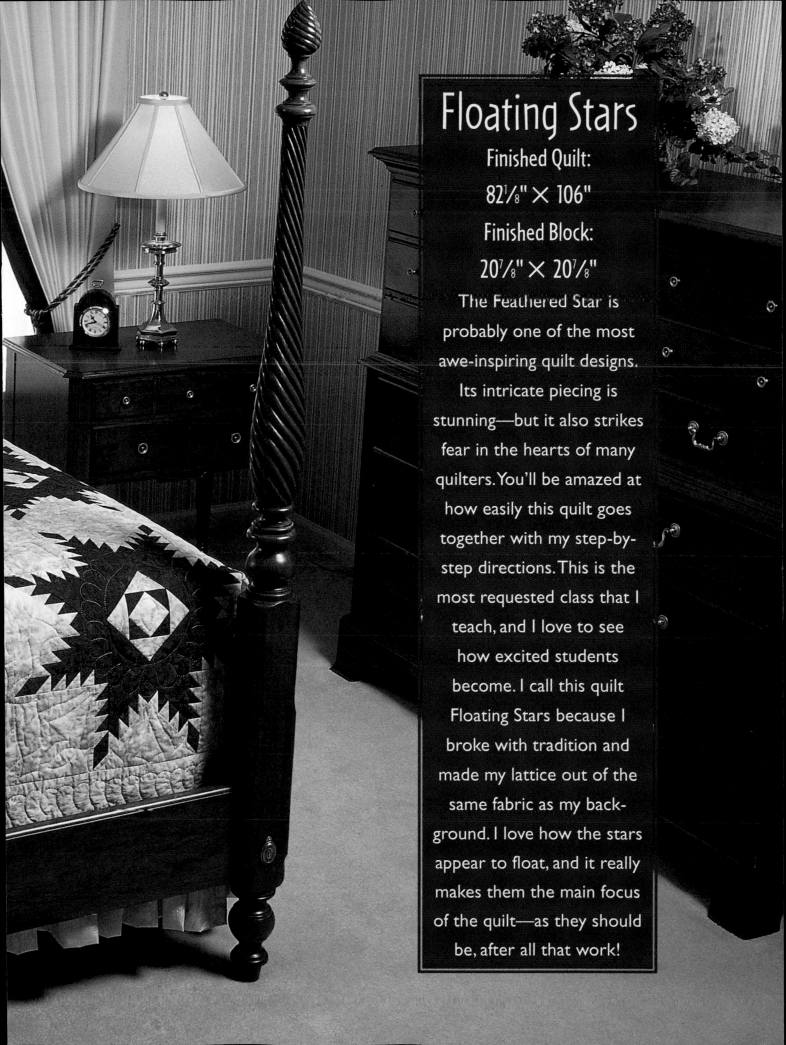

Floating Stars

Finished Quilt:
82⅛" × 106"

Finished Block:
20⅞" × 20⅞"

The Feathered Star is probably one of the most awe-inspiring quilt designs. Its intricate piecing is stunning—but it also strikes fear in the hearts of many quilters. You'll be amazed at how easily this quilt goes together with my step-by-step directions. This is the most requested class that I teach, and I love to see how excited students become. I call this quilt Floating Stars because I broke with tradition and made my lattice out of the same fabric as my background. I love how the stars appear to float, and it really makes them the main focus of the quilt—as they should be, after all that work!

Materials and Cutting Chart

Fabric	Used For	Strips to Cut		First Cut			Second Cut	
		Number	Size	Number	Shape	Size	Number	Shape
Dark 3¾ yards	A	15	2" × 40"	288	(37)	2" × 2"	576	(38)
	C	6	1⅝" × 40"	96	(48)	1⅝"	—	—
	D	4	1⅝" × 40"	96	(37)	1⅝" × 1⅝"	—	—
	E	4	5⅜" × 40"	24	(37)	5⅜" × 5⅜"	48	(38)
	F	4	5⅜" × 40"	24	(37)	5⅜" × 5⅜"	48	* (40)
	J	2	2⅝" × 40"	24	(37)	2⅝" × 2⅝"	48	(38)
	L	3	4¼" × 40"	24	(37)	4¼" × 4¼"	48	(38)
	Cornerstones	1	3½" × 40"	6	(37)	3½" × 3½"	—	—
Light 7¾ yards	B	20	2" × 40"	384	(37)	2" × 2"	768	(38)
	G	8	6⅝" × 40"	48	(37)	6⅝" × 6⅝"	—	—
	H	3	9⅞" × 40"	12	(37)	9⅞" × 9⅞"	48	(39)
	I	1	2¾" × 40"	12	(37)	2¾" × 2¾"	—	—
	K	2	3¼" × 40"	24	(37)	3¼" × 3¼"	48	(38)
	Lattice†	3	3½" × 130"	17	(44)	3½" × 21"	—	—
	Border†	2	7" × 95"	—	—	—	—	—
		2	7" × 86"	—	—	—	—	—

Batting 90" × 108"	Backing 88" × 112"	Binding Included in dark yardage

Note: Yardages are based on 40-inch-wide fabric after preshrinking. Page numbers in parentheses indicate where to find instructions for rotary cutting individual shapes.

*Left-handed quilters must cut the kites with the *wrong* side of the fabric facing up. Right-handed quilters must have the *right* side of the fabric facing up.

†Cut lattice and border strips on the lengthwise grain.

Floating Stars

The sky's the limit here: Make each star-point different from the rest of the star; make the feathers and the point the same but different from the star body; or have the point, the feathers, and the star body all different. Simplify the block by using a solid center square, then add pizzazz by appliquéing your favorite motif!

Block Diagram

Shapes Used

▪	(page 37)
◣	(page 38)
◥	(page 48)
▸	(page 40)
◒	(page 39)
▬	(page 44)

Techniques Used

Sewing Half-Square
Triangles (page 76)

Sewing Partial Seams
(page 86)

Sewing 4 Triangles to a
Square (page 87)

Squaring-Up Blocks
(page 90)

Attaching Lattice Strips
and Borders (page 91)

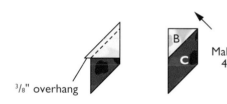

Diagram 2

Piecing the Block

Step 1
Sew an A triangle to a B triangle, as shown in **Diagram 1.** Trim the dog ears (page 77), and press toward A. Make a total of 48 AB Units.

❖ AB Units should measure 1⅝" × 1⅝".

Make 48

Diagram 1

Step 2
Sew a B triangle to a C diamond, placing them exactly as shown in **Diagram 2.** Press toward B, and trim the dog ears. Make four BC Units.

❖ BC Units should measure 1⅝" × 3⅝".

Step 3
Sew together three AB Units, as shown in **Diagram 3.** Add one of the BC Units you made in Step 2 to the bottom, as shown. Press as indicated by the arrow. Make four of Strip 1.

Strip 1

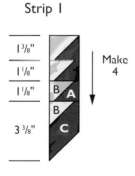

Diagram 3

Step 4

Sew a B triangle to a C diamond, placing them exactly as shown in **Diagram 4.** Press toward B, and trim the dog ears. Make four BC Units.

❖ BC Units should measure 1⅝" × 3⅝".

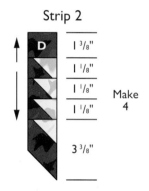

3/8" overhang

Diagram 4

Step 5

Sew together three AB Units, as shown in **Diagram 5.** Add a D square to the top and a BC Unit to the bottom, as shown. Press as indicated by the arrows. Make four of Strip 2.

Strip 2

D	1 ³/₈"
	1 ¹/₈"
	1 ¹/₈"
	1 ¹/₈"
	3 ³/₈"

Make 4

Diagram 5

Step 6

Align and pin Strip 1 to the right side of a G square, as shown in **Diagram 6.** The C diamond will hang over the G square by ⅜ inch. Sew, then press toward G. Do *not* trim the dog ear. In the same way, add Strip 2 to the top of G. Make four of Unit 1.

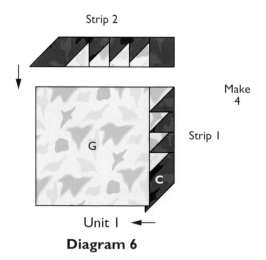

Strip 2

Make 4

Strip 1

G

C

Unit 1 ←

Diagram 6

Step 7

Sew together three AB Units, as shown in **Diagram 7.** Add a B triangle to the bottom. Press toward B. Make four of Strip 3.

Strip 3

1 ³/₈"	
1 ¹/₈"	
1 ¹/₈"	B A
1 ³/₄"	B

Make 4

Diagram 7

Step 8

Sew together three AB Units, as shown in **Diagram 8.** Add a D square to the top and a B triangle to the bottom. Press as indicated by the arrows. Make four of Strip 4.

Strip 4

D	1 ³/₈"
A B	1 ¹/₈"
	1 ¹/₈"
	1 ¹/₈"
B	1 ³/₄"

Make 4

Diagram 8

Step 9

Measure 4 inches up each short side of an H triangle, starting at the very tips, as shown in **Diagram 9.** Make a small pencil mark at each 4-inch point. Mark four H triangles.

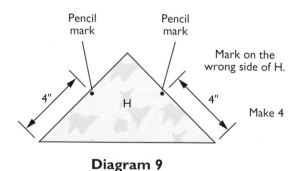

Pencil mark

Pencil mark

Mark on the wrong side of H.

4"

H

4"

Make 4

Diagram 9

Step 10

Align Strip 3 with the right side of the H triangle, as shown in **Diagram 10** on the opposite page. Make sure the bottom edge of the B triangle is 1⅛ inches from the bottom edge of the H triangle. Sew from the top of the unit until you reach the pencil mark. Press toward H. Make four sets.

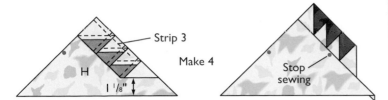

Diagram 10

Step 11

Align Strip 4 with the left side of the H triangle, as shown in **Diagram 11.** The bottom edge of the B triangle will be 1⅛ inches from the bottom edge of H. Sew from the top of the unit to the pencil mark. Press toward H. Make four sets.

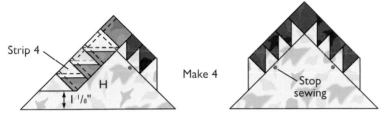

Diagram 11

Step 12

Sew an F kite to the right side of Strip 3, as shown in **Diagram 12.** Press toward F, and trim the dog ear. Make four sets.

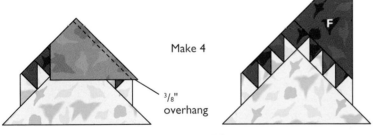

Diagram 12

Step 13

Sew an E triangle to the left side of Strip 4, as shown in **Diagram 13.** Press toward E, and trim the dog ears. Make four of Unit 2.

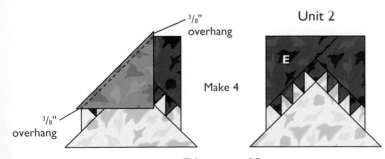

Diagram 13

Step 14

Sew J triangles to opposite sides of an I square, as shown in **Diagram 14A.** Press toward J and trim the dog ears. Sew J triangles to the remaining sides of I, as shown in **14B.** Press toward J, and trim the dog ears. The J triangles are oversize, so square up the unit.

❖ IJ Unit should measure 3¹¹⁄₁₆" × 3¹¹⁄₁₆" (between 3⅝" and 3¾" on your rotary ruler).

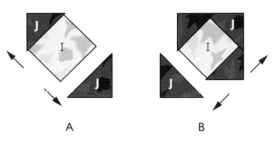

Diagram 14

Step 15

Sew K triangles to the IJ Unit, as shown in **Diagram 15.** Follow the directions for attaching the triangles in Step 14.

❖ IJK Unit should measure 5" × 5".

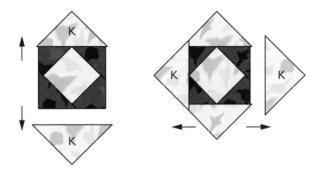

Diagram 15

Step 16

Similarly, sew L triangles to the IJK Unit, as shown in **Diagram 16.** The L triangles are oversize, so square up the Center Unit.

❖ Center Unit should measure 6⅞" × 6⅞".

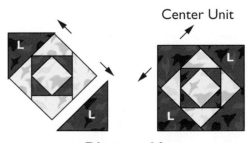

Diagram 16

Step 17

Pin and sew a Unit 1 to each side of a Unit 2, as shown in **Diagram 17**. The B triangles in Unit 2 will hang over the C diamonds in each Unit 1 by ⅜ inch. When sewing, pull the H triangles out of the way so they don't get caught in the seams—the partial seams will be sewn later. Press toward Unit 2. Make two of Row 1.

Row 1

Unit 1 → Unit 2 ← Unit 1

Make 2

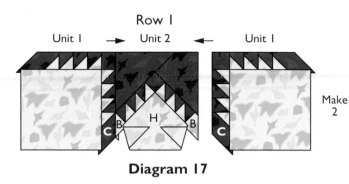

Diagram 17

Step 18

Pin and sew a Unit 2 to each side of the Center Unit, as shown in **Diagram 18**. Press away from the Center Unit. Make one of Row 2.

Row 2

Unit 2 ← Center Unit → Unit 2

Make 1

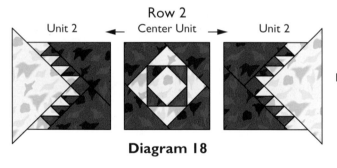

Diagram 18

Step 19

Butt (page 69) and pin a Row 1 to each side of Row 2, as shown in **Diagram 19**. The B triangles in Unit 2 will hang over the C diamonds in each Row 1 by ⅜ inch. When sewing, pull the H triangles out of the way so they don't get caught in the seams. Press toward Row 2.

Row 1

Row 2

Row 1

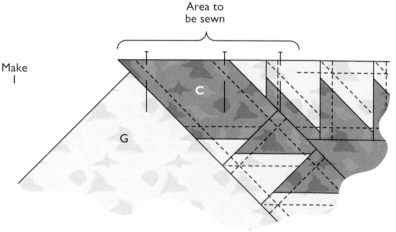

Diagram 19

Step 20

Match the tips of the C diamonds with the tips of the H triangles, and pin and sew the partial seams, as shown in **Diagram 20**. Repeat Steps 1 through 20 to make a total of 12 blocks.

Area to be sewn

Diagram 20

Assembling the Quilt Top

Step 1

Measure the star blocks and cut the 3½-inch lattice strips to match the length of the block edge (page 91). You need a total of 17 lattice strips.

Step 2

Referring to the **Quilt Diagram** on the opposite page, arrange the star blocks, cornerstones, and lattice strips into rows. Butt (page 69), pin, and sew the rows together. Press the seams toward the lattice.

Quilt Diagram

Adding the Borders

Step 1
Measure the quilt for the side borders (page 103), and trim the two longer border strips to fit. Pin and sew the borders to the sides (page 103). Press toward the borders.

Step 2
Measure for the top and bottom borders, and trim the remaining two strips to fit. Pin and sew the borders to the top and bottom. Press toward the borders.

Finishing the Quilt

Step 1
Layer the backing, batting, and quilt top. Quilt as desired. This quilt was machine quilted in the ditch around the stars and with feathers in the border.

Step 2
Square up the quilt top (page 104). Make and attach double-fold binding (page 107).

Pine Tree Delight

Finished Wallhanging:

55" × 55"

Finished Block:

17¾" × 17¾"

I just love this pattern because the stars and pine trees make me think of the woods where I live. The Pine Tree is a very versatile block that never fails to create a bold, graphic look. Here I've accented the pine trees with stars created by the lattice. This quilt is sure to be a show-stopper and will undoubtedly make your family and friends think you're a genius!

Materials and Cutting Chart

Fabric	Used For	Strips to Cut Number	Strips to Cut Size	First Cut Number	First Cut Shape	First Cut Size	Second Cut Number	Second Cut Shape
Light ⅞ yard	A	1	8¼" × 40"	4	■ (37)	8¼" × 8¼"	8	▶ * (40)
	B	1	5" × 21"	4	■ (37)	5" × 5"	8	◹ (38)
	C	1	1¾" × 22"	12	■ (37)	1¾" × 1¾"	—	—
	D	4	2⅛" × 40"	72	■ (37)	2⅛" × 2⅛"	144	◹ (38)
Red† ⅜ yard	E	2	2⅛" × 40"	21	■ (37)	2⅛" × 2⅛"	42	◹ (38)
	F	—	—	1	■ (37)	6⅝" × 6⅝"	2	◹ (38)
	G	—	—	1	▬ (44)	2½" × 9"	1	▶ (50)
Gold 1¼ yard	H	3	10½" × 40"	8	■ (37)	10½" × 10½"	16	◹ (38)
Navy Blue ½ yard	I	2	2⅛" × 40"	36	■ (37)	2⅛" × 2⅛"	72	◹ (38)
	J	1	3" × 30"	9	■ (37)	3" × 3"	—	—
	O	1	5" × 21"	4	■ (37)	5" × 5"	—	—
Tan/Taupe 1 yard	K	6	3" × 40"	—	—	—	—	—
	L	4	1¾" × 40"	—	—	—	—	—
	M	1	3¾" × 12"	3	■ (37)	3¾" × 3¾"	12	⊠ (39)
	N	1	1¾" × 9"	4	■ (37)	1¾" × 1¾"	—	—
Dark Brown 1½ yards‡	Outer Border	4	5" × 49"	—	—	—	—	—

Batting 59" × 59"	Backing 59" × 59"	Binding ½ yard

Note: Yardages are based on 40-inch-wide fabric after preshrinking. Page numbers in parentheses indicate where to find instructions for rotary cutting individual shapes.

*Cut kites with half-square triangles positioned with wrong sides together.

†Fabric amounts and cutting directions are for *one* tree block. Purchase and cut *four* different reds to make the quilt shown.

‡Cut outer border strips on the lengthwise grain. If you don't mind piecing your outer border, purchase only ⅞ yard.

Pine Tree Delight

Here's a place to use those gradated fabrics you've looked at but couldn't imagine how to use. I started with the lightest shades from Benartex's Barn Dance collection in the lattice, then continued with the medium in the borders and the dark in the binding.

Shapes Used

- (page 37)
- (page 40)
- (page 38)
- (page 44)
- (page 50)
- (page 39)
- (page 51)

Techniques Used

Sewing Half-Square Triangles (page 76)

Sewing 4 Triangles to a Square (page 87)

Making Flying Geese (page 89)

Squaring-Up Blocks (page 90)

Attaching Lattice Strips and Borders (page 91)

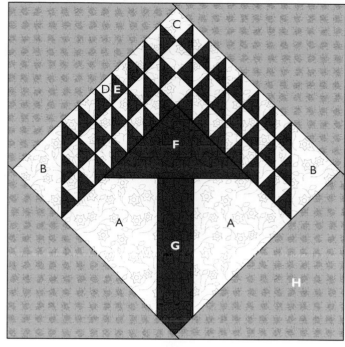

Block Diagram

See pages 130–133 for placement of pieces I through N.

Piecing the Blocks

Step 1
Sew the bias edge of an A kite to opposite sides of a G prism, as shown in **Diagram 1.** Press toward G.

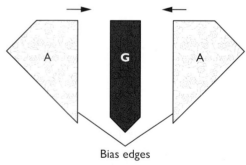

Bias edges

Diagram 1

Step 2
Sew an F triangle to the top of the AG Unit, as shown in **Diagram 2.** The tips of F will hang past the AG Unit by ⅜ inch on each end. (Discard the extra F triangle, or save it to use in another project.) Press toward F, and trim the dog ears. Square up if necessary (page 90).

❖ AGF Unit should measure 9¼" × 9¼".

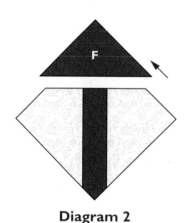

Diagram 2

Step 3
Sew a D triangle to an E triangle, as shown in **Diagram 3.** Trim the dog ears, and press toward E. Make 36 DE Units.

❖ DE Units should measure 1¾" × 1¾".

Make 36

Diagram 3

Step 4

Following **Diagram 4,** sew six DE Units together, then add an E triangle to one end of each row. Sew C squares to the opposite ends of rows 2, 4, and 6. Press as indicated by the arrows.

❖ C squares should now measure 1½" × 1¾".

❖ DE Units should now measure 1¼" × 1¾".

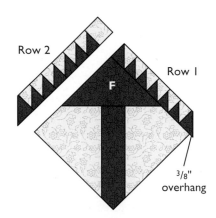

Diagram 5

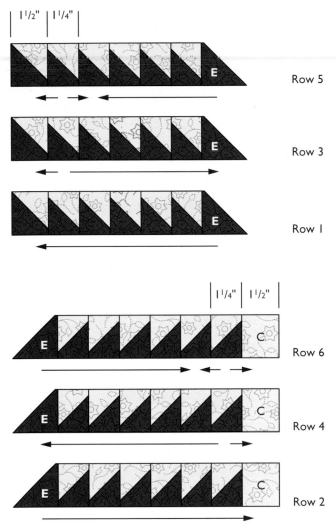

Diagram 4

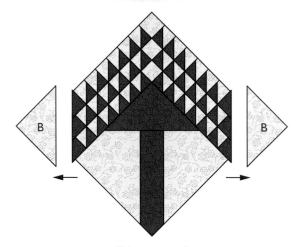

Diagram 6

Step 5

Sew Row 1 to the top right side of the AGF Unit, as shown in **Diagram 5.** The tip of the E triangle will hang over the edge of the unit by ⅜ inch. Press toward F. Add Row 2, and press toward F. Add rows 3, 4, 5, and 6, stopping after each row to press toward F.

Step 6

Sew B triangles to the sides of the block, as shown in **Diagram 6.** Press toward B. The B triangles are oversize, so square up the block (page 90).

❖ Block should measure 13" × 13".

Step 7

Sew H triangles to opposite sides of the block, as shown in **Diagram 7.** Press toward H. Sew H triangles to the two remaining sides. Press. The H triangles are oversize, so square up the block (page 90). Repeat Steps 1 through 7 to make a total of four Pine Tree blocks.

❖ Block should measure 18¼" × 18¼".

Diagram 7

Making and Attaching the Lattice

Measure the Pine Tree blocks for lattice (page 91). They should all be 18¼ inches square, but measure each one just to be certain. Cut the 3-inch-wide K strips to the measured length plus ¼ inch (because a double prism's length is cut size + ¾ inch; page 51). You will need 12 K rectangles. Cut the rectangles into double prisms (page 51). Cut the 1¾-inch-wide L strips to the measured length of the block. You will need eight L rectangles.

Step 1

Sew I triangles to K prisms, as shown in **Diagram 8.** There will be a ⅜-inch dog ear on both ends of each I triangle. Press toward I. Sew another I to the other side of the K triangle. Press toward I, and trim the dog ears. Repeat on the other end of K. Make 12 sets.

❖ IK Unit length should match the block length.

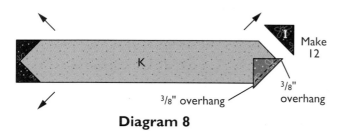

3/8" overhang   3/8" overhang

Diagram 8

Step 2

Make an IM Flying Geese block (page 89). Sew an I triangle to an M triangle, as shown in **Diagram 9.** Press toward I, and trim the dog ears. Repeat on the other side of M. Make a total of 12 IM Flying Geese.

❖ Flying Geese Unit should measure 1¾" × 3".

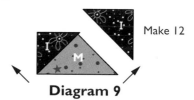

Make 12

Diagram 9

Step 3

Arrange and sew together N squares, IM Flying Geese Units, and L strips to make two of Lattice Row 1, as shown in **Diagram 10.** Arrange and sew together IM Flying Geese Units, J squares, and IK Units to make three of Lattice Row 2, as shown in the diagram. Press as indicated by the arrows.

Assembling the Wallhanging

Step 1

Sew together the Pine Tree blocks, IK Units, and L strips, as shown in **Diagram 11.** Press as indicated by the arrows. Make a total of two rows.

Row 1

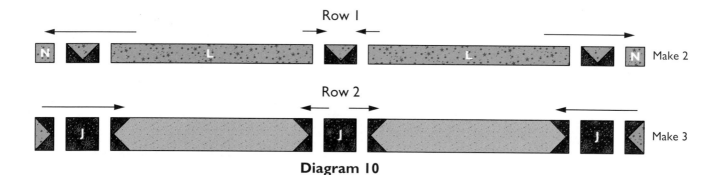

N   L   L   N   Make 2

Row 2

J   J   J   Make 3

Diagram 10

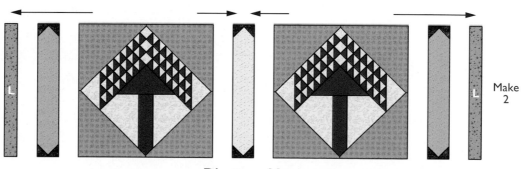

L   L   Make 2

Diagram 11

Step 2

Referring to **Diagram 12,** butt (page 69), pin, and sew lattice rows 1 and 2 to the block rows. Press as indicated by the arrows.

Adding the Borders

Step 1

Measure the wallhanging for side, top, and bottom borders (page 103). Cut all four of the 5-inch-wide outer border strips to this length, piecing them if necessary. Pin and sew the borders to the sides, as shown in **Diagram 13.** Press toward the borders.

Step 2

Sew an O square to each end of the two remaining border strips, as shown in **Diagram 13.** Press toward the border. Butt (page 69), pin, and sew these borders to the top and bottom, as shown in the **Quilt Diagram** on the opposite page. Press toward the borders.

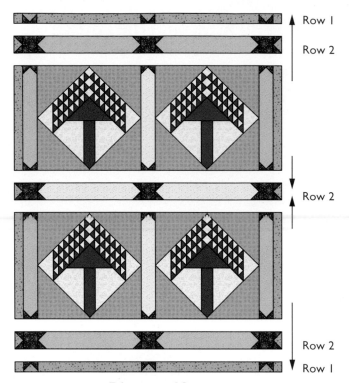

Diagram 12

Finishing the Wallhanging

Step 1

Layer the backing, batting, and wallhanging. Quilt as desired. This wallhanging was machine quilted in the ditch around all the tree's "leaves," and it has heart and leaf motifs quilted throughout the background, setting triangles, lattice, and borders.

Step 2

Square up the wallhanging (page 104). Make and attach double-fold binding (page 107).

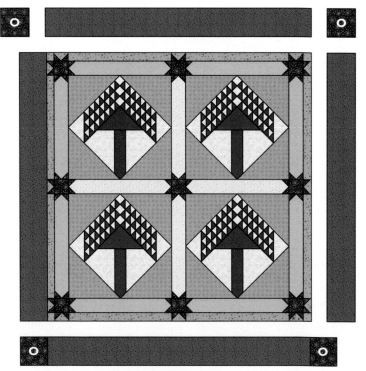

Diagram 13

Quilt Diagram

Campbell House

Finished Wallhanging:
24" × 35½"

Finished House: 6" × 6"

I like to name my quilt designs after special people, and this one is named for my friend Bonnie Campbell, who always knows when I need bailing out. The house resembles her former home, complete with a white picket fence. This wallhanging is a natural to make as a very special housewarming gift.

Materials and Cutting Chart

Fabric	Used For	Strips to Cut		First Cut			Second Cut	
		Number	Size	Number	Shape	Size	Number	Shape
House* Fat Eighth (8" × 22")	A	2	1" × 22"†	4	▬ (44)	1" × 2½"	—	—
	E			1	▬ (44)	1" × 5½"	—	—
	G			2	■ (37)	1" × 1"	—	—
	H			8	▬ (44)	1" × 2"	—	—
	C	1	1¼" × 4"	2	▬ (11)	1¼" × 1½"	—	—
Windows* Scraps	B	1	1½" × 4"	2	▬ (44)	1½" × 1¾"	—	—
	F	1	1" × 5"	4	■ (37)	1" × 1"	—	—
Door* Scraps	D	—	—	1	▬ (44)	1½" × 2½"	—	—
Sky ⅜ yard	I	2	1" × 40"	10	▬ (44)	1" × 4½"	—	—
	J	1	2⅛" × 12"	5	■ (37)	2⅛" × 2⅛"	10	◹ (38)
	L	1	1¼" × 40"‡	10	▬ (44)	1¼" × 1¾"	—	—
	N			5	▬ (44)	1¼" × 2½"	—	—
	V1	1	6½" × 40"§	1	▬ (44)	6½" × 7½"	—	—
	V2			1	■ (37)	6½" × 6½"	—	—
	V3			1	▬ (44)	6½" × 5½"	—	—
	V4			1	▬ (44)	6½" × 4½"	—	—
	V5			1	▬ (44)	6½" × 3½"	—	—
Roof* Scraps	K	1	1¾" × 7¼"	1	◢ (46)	1¾" × 7¼"	—	—
Chimney* Scraps	M	1	1¼" × 3"	2	■ (37)	1¼" × 1¼"	—	—
Grass ¼ yard	O	1	2¼" × 40"	5	▬ (44)	2¼" × 6½"	—	—
	P	2	1" × 40"	—	—	—	—	—
Fence ⅛ yard	Q	1	1" × 40"	—	—	—	—	—
	R	1	2" × 40"	30	▬ (44)	1" × 2"	—	—
Ground Fat Eighth	S	2	1¾" × 22"	5	▬ (44)	1¾" × 6½"	—	—
Water Fat Eighth	T1	1	6½" × 22"‖	1	▬ (44)	6½" × 1½"	—	—
	T2			1	▬ (44)	6½" × 2½"	—	—
	T3			1	▬ (44)	6½" × 3½"	—	—
	T4			1	▬ (44)	6½" × 4½"	—	—
	T5			1	▬ (44)	6½" × 5½"	—	—
Border ⅓ yard	Border	3	3" × 40"	—	—	—	—	—

Batting 30" × 41"	Backing 30" × 41"	Binding ¼ yard

Note: Yardages are based on 40-inch-wide fabric after preshrinking. Page numbers in parentheses indicate where to find instructions for rotary cutting individual shapes.

*Fabric amounts and cutting directions are for *one* house. Purchase and cut *five* of each of these fabrics to make the quilt shown.

†Cut all A, E, G, and H pieces from these strips.

‡Cut all L and N pieces from this strip.

§Cut all V pieces from this strip.

‖Cut all T pieces from this strip.

Campbell House

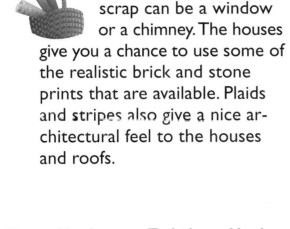

What a great project for your scrap bin! The tiniest scrap can be a window or a chimney. The houses give you a chance to use some of the realistic brick and stone prints that are available. Plaids and stripes also give a nice architectural feel to the houses and roofs.

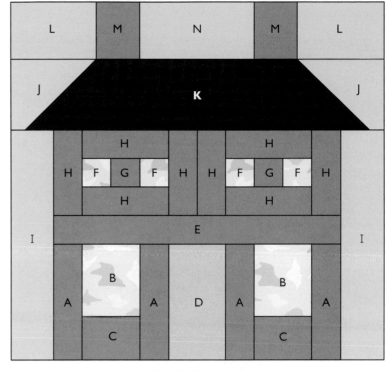

Block Diagram

See pages 138–141 for placement of pieces O through V.

Shapes Used

(page 44)
(page 37)
(page 38)
(page 46)

Techniques Used

Strip Piecing
(page 81)
Making Flying Geese
(page 89)

Piecing the House Blocks

Step 1
Sew a B rectangle to a C rectangle, as shown in **Diagram 1.** Press toward C. Make two BC Units.

❖ BC Unit should measure 1½" × 2½".

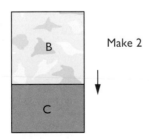

Make 2

Diagram 1

Step 2
Sew an A rectangle to each side of each BC Unit, as shown in **Diagram 2.** Press toward A. Make two ABC Units.

❖ ABC Unit should measure 2½" × 2½".

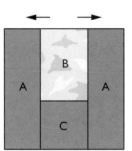

Make 2

Diagram 2

Step 3
Sew an ABC Unit to each side of a D rectangle, as shown in **Diagram 3.** Press toward D.

❖ ABCD Unit should measure 2½" × 5½".

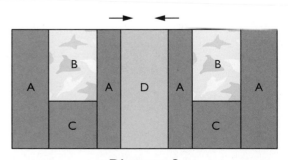

Diagram 3

Step 4

Add an E rectangle to the top of the ABCD Unit, as shown in **Diagram 4.** Press toward E.

❖ Unit should measure 3" × 5½".

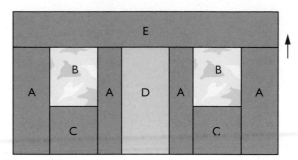

Diagram 4

Step 5

Sew F squares to opposite sides of a G square, as shown in **Diagram 5.** Press toward G. Make two FG Units.

❖ FG Units should measure 1" × 2".

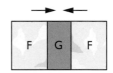

Make 2

Diagram 5

Step 6

Sew an H rectangle to the top and bottom of each FG Unit, as shown in **Diagram 6.** Press toward H. Make two FGH Units.

❖ FGH Units should measure 2" × 2".

Make 2

Diagram 6

Step 7

Arrange and sew H rectangles and FGH Units as shown in **Diagram 7.** Press toward H. Press the center seam in either direction.

❖ Unit should measure 2" × 5½".

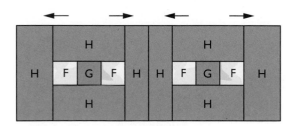

Diagram 7

Step 8

Sew this new FGH Unit to the ABCD Unit from Step 4, as shown in **Diagram 8.** Press toward E.

❖ Unit should measure 4½" × 5½".

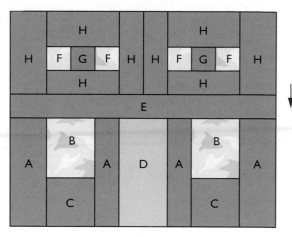

Diagram 8

Step 9

Sew an I rectangle to each side of the unit from Step 8, as shown in **Diagram 9.** Press toward I.

❖ House Unit should measure 4½" × 6½".

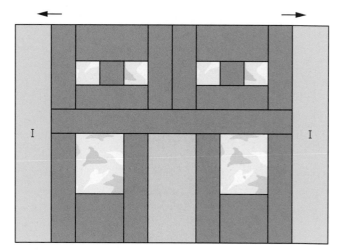

House Unit
Diagram 9

Step 10

Sew J triangles to each side of a K trapezoid as for a Flying Geese block (page 89), as shown in **Diagram 10** on the opposite page. Press toward J, and trim the dog ears (page 77).

❖ Roof Unit should measure 1¾" × 6½".

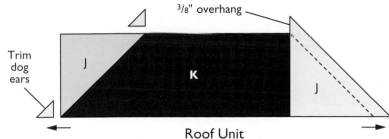

³/₈" overhang

Trim dog ears

J

K

J

Roof Unit
Diagram 10

Diagram 13

Step 11

Sew the Roof Unit to the top of the House Unit, as shown in **Diagram 11.** Press toward the roof.

❖ House and Roof Unit should measure 5¾" × 6½".

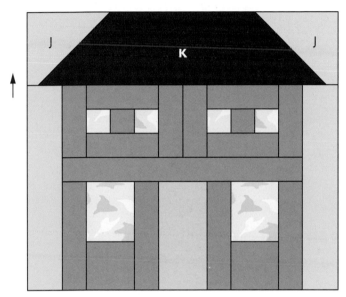

J K J

Diagram 11

Piecing the Grass and Fence

Step 1

Make a PQP strip set (page 81), as shown in **Diagram 14.** Press toward Q.

❖ PQP strip set should measure 2" wide.

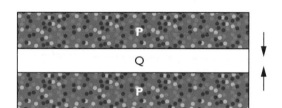

P

Q

P

Diagram 14

Step 12

Arrange and sew L, M, and N pieces as shown in **Diagram 12.** Press toward M.

❖ Chimney Unit should measure 1¼" × 6½".

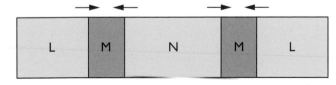

L M N M L

Chimney Unit
Diagram 12

Step 2

Cut the strip set into thirty 1-inch segments, as shown in **Diagram 15.**

❖ Segments should measure 1" × 2".

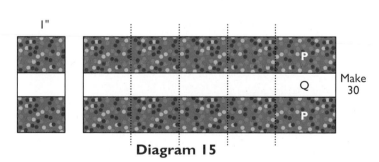

1"

P

Q

P

Make 30

Diagram 15

Step 13

Sew the Chimney Unit to the House and Roof Unit, as shown in **Diagram 13.** Press toward the Chimney Unit. Repeat Steps 1 through 13 to make a total of five houses.

❖ Block should measure 6½" × 6½".

Step 3
Arrange and sew six PQP segments and six R rectangles, as shown in **Diagram 16.** Press toward R. Make five Fence Units.

❖ Fence Units should measure 2" × 6½".

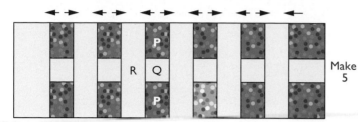

Diagram 16

Step 4
Sew an O rectangle to the top of the Fence Unit and an S rectangle to the bottom, as shown in **Diagram 17.** Press away from the fence. Make five units.

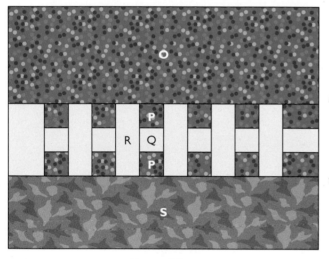

Fence Unit

Diagram 17

Assembling the Wallhanging

Refer to the **Quilt Diagram** on the opposite page for the following steps.

Step 1
Sew the houses to the fence units. Press toward the fence units.

Step 2
Lay the houses out in the order you want them to be in the wallhanging. Sew the appropriate T pieces to the bottoms of the Fence Units, and the appropriate V pieces to the tops of the House Units. Press the seams in either direction.

Step 3
Sew the houses together. Press the seams in either direction.

Adding the Borders

Step 1
Cut one border strip in half. Measure the wallhanging for the side borders (page 103) and trim the shorter border strips to fit. Pin and sew the borders to the sides (page 103). Press toward the borders.

Step 2
Measure for the top and bottom borders, and trim the longer strips to fit. Pin and sew the borders to the top and bottom. Press toward the borders.

Finishing the Wallhanging

Step 1
Layer the backing, batting, and top. Quilt as desired. This wallhanging was machine quilted in the ditch around the houses and fences, with random stippling in the sky, leaves on the ground, apples in the grass, and lucky clovers in the water and border.

Step 2
Square up the wallhanging (page 104). Make and attach double-fold binding (page 107).

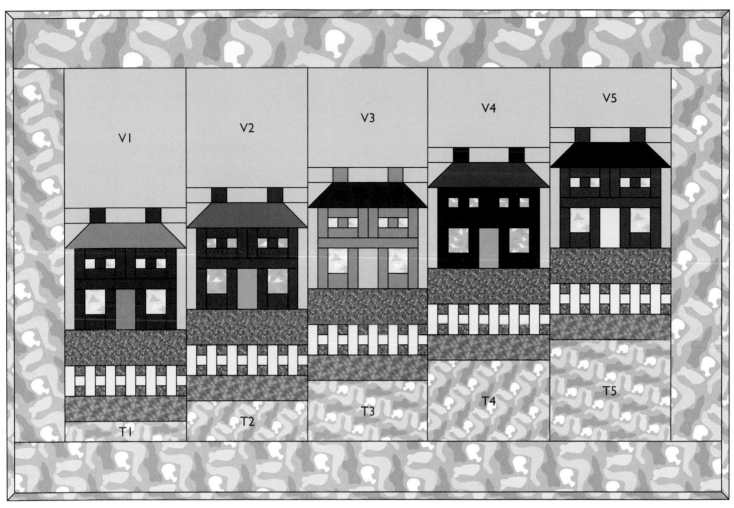

Quilt Diagram

Color Variation

The wallhanging shown on page 134 is my "California Beach House" version of the Campbell House. I made it one winter when there was three feet of snow in my driveway, and I was dreaming about being on the beach. The version shown here is a little more traditional, and it looks more like the houses you'd find in town. It was made by Ruth Lindhagen, who collects house quilts.

Monkey Wrench Times 2

Finished Wallhanging:
49½" × 49½"

Finished Blocks: 12" × 12"

This quilt is quintessential country, with its scrappy mix of 9 different backgrounds and 27 different plaids and stripes. The real crowd-pleaser is the way the center of the quilt extends out into the border. I didn't want to fence-in this explosion of plaids by just bordering it with four strips of fabric, so I designed a border that blended with the background and continued the design. Believe me…this just *looks* tricky. It's very easy to piece.

—

Materials and Cutting Chart

Fabric	Used For	Strips to Cut — Number	Strips to Cut — Size	First Cut — Number	First Cut — Shape	First Cut — Size	Second Cut — Number	Second Cut — Shape
Lights* 8" × 28" scrap	A	1	3⅞" × 9"	2	■ (37)	3⅞" × 3⅞"	4	◣ (38)
	C	1	2" × 28"	—	—	—	—	—
6" × 12" scrap	A1	1	2⅞" × 7"	2	■ (37)	2⅞" × 2⅞"	4	◣ (38)
	C1	1	1½" × 12"	—	—	—	—	—
3" × 24" strip	E	1	2½" × 24"	9	■ (37)	2½" × 2½"	—	—
Scraps	A2	—	—	14	■ (37)	3⅞" × 3⅞"	28	◣ (38)
Mediums/ Darks* 8" × 28" scrap	B	1	3⅞" × 9"	2	■ (37)	3⅞" × 3⅞"	4	◣ (38)
	D	1	2" × 28"	—	—	—	—	—
6" × 12" scrap	B1	1	2⅞" × 7"	2	■ (37)	2⅞" × 2⅞"	4	◣ (38)
	D1	1	1½" × 12"	—	—	—	—	—
Medium-Dark Tan Print 1¼ yards	Border 1	4	1¾" × 40"	—	—	—	—	—
	Border 3	4	1¼" × 40"	—	—	—	—	—
	Border 4	5	4" × 40"	—	—	—	—	—
	F	1	1¼" × 40"	8	▬ (44)	1¼" × 4¼"	8	▰ (46)
Dark Red ⅓ yard	Border 2	4	1½" × 40"	—	—	—	—	—
	G	1	2¾" × 6"	2	■ (37)	2¾" × 2¾"	8	✕ (39)

Batting 54" × 54"	Backing 54" × 54"	Binding ⅜ yard

Note: Yardages are based on 40-inch-wide fabric after preshrinking. Page numbers in parentheses indicate where to find instructions for rotary cutting individual shapes.

*Fabric amounts and cutting directions are for *one* block. Purchase and cut *nine* lights and *nine* mediums/darks to make the quilt shown.

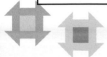

Monkey Wrench Times 2

Scrappy backgrounds are a lot of fun, but make sure your background fabrics don't fight with each other. They should vary in shade but stay similar in scale. You don't want one bold design to stand out—after all, it's called a background for a reason!

Shapes Used

(page 37)
(page 38)
(page 39)
(page 44)
(page 46)

Techniques Used

Sewing Half-Square
  Triangles (page 76)
Strip Piecing (page 81)
Making Flying Geese
  (page 89)

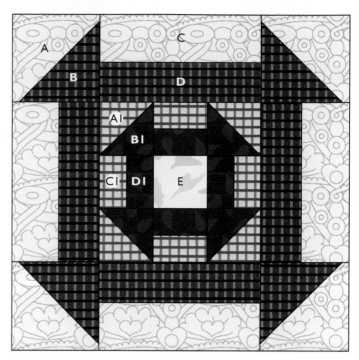

Block Diagram

See pages 148–149 for placement of pieces F and G.

Piecing the Blocks

Step 1

Sew an AI triangle to a BI triangle, as shown in **Diagram 1.** Trim the dog ears, and press toward BI. Repeat to make a total of four AIBI Units.

❖ AIBI Units should measure 2½" × 2½".

Make 4

Diagram I

Step 2

Make a CIDI strip set (page 81), as shown in **Diagram 2.** Press toward DI. Cut four 2½-inch segments.

❖ CIDI segments should measure 2½" × 2½".

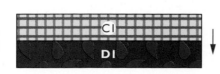

Diagram 2

Step 3

Pin, sew, and press the AIBI Units, CIDI segments, and an E square into rows, as shown in **Diagram 3.** Butt, pin, and sew the rows together into a Block Center. Press the seams in either direction.

❖ Block Center should measure 6½" × 6½".

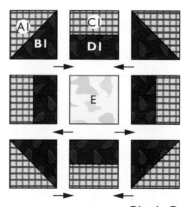
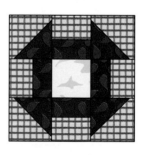

Block Center

Diagram 3

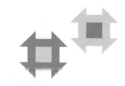

Step 4

Sew an A triangle to a B triangle. Do *not* press the seam yet. Repeat to make a total of four AB Units.

❖ AB Units should measure 3½" × 3½".

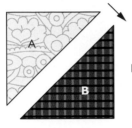

Diagram 4

Make 4

Step 5

Make a CD strip set (page 81), as shown in **Diagram 5.** Press toward D. Cut four 6½-inch segments.

❖ CD segments should measure 3½" × 6½".

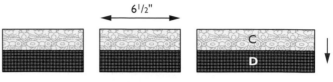

6½"

Diagram 5

Step 6

Repeat Steps 1 through 5 with different fabrics to make a total of nine sets of Block Centers, AB Units, and CD segments.

Assembly Diagram

Assembling the Wallhanging

The secret to this wallhanging is in the pressing. In order to get a perfectly square wallhanging, you have to butt all your seams. Follow the **Assembly Diagram** on the opposite page carefully, and you'll be pleased with your beautiful results!

Step 1
Hang a flannel sheet or a large piece of cotton batting on a wall, and arrange your Block Centers, CD segments, and AB Units as shown in the **Assembly Diagram.** Refer to the photograph on page 142 as needed for color placement.

Step 2
The top consists of four piecing units: Block Centers (see **Diagram 3** on page 145), Vertical Units, Horizontal Units, and Pieced Squares. Referring to **Diagram 6,** assemble and press the units.

Vertical Unit

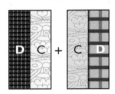

Make 6.
Refer to **Assembly Diagram** for pressing direction.

Horizontal Unit

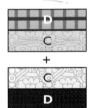

Make 6.
Refer to **Assembly Diagram** for pressing direction.

Pieced Square

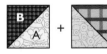

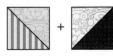

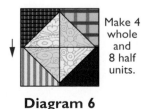

Make 4 whole and 8 half units.

Refer to **Assembly Diagram** for pressing direction.

Diagram 6

Step 3
Assemble the top into rows, referring to the **Assembly Diagram** on the opposite page. Press toward the Horizontal and Vertical Units. Sew the rows together.

Adding the Borders

Step 1
Sew together the Border 1 strips and the Border 2 strips. Press toward Border 2. Add the Border 3 strip, as shown in **Diagram 7.** Press toward Border 2. Repeat to make a total of four strip sets. Cut the strip sets into twelve 13¼-inch border segments.

❖ Border segments should measure 3½" × 13¼".

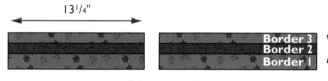

Diagram 7

Step 2
Cut the segments into trapezoids (page 46), as shown in **Diagram 8.** Be sure to place the narrow border strip (Border 3) at the *bottom* of the trapezoid.

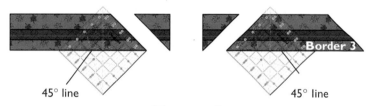

Diagram 8

Step 3
Sew an A2 triangle to each end of each trapezoid, as for a Flying Geese Unit (page 89). See **Diagram 9.** Press toward the trapezoid on eight units and toward the triangles on four units.

❖ Border Units should measure 3½" × 12½".

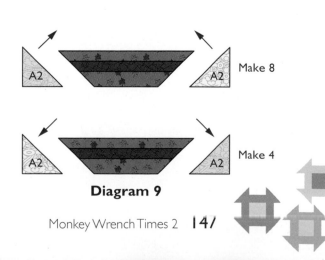

Make 8

Make 4

Diagram 9

Step 4

Sew a G triangle to an F trapezoid, as shown in **Diagram 10.** Repeat to make a total of eight FG Units. Press toward F on four units and toward G on four units.

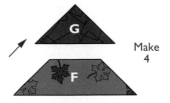

Make 4

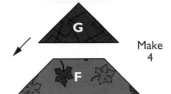

Make 4

3/8" overhang

Diagram 10

Step 5

Butt, pin, and sew opposite-pressed FG Units together into sets, as shown in **Diagram 11A.** Press the seam in either direction. Sew an A2 triangle to each FG set, as shown in **11B.** Press toward A2. Make four Corner Units.

❖ Corner Units should measure 3½" × 3½".

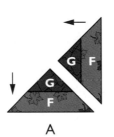

A

A2

B

Corner Unit

Diagram 11

Step 6

Referring to the **Quilt Diagram** on the opposite page and the pressing arrows in **Diagram 12,** arrange the Border Units and Corner Units into rows. Butt, pin, and sew the side borders on, and press toward the border. Butt, pin, and sew the top and bottom borders on, and press toward the borders.

Bottom Border

Top Border

Left Side Border

Right Side Border

Diagram 12

Step 7

Cut one Border 4 strip into four equal pieces and sew each piece to a long border strip. Measure the quilt top for the side borders (page 103), and trim two border strips to fit. Pin and sew the borders to the sides (page 103). Press toward Border 4. Measure for the top and bottom borders, and trim the remaining two strips to fit. Pin and sew the borders to the top and bottom. Press toward Border 4.

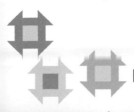

Finishing the Wallhanging

Step 1 Layer the backing, batting, and top. Quilt as desired. This wallhanging was machine quilted with heart-and-leaf patterns in the blocks and borders.

Step 2 Square up your wallhanging (page 104). Make and attach double-fold binding (page 107).

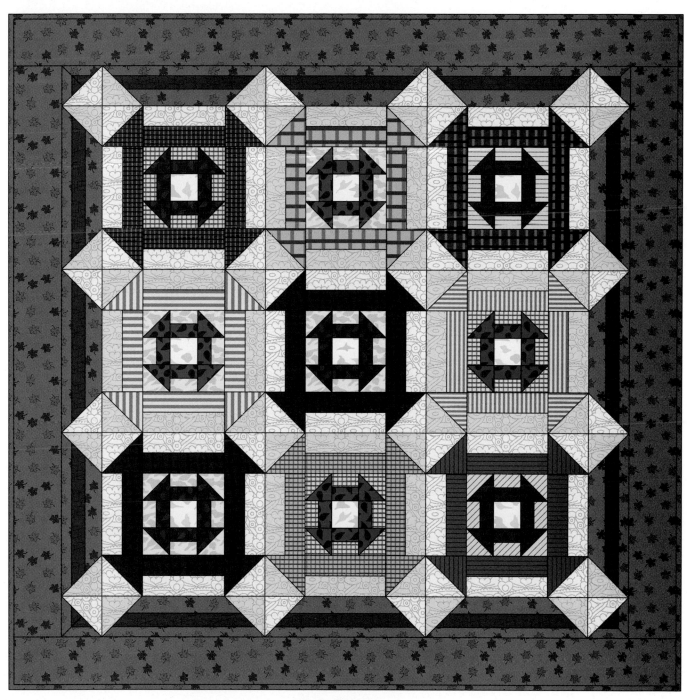

Quilt Diagram

Indian Puzzle

Finished Quilt: 73" × 73"

Finished Piecing Units: 4" × 4"

Who would believe you could get so much movement and variety from only two basic shapes—a square and a triangle. I like to call the smaller wallhanging on page 154 the Country version, and this bed topper (made by my friend Janet McCarroll) the Rock 'n Roll version. The larger quilt is made of bigger blocks—an easy shortcut to make a bed-size quilt without making four times as many blocks.

Materials and Cutting Chart

Fabric	Used For	Strips to Cut		First Cut			Second Cut	
		Number	Size	Number	Shape	Size	Number	Shape
Light 3¼ yards	A	6	2½" × 40"	96	■ (37)	2½" × 2½"	—	—
	B	5	4⅞" × 40"	40	■ (37)	4⅞" × 4⅞"	80	◨ (38)
	C	2	4½" × 40"	16	■ (37)	4½" × 4½"	—	—
	Borders	8	6¾" × 40"	—	—	—	—	—
Medium-Light 1 yard	A	4	2½" × 40"	60	■ (37)	2½" × 2½"	—	—
	B	3	4⅞" × 40"	22	■ (37)	4⅞" × 4⅞"	44	◨ (38)
	C	1	4½" × 40"	8	■ (37)	4½" × 4½"	—	—
Brights* 10" × 15" scrap	A	1	2½" × 11"	4	■ (37)	2½" × 2½"	—	—
	B	1	4⅞" × 11"	2	■ (37)	4⅞" × 4⅞"	4	◨ (38)
	C	—	—	1	■ (37)	4½" × 4½"	—	—

Batting 81" × 81"	Backing 81" × 81"	Binding ⅔ yard

Note: Yardages are based on 40-inch-wide fabric after preshrinking. Page numbers in parentheses indicate where to find instructions for rotary cutting individual shapes.

*Fabric amounts and cutting directions are for one "spider." Purchase and cut twenty-five different brights to make the quilt shown.

Indian Puzzle

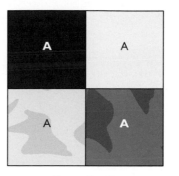

Scrapoholics—pay attention! You can use the tiny scraps in your bin and feel so virtuous. Each large "spider" in the bed quilt takes about a 10 × 15-inch scrap, and each small one in the wallhanging (page 154) takes about an 8 × 8-inch piece. A design wall is the key to making this quilt. Testing different color placements is easier when you can look at them on a wall.

Shapes Used
■ (page 37)
◩ (page 38)

Techniques Used
Sewing Half-Square Triangles (page 76)

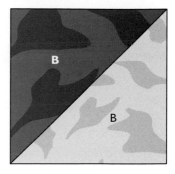

| Four Patch | Half-Square |

Piecing Units

Piecing the Units

Step 1 Cut out all the A, B, and C pieces, and arrange them on your design wall, as shown in the **Assembly Diagram.** Make sure that all the half-square triangles are going in the correct directions and that you are happy with the color arrangement.

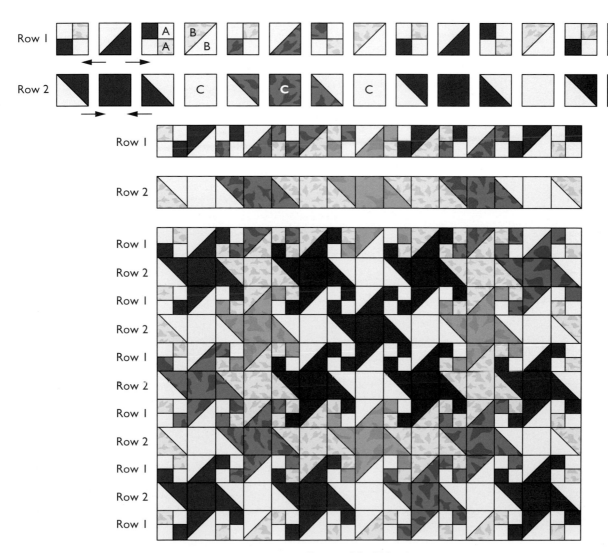

Assembly Diagram

Step 2

Make the Four Patch Units. Remove the A squares from your design wall two pairs at a time, sew each pair, and press the seams in opposite directions, as shown in **Diagram 1.** Butt, pin, and sew (page 69) the pairs into Four Patches. Press the center seam in either direction. Make a total of 64 Four Patch Units. Return them to their positions on the design wall as you sew them.

❖ Four Patch Units should measure 4½" × 4½".

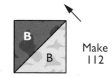

Make
64

Diagram 1

Step 3

Remove the half-square triangles from your design wall one pair at a time, sew each pair, trim the dog ears (page 77), and press toward the darker fabric. See **Diagram 2.** Make a total of 112 Half-Square Units.

❖ Half-Square Units should measure 4½" × 4½".

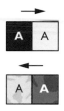

Make
112

Diagram 2

Assembling the Quilt

Step 1

Sew the Four Patch Units, Half-Square Units, and C squares together into rows, referring to the **Assembly Diagram** on page 153.

❖ Row 1: Four Patch Units and Half-Square Units; press toward Four Patch Units. Make eight rows.

❖ Row 2: Half-Square Units and C squares; press toward C. Make seven rows.

Step 2

Butt, pin, and sew (page 69) the rows together. Press all seams toward the bottom of the quilt.

Adding the Borders

Step 1

Sew the border strips together along one short edge into four sets of two. Measure the quilt for the side borders (page 91) and trim two of the border strips to fit. Pin and sew the borders to the sides, as shown in the **Quilt Diagram** on the opposite page. Press toward the borders.

Step 2

Measure for the top and bottom borders, and trim the remaining two strips to fit. Pin and sew the borders to the top and bottom. Press toward the borders.

Indian Puzzle Wallhanging

This 29½" × 29½" wallhanging has fewer piecing units, each made of smaller pieces: The A square is 1½" × 1½"; the B half-square triangles are cut from 2⅞" × 2⅞" squares; and the C squares are 2½" × 2½". Fabric requirements are below.

Fabric	Amount
Blue	Nine 8" × 8" squares
Red	Four 8" × 8" squares
Medium light	18" × 22" scrap
Light	9" × 16"

Border/Binding	1 yard	Batting	34" × 34"
Backing		34" × 34"	

Finishing the Quilt

Step 1 Layer the backing, batting, and quilt top. Quilt as desired. This quilt has feathers in the borders and vines in the "spiders."

Step 2 Square up your quilt top (page 104). Make and attach double-fold binding (page 107).

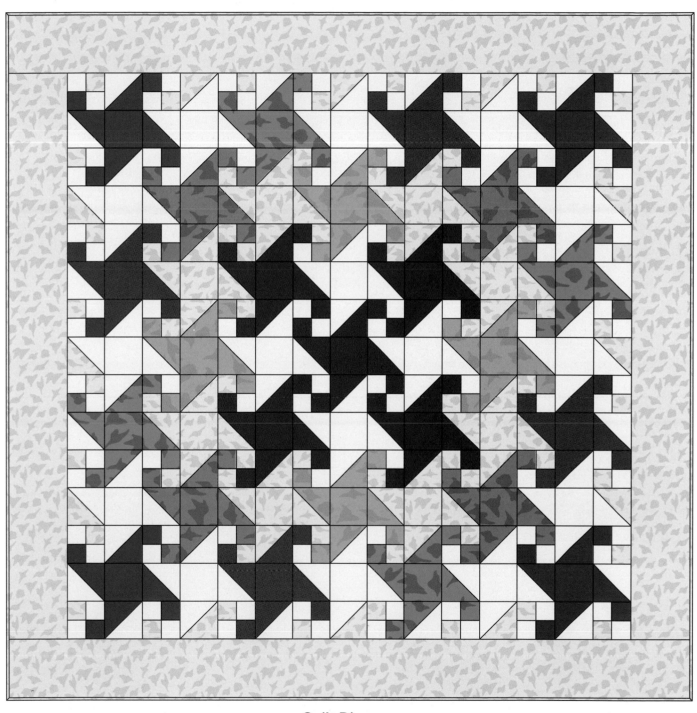

Quilt Diagram

Ferris Wheel Flowers

Finished Wallhanging:
26⅞" × 36½"
Finished Short Flower Block:
7" × 15⅞"
Finished Tall Flower Block:
6" × 15⅞"

These perky little flowers are sure to brighten up any room and make you think of spring. The ground-and-grass strip is a good place to use up green and brown scraps to give the quilt a realistic garden look. Cutting the strips at 45 degree angles helps to soften up the ground when it would other-wise look boxy and unnatural.

Materials and Cutting Chart

Fabric	Used For	Strips to Cut		First Cut			Second Cut	
		Number	Size	Number	Shape	Size	Number	Shape
Flower Tops* 2½" × 25" scrap of each shade	A1 (medium dark)	1	1⅜" × 25"	—	—	—	—	—
	A2 (medium light)	1	1⅜" × 25"	—	—	—	—	—
	B (dark)	1	2⅛" × 9"	4	■ (37)	2⅛" × 2⅛"	8	◪ (38)
Light 1 yard	C	1	2⅝" × 22"	8	■ (37)	2⅝" × 2⅝"	16	◪ (38)
	D	2	3⅛" × 40"†	4	▬ (44)	3⅛" × 4⅛"	—	—
	E			2	▬ (44)	3⅛" × 2⅛"	—	—
	I			4	▬ (44)	3⅛" × 3½"	—	—
	J			4	▬ (44)	3⅛" × 2"	—	—
	F	1	2⅛" × 11"	5	■ (37)	2⅛" × 2⅛"	10	◪ (38)
	G	1	1⅞" × 40"‡	4	▬ (44)	1⅞" × 3½"	4	◣ (47)
	H			6	▬ (44)	1⅞" × 3½"	6	◢ (47)
	K	1	4¾" × 15"	2	▬ (44)	4¾" × 7½"	—	—
	L	2	1½" × 40"§	1	▬ (44)	1½" × 16⅜"	—	—
	M			2	▬ (44)	1½" × 12⅛"	—	—
	Inner border	2	2" × 40"	—	—	—	—	—
Stems and Leaves green scraps	N	—	—	10	▬ (44)	1½" × 5"	10	▱ (46)
	O1	—	—	2	▬ (44)	1¼" × 10⅜"	—	—
	O2	—	—	2	▬ (44)	1¼" × 6⅛"	—	—
	P	—	—	5	■ (37)	2⅛" × 2⅛"	10	◪ (38)
Ground and Grass green and brown scraps	Q	13–17	1½" × 6" to 1½" × 12"	—	▱ (49)	—	—	—
Dark ½ yard	Outer border	2	3½" × 24"	—	—	—	—	—
		2	3½" × 40"	—	—	—	—	—

Batting 32" × 42"	Backing 32" × 42"	Binding ¼ yard

Note: Yardages are based on 40-inch-wide fabric after preshrinking. Page numbers in parentheses indicate where to find instructions for rotary cutting individual shapes.

*Fabric amounts and cutting directions are for *one* flower. Purchase and cut *four* of each shade to make the quilt shown.

†Cut all the D, E, I, and J pieces from these two strips.

‡Cut all the G and H pieces from this strip.

§Cut all the L and M pieces from these two strips.

Ferris Wheel Flowers

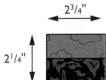
These flowers are a great place to use your brightly colored scraps! Use a variety of medium-light, medium-dark, and dark fabrics for the flower tops, and accent them with plaids and stripes of similar values in the stems and leaves.

Block Diagram

See pages 160–163 for placement of pieces D through Q.

Shapes Used

(page 37)
(page 38)
(page 44)
(page 46)
(page 47)
(page 47)
(page 49)

Techniques Used

Strip Piecing (page 81)
Piecing 45 Degree Angle Shapes (page 88)

Piecing the Flower Tops

Step 1
Make an A1A2 strip set (page 81), as shown in **Diagram 1.** Press toward A1. Cut the strip set into eight 2¾-inch segments.

❖ Segments should measure 2¾" × 2¼".

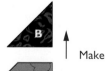

Diagram 1

Step 2
Cut each segment into a single prism (page 50), as shown in **Diagram 2.** Discard the triangle tips. Keep the color you want on the outside of the flower to the *left* when cutting the prism.

Diagram 2

Step 3
Sew a B triangle to the prism, as shown in **Diagram 3.** Press toward B. Trim the dog ears. Repeat to make a total of eight flower units.

Make 8

Diagram 3

Step 4
Sew two flower units together, as shown in **Diagram 4.** Press and trim the dog ears (page 77). Repeat to make a total of four pairs.

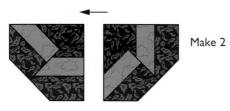

Make 4

Diagram 4

Step 5
Butt (page 69), pin, sew, and press two pairs together to make a half-flower, as shown in **Diagram 5.** Repeat to make two halves.

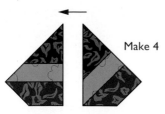

Make 2

Diagram 5

Step 6
Butt (page 69), pin, and sew the two halves together (page 69), as shown in **Diagram 6.** Press the center seam in either direction. Sew a C triangle to each corner, as shown. Press toward C, and trim the dog ears. Repeat Steps 1 through 6, using different fabrics, to make a total of four flowers.

❖ Flower Unit should measure 6½" × 6½".

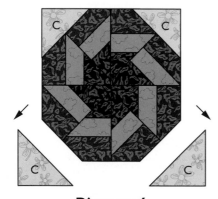

Diagram 6

Piecing the Leaf Units

Step 1
Pin and sew an F triangle to an N trapezoid, as shown in **Diagram 7.** Press toward N, and trim the dog ears (page 77). Make a total of ten sets.

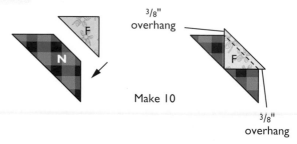

³⁄₈" overhang

³⁄₈" overhang

Make 10

Diagram 7

Step 2
Pin and sew a P triangle to a G half-trapezoid to make the left leaf, as shown in **Diagram 8A.** Pin and sew a P triangle to an H half-trapezoid to make the right leaf, as shown in **8B.** Press toward P, and trim the dog ears (page 77). Repeat to make a total of four left leaves and six right leaves.

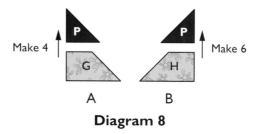

Make 4

Make 6

A

B

Diagram 8

Step 3
Sew the FN sets to the PG and PH sets to make Leaf Units, as shown in **Diagram 9.** Press toward N, and trim the dog ears (page 77).

❖ Leaf Units should measure 3⅛" × 3⅛".

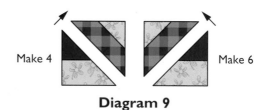

Make 4

Make 6

Diagram 9

Step 4
Referring to **Diagram 10** on the opposite page, sew and press the leaf units to the proper D, E, I, and J background pieces. Add these new units to each side of the O1 and O2 stems.

❖ Tall Flower Unit should measure 6½" × 10⅜".

❖ Short Flower Unit should measure 6½" × 6⅛".

Tall Flower Unit

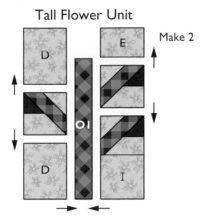

Make 2

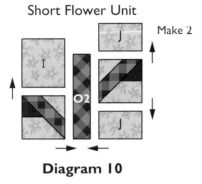

Short Flower Unit

Make 2

Diagram 10

Assembling the Flowers

Step 1

Referring to **Diagram 11,** sew the flowers to the Tall and Short Flower Units. Press toward the flowers. Sew an M strip to the left side of each short flower; press toward M. Sew a K rectangle to the top of each short flower; press

toward K. Sew the flowers into pairs, then sew each pair to one side of the L strip. Press as indicated by the arrows.

Step 2

Cut one of the inner border strips in half. Measure the wallhanging for the side borders (page 103) and trim the shorter border strips to fit. Pin and sew the borders to the sides (page 103). Press toward the borders. Measure for the top and bottom borders. Pin and sew the borders to the top. Press toward the border. See the **Quilt Diagram** on page 163.

Piecing the Ground-and-Grass Strip

Step 1

Using the Q strips (1½-inch strips of varying lengths), cut both ends of each strip at a 45 degree angle, as you would for binding strips (page 107). Trim the ⅜-inch-tip from each end, as shown in **Diagram 12.**

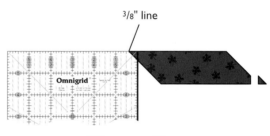

3/8" line

Diagram 12

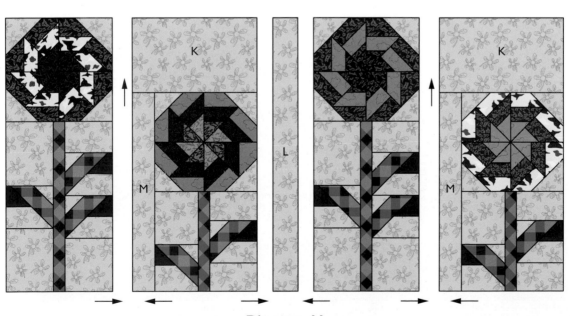

Diagram 11

Step 2

Position the strips right sides together, as shown in **Diagram 13.** Sew them together and press the seams in either direction. Make three strips, each at least 32 inches long.

Diagram 13

Step 3

Sew the three strips together, as shown in **Diagram 14.** Press the seams in either direction.

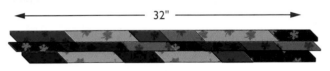

← 32" →

Diagram 14

Step 4

Sew this ground-and-grass section to the flower section, as shown in **Diagram 15.** Press toward the grass. Trim the ends of the grass section even with the flower section, as shown.

Adding the Borders

Step 1

Measure the wallhanging for the side borders (page 103), and trim the two shorter border strips to fit. Pin and sew the borders to the sides (page 103). Press toward the borders.

Step 2

Measure for the top and bottom borders, and trim the remaining two strips to fit. Pin and sew the borders to the top and bottom. Press toward the borders.

Finishing the Wallhanging

Step 1

Layer the backing, batting, and top. Quilt as desired. This wallhanging was machine quilted in the ditch around the flowers and leaves. In the background, variegated blue thread forms a daisy chain, and a clover pattern winds its way through the border.

Step 2

Square up your wallhanging (page 104). Make and attach double-fold binding (page 107).

Trim

Trim

Diagram 15

Quilt Diagram

 Variation

If you can't find the right background fabric, make one yourself! The larger version of this wallhanging (shown on page 105) has a pieced background that I made out of scraps. I sewed small pieces of fabric together into large rectangles, then cut them into the background shapes. Because the background had so much movement, I eliminated one of the leaves on the tall flowers.

Dancing Star Table Runner

Finished Size: 15⅞" × 57"

Believe it or not, this block is made from only one shape: the 60 degree diamond. Easy strip piecing allows you to create two different stars without endlessly arranging and piecing tiny diamonds. Once you start the easy piecing, you'll want to keep going until you've made a runner for every table in your house!

Materials and Cutting Chart

Fabric	Used For	Strips to Cut		First Cut			Second Cut	
		Number	Size	Number	Shape	Size	Number	Shape
Light 1¼ yards	B	5	2" × 40"	—	—	—	—	—
	D	3	3½" × 40"*	14	(52)	3½"	—	—
	E1			2	(44)	3½" × 8"	2	(47)†
	E2			2	(44)	3½" × 8"	2	(47)†
	Outer border	4	2½" × 26"	—	—	—	—	—
	I	1	4½" × 40"	—	—	—	—	—
Medium 1 ⅜ yard	C	4	2" × 40"	—	—	—	—	—
Medium 2 ⅜ yard	A	2	2" × 40"	—	—	—	—	—
	Inner border	4	1¼" × 40"	—	—	—	—	—

Batting 22" × 64"	Backing 22" × 64"	Binding ⅜ yard

Note: Yardages are based on 40-inch-wide fabric after preshrinking. Page numbers in parentheses indicate where to find instructions for rotary cutting individual shapes.

*Cut all the D and E pieces from these strips.

†Cut these half-trapezoids using the 60 degree line on your ruler.

Dancing Star Table Runner

Heighten the drama by choosing a dark background fabric and mediums and lights for the stars. Choose a quilting thread that contrasts with the color of the fabric to highlight the quilting stitches.

Block Diagram

See pages 170–171 for placement of pieces D and E.

Shapes Used

(page 52)
(page 44)
(page 47)
(page 47)

Techniques Used

Setting In Seams
  (page 72)
Strip Piecing (page 81)
Squaring-Up Blocks
  (page 104)

Piecing the Star Blocks

Step 1
Make one AB strip set and three BC strip sets (page 81) from the 2-inch strips, as shown in **Diagram 1.** Offset the strips by 2 inches. Press as indicated by the arrows.

❖ Strip sets should measure 3½" high.

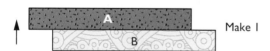

Make 1

Make 3

(Left-handed quilters see page 84 for assembly diagrams.)

Diagram 1

Step 2
Align your ruler's 60 degree line on the sewn seam, as shown in **Diagram 2.** (Your ruler will be upside down.) Cut off and discard the end. Move the ruler so the 2-inch line on the ruler

lines up with the freshly cut edge, and cut a 2-inch diagonal strip. Cut a new 60 degree angle after every three cuts.

❖ Cut 18 AB segments and 54 BC segments.

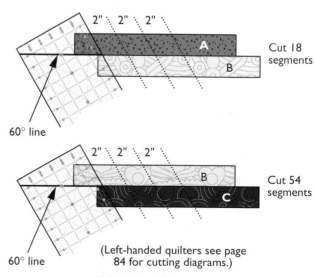

Cut 18 segments

Cut 54 segments

(Left-handed quilters see page 84 for cutting diagrams.)

Diagram 2

Step 3

Sew together 18 AB and 18 BC segment pairs into diamonds, as shown in **Diagram 3.** Press as indicated by the arrows. Trim the dog ears.

❖ Diamonds should measure 3½" wide.

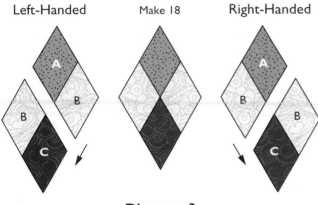

Left-Handed   Make 18   Right-Handed

Diagram 3

Step 4

Butt (page 69), pin, and start sewing two diamonds together, as shown in **Diagram 4.** Stop sewing ¼ inch from the edge, as indicated by the dot, and backtack (page 70). Press to the right. Do *not* trim the dog ear.

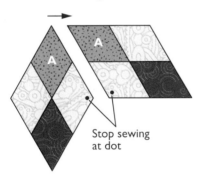

Stop sewing
at dot

Diagram 4

Step 5

Butt (page 69), pin, and sew another diamond to this unit, as shown in **Diagram 5.** Stop sewing ¼ inch from the bottom, and backtack. Press to the left. Trim all the dog ears. Repeat to make six half-stars.

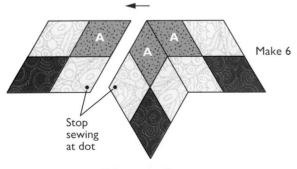

Make 6

Stop
sewing
at dot

Diagram 5

Step 6

Butt (page 69) and pin two halves, as shown in **Diagram 6.** Start sewing ¼ inch from the edge, backtack, continue sewing, stop ¼ inch from the other end, and backtack. Press the seam in either direction. Make a total of three stars.

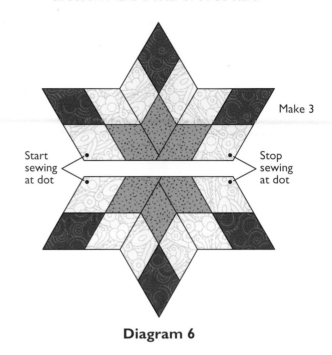

Make 3

Start
sewing
at dot

Stop
sewing
at dot

Diagram 6

Piecing the Diamonds

Step 1

Sew together the remaining BC segments to form 18 diamonds, as shown in **Diagram 7.** Press the seam in the direction of the arrow.

❖ Diamonds should measure 3½" wide.

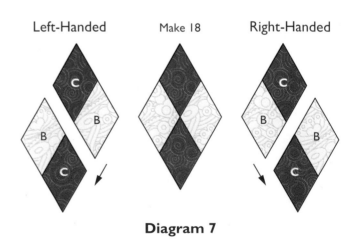

Left-Handed   Make 18   Right-Handed

Diagram 7

Step 2

Set in (page 72) four BC diamonds around each of the three stars, as shown in **Diagram 8.** Press away from the star. Reserve the remaining six BC diamonds for later use.

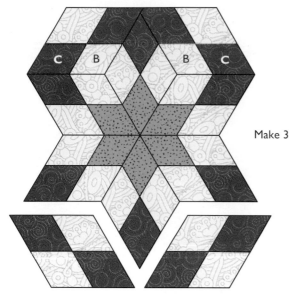

Make 3

Diagram 8

Piecing the Half-Stars

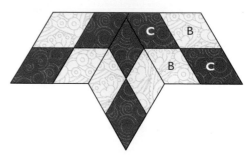

Half-Star Diagram

Step 1 Butt, pin, and start sewing together two BC diamonds, as shown in **Diagram 10.** Stop sewing ¼ inch from the edge, and backtack. Press to the right. Do *not* trim the dog ear.

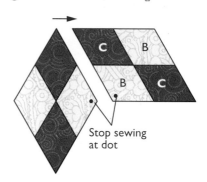

Stop sewing at dot

Diagram 10

Step 3 Sew the three star units together, as shown in **Diagram 9.** Start sewing ¼ inch from the edge, backtack, sew to ¼ inch from the other end, and backtack. Press the seams in either direction.

Step 2 Butt, pin, and start sewing a third diamond to this unit, as shown in **Diagram 11.** Stop sewing ¼ inch from the edge, and backtack. Press to the left. Trim all the dog ears. Make two half-stars.

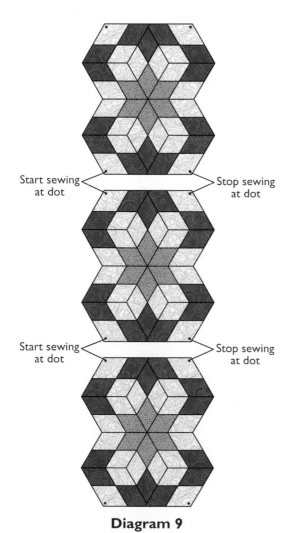

Start sewing at dot — Stop sewing at dot

Start sewing at dot — Stop sewing at dot

Diagram 9

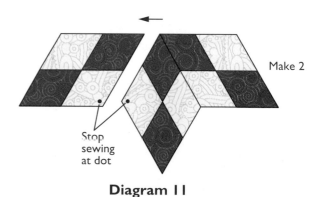

Make 2

Stop sewing at dot

Diagram 11

Assembling the Table Runner

Step 1
Sew one half-star onto one end of the runner and one onto the other end, as shown in **Diagram 12.** Remember to start sewing ¼ inch from the edge, backtack, continue sewing, stop ¼ inch from the other end, and backtack. Press the seams in either direction.

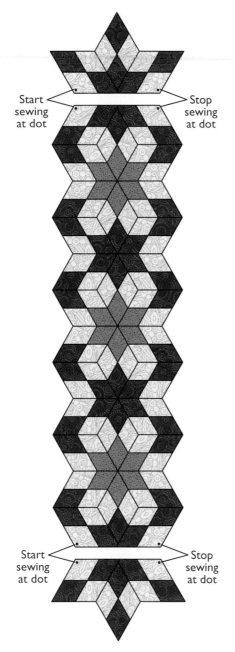

Start sewing at dot   Stop sewing at dot

Start sewing at dot   Stop sewing at dot

Diagram 12

Step 2
Set in (page 72) the D side diamonds, as shown in **Diagram 13.** Press the seams toward the D diamonds. Set in the E1 and E2 half-trapezoids. Press toward the half-trapezoids.

Diagram 13

Step 3
Square up the table runner (page 104), as shown in **Diagram 14.** Align the ¼-inch line on your ruler with the outside points of the stars so that you leave a ¼-inch seam allowance around the outside dark diamond points.

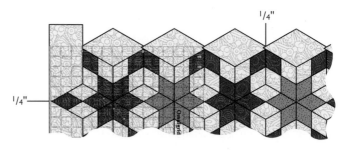

Diagram 14

Adding the Borders

Refer to the **Quilt Diagram** for the following steps.

Step 1
Cut one of the 1¼-inch inner border strips in half. Sew each half to one long inner border strip. Measure the runner for the side borders (page 103), and trim these pieced border strips to fit. Pin and sew the borders to the sides (page 103). Press toward the borders.

Step 2
Cut the remaining inner border strip in half. Measure for the end borders (page 103), and trim these strips to fit. Pin and sew the borders to the ends (page 103). Press toward the borders.

Step 3
Sew the 2½-inch outer border strips together in pairs to make two long outer border strips. Measure the runner for the side borders (page 103), and trim these border strips to fit. Pin and sew the borders to the sides (page 103). Press toward the outer borders.

Step 4
Cut the 4½-inch outer border strip in half. Measure for the end borders (page 103), and trim these strips to fit. Pin and sew the borders to the ends (page 103). Press toward the outer borders.

Finishing the Table Runner

Step 1
Layer the backing, batting, and top. Quilt as desired. This table runner has a clover-and-leaf design in the center, straight-line quilting in the inner border, and a heart pattern in the outer border.

Step 2
Square up your table runner (page 104). Make and attach double-fold binding (page 107).

Quilt Diagram

Square within a Square Miniature

Finished Wallhanging:
27" × 27"

Finished Block: $2\frac{7}{8}$" × $2\frac{7}{8}$"

This sweet little quilt is the result of a challenge: A representative from Mission Valley Fabrics invited me to incorporate their summer line of light plaids and stripes with their existing darker line. I pieced the center, then turned it different ways to see how it looked (something I always do as I'm designing). When I turned the center on point, I knew instantly that was the setting to use.

Materials and Cutting Chart

Fabric	Used For	Strips to Cut		First Cut			Second Cut	
		Number	Size	Number	Shape	Size	Number	Shape
Light Plaid* Scraps	A	—	—	I	■ (37)	2½" × 2½"	—	—
Dark Plaid* Scraps	B	I	2⅜" × 6"	2	■ (37)	2⅜" × 2⅜"	4	(38)
Medium Plaid 1½" × 15"	C	I	1¼" × 13"	9	■ (37)	1¼" × 1¼"	—	—
Light ⅔ yard	D	3	1¼" × 40"	24	▬ (44)	1¼" × 3⅜"	—	—
	E	I	11½" × 24"	2	■ (37)	11½" × 11½"	4	◤ (38)
	Inner border	4	1½" × 25"	—	—	—	—	—
Stripe ½ yard	Outer border	2	3" × 25"	—	—	—	—	—
		2	3" × 33"	—	—	—	—	—

Batting 30" × 30"	Backing 30" × 30"	Binding ¼ yard

Note: Yardages are based on 40-inch-wide fabric after preshrinking. Page numbers in parentheses indicate where to find instructions for rotary cutting individual shapes.

*Fabric amounts and cutting directions are for *one* block. Cut *sixteen* different plaids to make the quilt shown.

Square within a Square Miniature

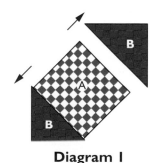

Play with the scale of your fabrics. A lot of visual interest comes from combining large- and small-scale plaids. Choose a very restful background fabric so that the individual blocks stand out on their own without competing with each other.

Shapes Used
■ (page 37)
◩ (page 38)
▬ (page 44)

Techniques Used
Sewing 4 Triangles to a Square (page 87)
Squaring-Up Blocks (page 90)

Block Diagram

See pages 176–177 for placement of pieces C through E.

Piecing the Quilt

Step 1
Sew B triangles to opposite sides of an A square, as shown in **Diagram 1.** Press toward B, and trim the dog ears.

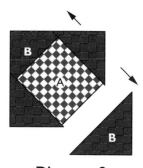

Diagram 2

Step 3
Arrange the blocks on your design wall. Following the **Assembly Diagram** on page 176, sew the blocks, D lattice strips, and C cornerstones into rows. Press as indicated by the arrows. Sew the rows together, and press toward the lattice.

Step 4
Referring to the **Quilt Diagram** on page 177, sew two E triangles to opposite sides of the assembled top. (These pieces are slightly oversize.) Press toward E. Add the remaining E triangles to the other two sides. Press toward E. Square up the wallhanging (page 104).

Diagram 1

Step 2
Sew B triangles to the remaining sides of the A square, as shown in **Diagram 2.** Press toward B, and trim the dog ears. Repeat to make a total of 16 blocks.

❖ Blocks should measure 3⅜" × 3⅜".

❖ Wallhanging should measure 20" × 20".

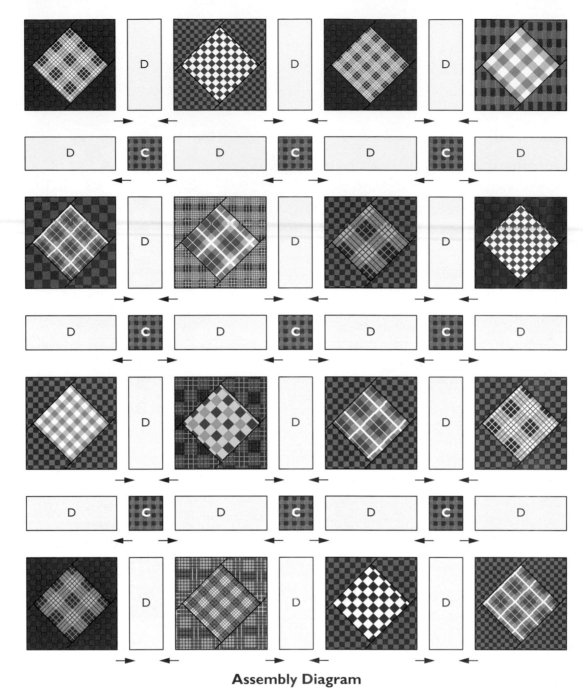

Assembly Diagram

Adding the Borders

Step 1
Measure the wallhanging for the side borders (page 103), and trim two of the inner border strips to fit. Pin and sew the borders to the sides (page 103). Press toward the borders.

Step 2
Measure for the top and bottom borders, and trim the remaining two strips to fit. Pin and sew the borders to the top and bottom. Press toward the borders. Repeat Steps 1 and 2 for the outer borders.

Finishing the Wallhanging

Step 1
Layer the backing, batting, and wallhanging. Quilt as desired. This miniature was machine quilted in the ditch around the blocks and with simple looping patterns in the background and border.

Step 2
Square up your wallhanging (page 104). Make and attach single-fold binding (page 107).

Quilt Diagram

Country Potpourri

Finished Wallhanging: 30¼" × 30¼"

Finished Block: 7½" × 7½"

I first made this wallhanging in Amish colors and was quite pleased with the results. But then I challenged myself to stretch my creative powers to see if I could come up with a totally different look. I used a warm gold palette with highlights of blue and green to remake it in a country mood. This pattern is a good baby step to take if you're interested in making miniature quilts but are afraid of tiny pieces. The pieces are small but they're basic, non-intimidating shapes that make it easy for you to get used to working on a smaller scale.

Materials and Cutting Chart

Fabric	Used For	Strips to Cut Number	Strips to Cut Size	First Cut Number	First Cut Shape	First Cut Size	Second Cut Number	Second Cut Shape
Light ½ yard	A	2	2" × 40"*	12	▪ (37)	2" × 2"	—	—
	B			8	▬ (44)	2" × 3½"	—	—
	C			2	▬ (44)	2" × 5"	—	—
	D	1	2⅜" × 40"	16	▪ (37)	2⅜" × 2⅜"	32	◥ (38)
	E	1	2¾" × 6"	2	▪ (37)	2¾" × 2¾"	8	⊠ (39)
	F	—	—	1	▪ (37)	3⅞" × 3⅞"	2	◥ (38)
	G	—	—	1	▪ (37)	5⅜" × 5⅜"	2	◥ (38)
Blue 9" × 15" scrap	I	1	2⅜" × 15"	5	▪ (37)	2⅜" × 2⅜"	10	◥ (38)
	K	—	—	1	▪ (37)	5⅜" × 5⅜"	2	◥ (38)
Orange 9" × 13" scrap	H	1	2" × 13"	5	▪ (37)	2" × 2"	—	—
	I	1	2⅜" × 13"	4	▪ (37)	2⅜" × 2⅜"	8	◥ (38)
	J	1	2¾" × 6"	2	▪ (37)	2¾" × 2¾"	8	⊠ (39)
Red 3" × 25" scrap	H	—	—	1	▪ (37)	2" × 2"	—	—
	I	1	2⅜" × 20"	8	▪ (37)	2⅜" × 2⅜"	16	◥ (38)
Green 5" × 20" scrap	H	1	2" × 20"	9	▪ (37)	2" × 2"	—	—
	I	1	2⅜" × 10"	4	▪ (37)	2⅜" × 2⅜"	8	◥ (38)
Medium Light ⅝ yard	L	—	—	1	▪ (37)	8" × 8"	—	—
	M	—	—	1	▪ (37)	11⅞" × 11⅞"	4	⊠ (39)
	N	1	6¼" × 13"	2	▪ (37)	6¼" × 6¼"	4	◥ (38)
	Middle border	4	1¼" × 40"	—	—	—	—	—
Dark ¾ yard	Inner border	4	1½" × 40"	—	—	—	—	—
	Outer border	4	3" × 40"	—	—	—	—	—

Batting	35" × 35"	Backing	35" × 35"	Binding	Included in dark yardage

Note: Yardages are based on 40-inch-wide fabric after preshrinking. Page numbers in parentheses indicate where to find instructions for rotary cutting individual shapes.

*Cut all A, B, and C pieces from these two strips.

Country Potpourri

Look for visually stimulating fabrics to add a little zing to your wallhanging. These are the simplest of borders—they're not even mitered!—but the texture of the fabric really adds excitement.

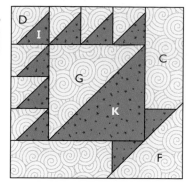
May Basket

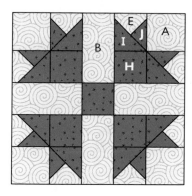
Duck Paddle

Shapes Used

- (page 37)
- (page 44)
- (page 38)
- (page 39)

Techniques Used

Sewing Half-Square Triangles (page 76)

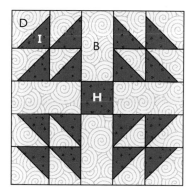
Birds in Flight

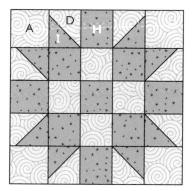
Sister's Choice

Block Diagrams

See pages 184–185 for placement of pieces L through N.

Piecing the May Basket Block

Step 1
Sew a D triangle to a blue I triangle, as shown in **Diagram 1**. Trim the dog ears and press toward I. Repeat to make a total of seven DI squares.

❖ DI squares should measure 2" × 2".

Make 7

Diagram 1

Step 2
Sew three DI squares together, as shown in **Diagram 2**. Press as indicated by the arrows.

❖ Unit should measure 2" × 5".

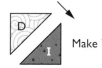

Diagram 2

Step 3
Sew four DI squares together, as shown in **Diagram 3**. Press as indicated by the arrows.

❖ Unit should measure 2" × 6½".

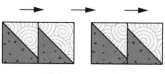

Diagram 3

Step 4
Sew a G triangle to a blue K triangle, as shown in **Diagram 4**. (You will have one extra each of G and K.) Trim the dog ears, and press toward K.

❖ GK square should measure 5" × 5".

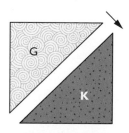

Diagram 4

Step 5
Sew a blue I triangle to a C rectangle, making two sets and orienting the I pieces as shown in **Diagram 5.** Press toward I and trim the dog ears. (You will have one extra I.)

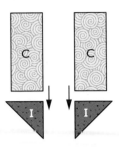

Diagram 5

Step 6
Sew the short row of DI squares to the right side of G, as shown in **Diagram 6.** Press toward G. Sew the long row of DI squares to the left side of G, as shown. Press toward G.

❖ Unit should measure 6½" × 6½".

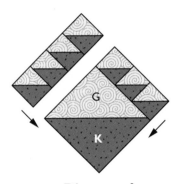

Diagram 6

Step 7
Sew the IC units to the basket unit, as shown in **Diagram 7.** Press toward C, and trim the dog ears after adding each unit.

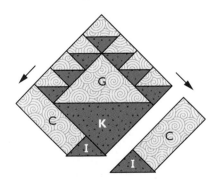

Diagram 7

Step 8
Sew an F triangle to the bottom of the basket, as shown in **Diagram 8.** Press toward F, and trim the dog ears.

❖ Block should measure 8" × 8".

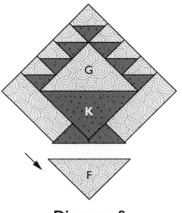

Diagram 8

Piecing the Duck Paddle Block

Step 1
Sew an E triangle to an orange J triangle, making two sets and orienting the pieces as shown in **Diagram 9.** Be careful to sew the correct edges together. Press toward J and trim the dog ears. Make four of each set.

Diagram 9

Step 2
Sew an orange I triangle to each EJ set, as shown in **Diagram 10.** Trim the dog ears, and press toward I. Make four of each unit.

❖ IEJ Unit should measure 2" × 2".

Diagram 10

Step 3
Sew A squares to four IEJ Units and H squares to four IEJ Units, making sure to match the placement shown in **Diagram 11.** Press toward the squares. Make four of each unit.

❖ Units should measure 2" × 3½".

Diagram 11

Step 4

Sew the Step 3 units together into pairs, as shown in **Diagram 12.** Press toward the A unit. Make four units.

❖ Units should measure 3½" × 3½".

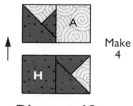

Diagram 12

Step 5

Sew and press the units from Step 4, B rectangles, and orange H square into rows, as shown in **Diagram 13.** Butt (page 69), pin, and sew the rows together. Press toward the center row.

❖ Block should measure 8" × 8".

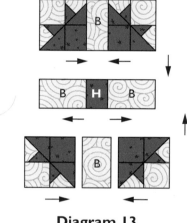

Diagram 13

Piecing the Birds In Flight Block

Step 1

Sew a D triangle to a red I triangle, as shown in **Diagram 14.** Trim the dog ears, and press toward I. Make a total of 16 DI Units.

❖ DI Units should measure 2" × 2".

Diagram 14

Step 2

Sew the DI Units together into sets, making two sets and orienting the pieces as shown in **Diagram 15.** Make four of each set.

❖ Sets should measure 2" × 3½".

Diagram 15

Step 3

Press the Step 2 sets as indicated by the arrows in **Diagram 16.** Sew the sets into units as shown. Press the units as indicated by the arrows. Make two of each unit.

❖ Units should measure 3½" × 3½".

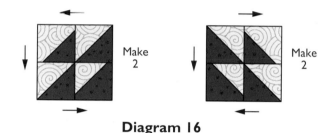

Diagram 16

Step 4

Sew and press the Step 3 units, B rectangles, and red H square into rows, as shown in **Diagram 17.** Butt (page 69), pin, and sew the rows together. Press toward the center row.

❖ Block should measure 8" × 8".

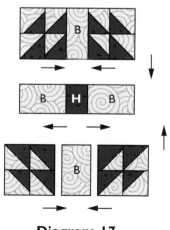

Diagram 17

Piecing the Sister's Choice Block

Step 1
Sew a D triangle to a green I triangle, as shown in **Diagram 18**. Trim the dog ears, and press toward I. Make eight DI Units.

❖ DI Units should measure 2" × 2".

Make 8

Diagram 18

Step 2
Sew and press the units from Step 1, A squares, and green H squares into rows, as shown in **Diagram 19**. Butt (page 69), pin, and sew the rows together. Press toward the center row.

❖ Block should measure 8" × 8".

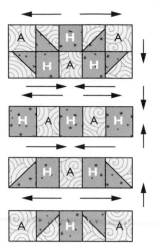

Diagram 19

Assembling the Top

Step 1
Referring to **Diagram 20,** arrange the blocks into diagonal rows, adding the L square and M triangles. Sew and press as indicated by the arrows. Trim the dog ears.

Step 2
Sew the rows together, then add the N corner triangles. Press toward N, and trim the dog ears.

Diagram 20

Adding the Borders

Refer to the **Quilt Diagram** for these steps.

Step 1
Sew the 1½-inch inner border strips to the 1¼-inch middle border strips. Press toward the inner border. Add the 3-inch outer border strip to the other side of the middle border. Press toward the outer border. Make four sets.

Step 2
Measure the wallhanging for the side borders (page 103), and trim two border units to fit. Pin and sew the borders to the sides of the wallhanging. Press toward the borders. Repeat for the top and bottom borders.

Finishing the Wallhanging

Step 1
Layer the backing, batting, and wallhanging. Quilt as desired. This sampler was machine quilted with variegated thread in the borders and blocks, and matching thread was used in the background.

Step 2
Square up the wallhanging (page 104). Make and attach double-fold binding (page 107).

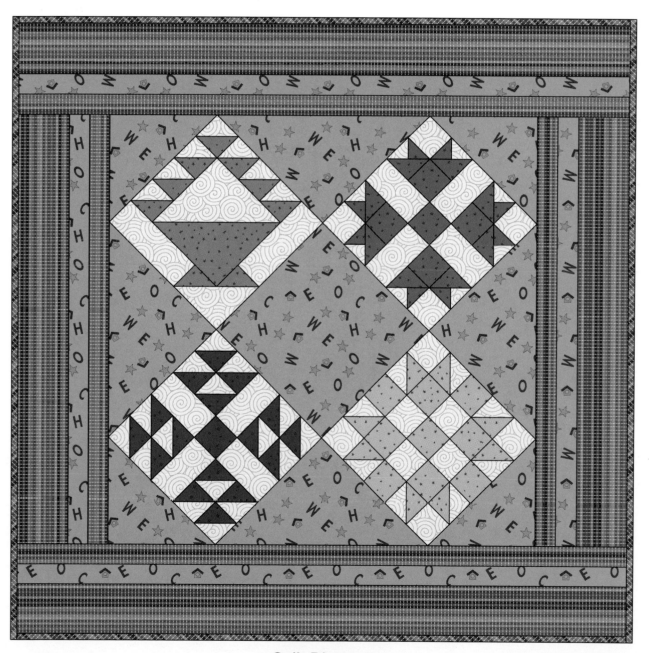

Quilt Diagram

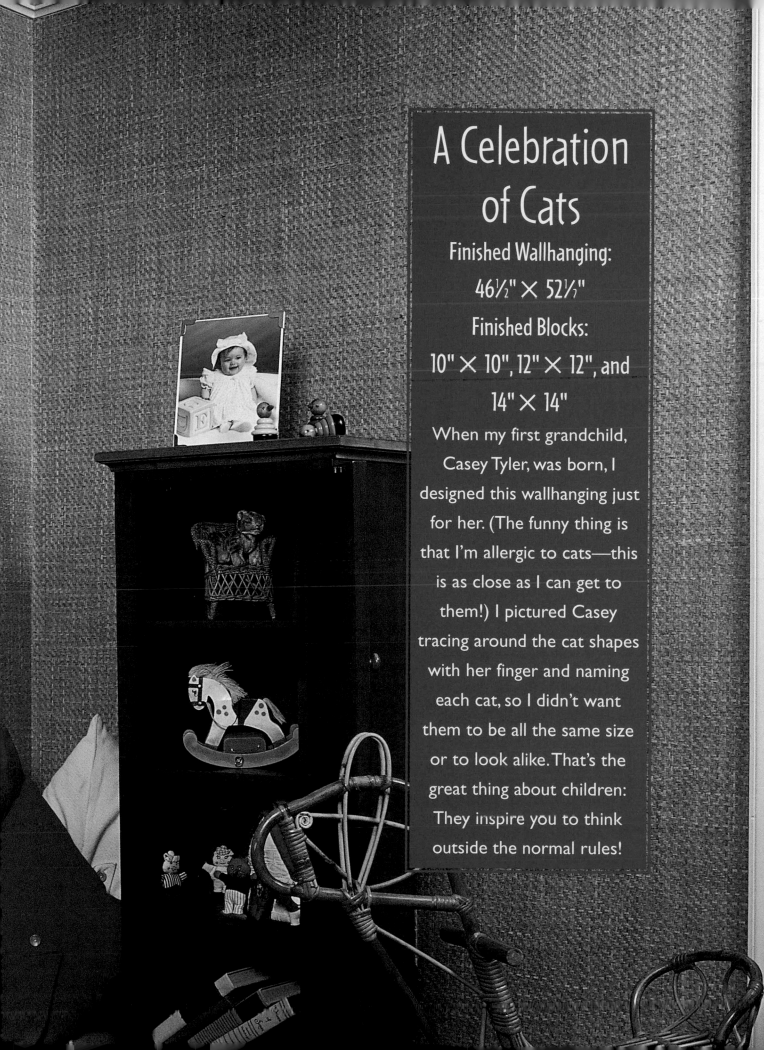

A Celebration of Cats

Finished Wallhanging:
46½" × 52½"

Finished Blocks:
10" × 10", 12" × 12", and
14" × 14"

When my first grandchild, Casey Tyler, was born, I designed this wallhanging just for her. (The funny thing is that I'm allergic to cats—this is as close as I can get to them!) I pictured Casey tracing around the cat shapes with her finger and naming each cat, so I didn't want them to be all the same size or to look alike. That's the great thing about children: They inspire you to think outside the normal rules!

Materials and Cutting Chart

Fabric	Used For	First Cut 10" Cat No.	Shape	Size	First Cut 12" Cat No.	Shape	Size	First Cut 14" Cat No.	Shape	Size	Second Cut Shape
Darks 9 different fabrics, each 18" × 22" (Quilter's Quarter)*	A	1	(37)	2⅜" × 2⅜"	1	(37)	2⅜" × 2⅜"	1	(37)	2⅞" × 2⅞"	(38)
	B	1	(44)	3" × 4½"	1	(44)	2¾" × 5"	1	(44)	3½" × 6½"	—
	C1†	1	(44)	3½" × 7⅞"	1	(44)	4¼" × 9⅛"	1	(44)	4½" × 10⅞"	(47)
	C2†	1	(44)	3½" × 7⅞"	1	(44)	4¼" × 9⅛"	1	(44)	4½" × 10⅞"	(47)
	D	1	(44)	3½" × 7½"	1	(44)	4¼" × 8¾"	1	(44)	4½" × 10½"	—
	E	1	(44)	1½" × 2½"	1	(37)	2½" × 2½"	1	(44)	2¼" × 2¾"	—
	F	1	(44)	1½" × 6¼"	1	(44)	2¼" × 7½"	1	(44)	2¼" × 11½"	—
	G	1	(44)	1½" × 2½"	1	(44)	1¾" × 2½"	1	(44)	2¼" × 2¾"	—
	Outer border‡	1	(44)	3½" × 10½"	—	—	—	—	—	—	—
		1	(44)	3½" × 12½"	—	—	—	—	—	—	—
		2	(44)	3½" × 14½"	—	—	—	—	—	—	—
		1	(44)	3½" × 15½"	—	—	—	—	—	—	—
		4	(44)	3½" × 16½"	—	—	—	—	—	—	—
		1	(44)	3½" × 17½"	—	—	—	—	—	—	—
		2	(44)	3½" × 19½"	—	—	—	—	—	—	—
Light 1⅝ yards	Inner border§	4	(44)	2½" × 44"	—	—	—	—	—	—	—
	H	3	(44)	2" × 5¼"	3	(44)	2" × 5¾"	3	(44)	2½" × 7¼"	(46)
	I1†	3	(44)	3½" × 7⅞"	3	(44)	4¼" × 9⅛"	3	(44)	4½" × 10⅞"	(47)
	I2†	3	(44)	3½" × 7⅞"	3	(44)	4¼" × 9⅛"	3	(44)	4½" × 10⅞"	(47)
	J	3	(44)	2½" × 4¼"	3	(44)	2½" × 4¼"	3	(44)	2¾" × 8"	—
	K	3	(44)	3½" × 4¾"	3	(44)	4¼" × 5½"	3	(44)	3½" × 4½"	—
	M1	—	—	—	3	(44)	2½" × 12½"	—	—	—	—
	M2	3	(44)	4½" × 10½"	—	—	—	—	—	—	—
Collar Scraps	L	—	—	—	1	(44)	1¼" × 5"	1	(44)	1½" × 6½"	—

Batting 52" × 58"	Backing 52" × 58"	Binding ⅜ yard

Note: Yardages are based on 40-inch-wide fabric after preshrinking. Page numbers in parentheses indicate where to find instructions for rotary cutting individual shapes.

*Make one cat from each Quilter's Quarter. Cut your strips along the *long* edge of your fabric.

†Refer to the **Block Diagrams** to determine whether to cut a C1 or a C2 and an I1 or an I2 piece for each cat block.

‡Wait to cut these until you have pieced the quilt top.

§Cut border strips *first* along lengthwise grain.

A Celebration of Cats

Go to town with this one! Look for fabrics that resemble fur, or use one of those fun cat prints. Embellish! Have fun putting rhinestones on the collars and buttons on for eyes. Just remember—if it's a baby quilt, don't put on anything that a child could pull off and eat.

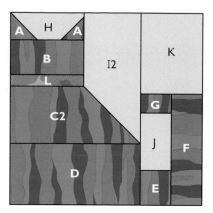
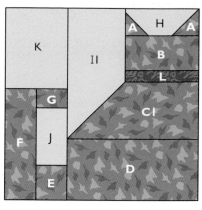

Left-Facing Cat   Right-Facing Cat

Block Diagrams

Shapes Used

(page 44)
(page 46)
(page 47)
(page 47)
(page 37)
(page 38)

Techniques Used

Setting In Seams
  (page 72)
Making Flying Geese
  (page 89)

Piecing the Blocks

To make the wallhanging shown, make:

❖ One left-facing and two right-facing 10-inch cats.

❖ One left-facing and two right-facing 12-inch cats.

❖ Two left-facing and one right-facing 14-inch cats.

Step 1 Sew an A triangle to each side of an H trapezoid, as shown in **Diagram 1.** This is the same technique used for making Flying Geese (page 89). Press toward A, and trim the dog ears (page 77). Make one AH Unit for each cat.

❖ AH Unit for 10-inch cat should measure 2" × 4½".

❖ AH Unit for 12-inch cat should measure 2" × 5".

❖ AH Unit for 14-inch cat should measure 2½" × 6½".

Diagram 1

Step 2 Sew the AH Unit to the top of a B rectangle, as shown in **Diagram 2.** Sew an L rectangle to the bottom of B. (Note: The 10-inch cat does not have an L piece.) Press as indicated by the arrow. Make one AHBL Unit for each cat.

❖ AHB Unit for 10-inch cat should measure 4½" × 4½".

❖ AHBL Unit for 12-inch cat should measure 5" × 5".

❖ AHBL Unit for 14-inch cat should measure 6½" × 6½".

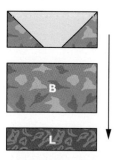

Diagram 2

Step 3

Refer to **Diagram 3** to sew the I and C pieces correctly for the right- and left-facing cats. For the left-facing cat, pin C2 to I2 with C2 on top. For the right-facing cat, pin I1 to C1 with I1 on top. Sew the angled seam, as shown in **Diagram 3,** stopping ¼ inch from the edge (page 70). Backtack three stitches. Wait until after you complete Step 4 to press and trim.

Left-Facing Cat

Wrong side of C2 facing you

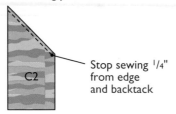

Stop sewing ¼" from edge and backtack

C2

Right-Facing Cat

Wrong side of I1 facing you

Stop sewing ¼" from edge and backtack

I1

Diagram 3

Step 4

Referring to **Diagram 4,** set in the head (AHBL Unit; page 72). For the left-facing cat, align the top and side of the head section with the I2 piece. For the right-facing cat, align the side and bottom of the head section with the C1 piece. Sew these seams, then pin and sew the adjoining seam. Press the side seam away from the head, the bottom seam toward the head, and the diagonal seam toward the light fabric. Trim the dog ears.

Left-Facing Cat   Right-Facing Cat

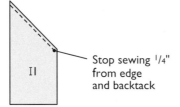

Side of head aligns with I2 here

Stop sewing ¹/₁₆" from diagonal seam

Bottom of head aligns with C1 here

Stop sewing ¹/₁₆" from diagonal seam

I2   C1

C2   I1

Diagram 4

Step 5

Sew a D rectangle to the bottom of the unit made in Step 4, as shown in **Diagram 5.** Press toward D to complete the Cat Unit.

❖ Unit for 10-inch cat should measure 7½" × 10½".

❖ Unit for 12-inch cat should measure 8¾" × 12½".

❖ Unit for 14-inch cat should measure 10½" × 14½".

Left-Facing Cat

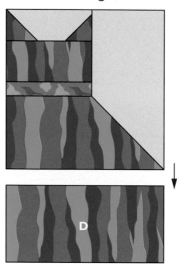

D

Right-Facing Cat

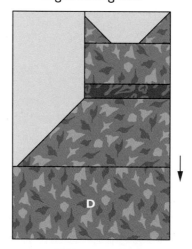

D

Diagram 5

Step 6

Sew G and E pieces to a J rectangle, referring to **Diagram 6** on the opposite page for proper placement for the left- and right-facing cats. Press away from J. Add an F rectangle. Press toward F.

❖ Unit for 10-inch cat should measure 3½" × 6¼".

❖ Unit for 12-inch cat should measure 4¼" × 7½".

❖ Unit for 14-inch cat should measure 4½" × 11½".

Left-Facing Cat   **Right-Facing Cat**

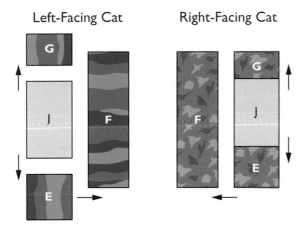

Diagram 6

Step 7

Sew a K rectangle to the unit made in Step 6, as shown in **Diagram 7.** Press toward K to complete the Tail Unit.

❖ Unit for 10-inch cat should measure 3½" × 10½".

❖ Unit for 12-inch cat should measure 4¼" × 12½".

❖ Unit for 14-inch cat should measure 4½" × 14½".

Left-Facing Cat   **Right-Facing Cat**

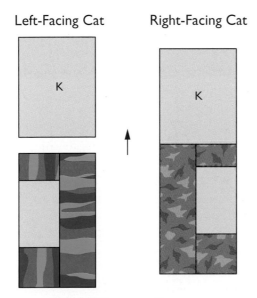

Diagram 7

Step 8

Sew the tail section to the body section, as shown in **Diagram 8.** Press toward the tail.

Left-Facing Cat

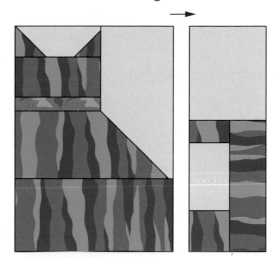

Right-Facing Cat

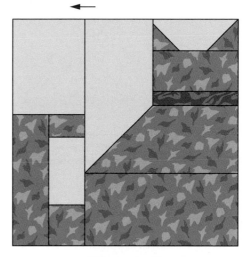

Diagram 8

Step 9

Referring to the **Assembly Diagram** on page 192, sew an M1 rectangle to the top of each 12-inch cat and an M2 rectangle to the top of each 10-inch cat. Press toward M1 and M2.

Step 10

Sew the cats into horizontal rows, arranging them as shown in the **Assembly Diagram** on page 192. Press either way. Sew the rows together. Press the seams in either direction.

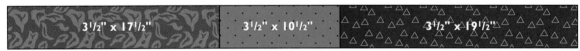

Assembly Diagram

Adding the Borders

Step 1 Measure for the side inner borders (page 103), cut the inner border strips to this length, and add them to the wallhanging (page 103). Press toward the border. Repeat for the top and bottom inner borders.

Step 2 Referring to the **Assembly Diagram,** measure and cut the outer border pieces. The seams on the borders should align visually with the

seams between the cat blocks. If you have arranged your cats a little differently than mine are here, your borders may have different measurements than I show here. *Remember to add ¼ inch to each end for seam allowances.* Cut, piece together, and sew the side borders on first, then cut and sew on the top and bottom, as shown in the **Quilt Diagram** on the opposite page. Don't forget to allow for the width of your side borders when measuring for the top and bottom pieces.

Finishing the Wallhanging

Step 1
Layer the backing, batting, and top. Quilt as desired. This wallhanging was machine quilted with parallel diagonal lines in the background (with a butterfly in the top corner for fun). Each cat has a different quilting pattern, and there's a wave pattern in the border.

Step 2
Square up the wallhanging (page 104). Make and attach double-fold binding (page 107).

Quilt Diagram

Black Star Eruption

Finished Wallhanging: 37½" × 37½"

Finished Checkered Stars: 6" × 6" and 12" × 12"

Finished Jacob's Ladder: 6" × 6"

Finished Nine Patch: 3" × 3"

Don't be afraid of using black! It makes a wonderful background fabric, since any color you put against it really pops out. I originally made this quilt as a way to use different size blocks (12-inch center star and 6-inch side stars). The creative challenge was to make them look like they belonged together. My solution was the Jacob's Ladder blocks that echo the shapes and extend into the center to visually tie the whole design together.

Materials and Cutting Chart

Fabric	Used For	Strips to Cut		First Cut			Second Cut	
		Number	Size	Number	Shape	Size	Number	Shape
Dark green Quilter's Quarter (18" × 22")	A	1	1¾" × 22"	2	▭ (44)	1¾" × 9"	—	—
	C2	1	1¾" × 14"	4	▭ (44)	1¾" × 3⅛"	2	▱ (47)
							2	▱ (47)
	D1	1	1¾" × 22"	4	▭ (44)	1¾" × 4⅜"	2	▱ (47)
							2	▱ (47)
	M	3	1½" × 22"	—	—	—	—	—
	Nine Patch	1	1½" × 26"	1	▭ (44)	1½" × 13"	—	—
				1	▭ (44)	1½" × 7"	—	—
Dark purple Fat eighth (9" × 22")	B	1	1¾" × 22"	2	▭ (44)	1¾" × 9"	—	—
	C1	1	1¾" × 14"	4	▭ (44)	1¾" × 3⅛"	2	▱ (47)
							2	▱ (47)
	D2	1	1¾" × 22"	4	▭ (44)	1¾" × 4⅜"	2	▱ (47)
							2	▱ (47)
Light green ⅓ yard	G	1	1⅛" × 40"	2	▭ (44)	1⅛" × 20"	—	—
	I2	1	1⅛" × 40"	16	▭ (44)	1⅛" × 2"	8	▱ (47)
							8	▱ (47)
	J1	2	1⅛" × 22"	16	▭ (44)	1⅛" × 2⅝"	8	▱ (47)
							8	▱ (47)
	P	1	2⅞" × 25"	8	▪ (37)	2⅞" × 2⅞"	16	◣ (38)
Light purple ¼ yard	H	1	1⅛" × 40"	2	▭ (44)	1⅛" × 20"	—	—
	I1	1	1⅛" × 40"	16	▭ (44)	1⅛" × 2"	8	▱ (47)
							8	▱ (47)
	J2	2	1⅛" × 22"	16	▭ (44)	1⅛" × 2⅝"	8	▱ (47)
							8	▱ (47)
Black 1¾ yards	E	—	—	1	▪ (37)	6¼" × 6¼"	4	⊠ (39)
	F	1	4" × 17"	4	▪ (37)	4" × 4"	—	—
	K	1	3¾" × 16"	4	▪ (37)	3¾" × 3¾"	16	⊠ (39)
	L	1	2¼" × 38"	16	▪ (37)	2¼" × 2¼"	—	—
	N	3	1½" × 22"	—	—	—	—	—
	O	1	2⅞" × 25"	8	▪ (37)	2⅞" × 2⅞"	16	◣ (38)
	Nine Patch	1	1½" × 26"	2	▭ (44)	1½" × 13"	—	—
		1	1½" × 14"	2	▭ (44)	1½" × 7"	—	—
	Background	2	6½" × 28"	8	▪ (37)	6½" × 6½"	—	—
	Lattice	2	3½" × 26"	4	▭ (44)	3½" × 12½"	—	—
	Borders	4	4" × 40"	—	—	—	—	—

Batting 42" × 42"	Backing 1 yard	Binding ⅜ yard

Note: Yardages are based on 40-inch-wide fabric after preshrinking. Page numbers in parentheses indicate where to find instructions for rotary cutting individual shapes.

Black Star Eruption

Hand-dyed sueded cottons are such a treat. They add a wonderful visual texture to any quilt. I love working with Cherrywood fabrics (I used them in this wallhanging). Position fabrics with strong visual textures carefully—you always want to make sure the quilt design is what pops out.

Shapes Used

(page 44)
(page 47)
(page 47)
(page 37)
(page 38)
(page 39)

Techniques Used

Setting In Seams (page 72)

Sewing Half-Square Triangles (page 76)

Strip Piecing (page 81)

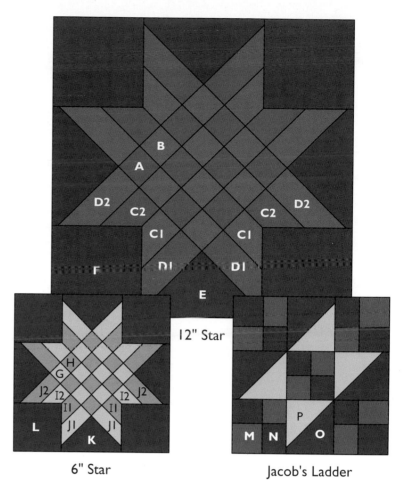

12" Star

6" Star

Jacob's Ladder

Star Block Diagrams

Piecing the Checkered Star Blocks

Step 1

Make AB and GH strip sets (page 81), as shown in **Diagram 1**. Press after adding each strip as indicated by the arrow.

❖ AB strip set should measure 5½" high.

❖ GH strip set should measure 3" high.

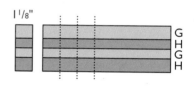

1¾"

A
B
A
B

1⅛"

G
H
G
H

Diagram 2

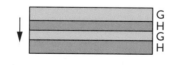

A
B
A
B

G
H
G
H

Diagram 1

Step 2

Cut the strip sets into segments, as shown in **Diagram 2.**

❖ Cut four 1¾-inch segments from the AB set.

❖ Cut sixteen 1⅛-inch segments from the GH set.

Step 3

Arrange the segments as shown in **Diagram 3**. Butt, pin, sew, and press as indicated by the arrow. Make one AB and four GH Units.

❖ AB Checkerboard Unit should measure 5½" × 5½".

❖ GH Checkerboard Unit should measure 3" × 3".

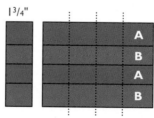

Make the 12" Star the same way

Diagram 3

Step 4

Sew a D2 and a C2 half-trapezoid together and a J2 and an I2 half-trapezoid together, as shown in **Diagram 4.** Sew a C1 to a D1 and an I1 to a J1. Sew the center (C1-C2 and I1-I2) seams, ending ¼ inch from the bottom edge (page 70). Backtack three stitches. Wait to press the seams. Make two CD Units and eight IJ Units.

❖ CD Unit should measure 5½" across.

❖ IJ Unit should measure 3" across.

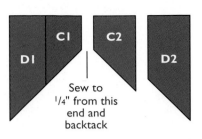

Sew to ¼" from this end and backtack

Sew to ¼" from this end and backtack

Diagram 6

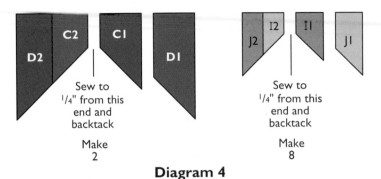

Sew to ¼" from this end and backtack

Make 2

Sew to ¼" from this end and backtack

Make 8

Diagram 4

Step 5

Lay out your CD and IJ Units next to your AB and GH Units, as shown in **Diagram 5.** Before sewing, press the seams in the CD and IJ Units so they fall in the opposite direction of their corresponding seams in the Checkerboard Units. Trim the dog ears. Butt, pin, and sew one unit to each end of the Checkerboard Unit. Press toward the Checkerboard Unit.

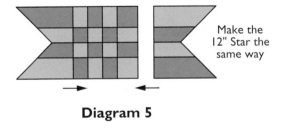

Make the 12" Star the same way

Diagram 5

Step 6

Sew a D1 and a C1 half-trapezoid together and a J1 and an I1 half-trapezoid together, as shown in **Diagram 6.** Sew a C2 to a D2 and an I2 to a J2. Sew the center (C1-C2 and I1-I2) seams, ending ¼ inch from the bottom edge. Backtack three stitches. Wait to press the seams. Make two CD Units and eight IJ Units.

❖ CD Unit should measure 5½" across.

❖ IJ Units should measure 3" across.

Step 7

Sew a black E triangle to each side of the CD Unit, and a black K triangle to each side of the IJ Units, as shown in **Diagram 7.** Press toward the black, and trim the dog ears. Make two CDE Units and eight IJK Units.

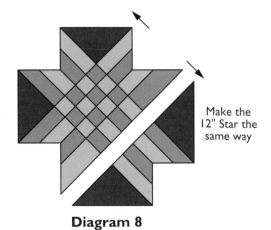

Make the 12" Star the same way

Diagram 7

Step 8

Lay out CDE and IJK Units next to the partially completed Star blocks from Step 5, as shown in **Diagram 8.** Before sewing, trim the dog ears and press the seams in the CDE and IJK Units so they fall opposite to their corresponding seams in the Checkerboard Units. Butt, pin, and sew one unit to each end of the Checkerboard Unit. Press toward the CDE and IJK Units.

Make the 12" Star the same way

Diagram 8

Step 9

Set in the black F and L squares, as shown in **Diagram 9** on the opposite page. Press toward the black. You should now have one complete large star block and four small star blocks.

❖ Small star should measure 6½" × 6½".

❖ Large star should measure 12½" × 12½".

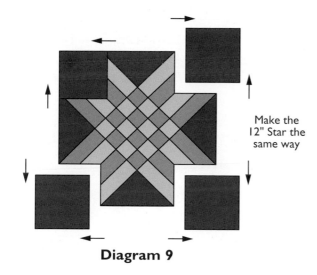

Make the 12" Star the same way

Diagram 9

Piecing the Jacob's Ladder Blocks

Jacob's Ladder Block Diagram

M N P O

Step 1

Sew together strips M and N, as shown in **Diagram 10.** Press toward N. Make three strip sets.

❖ Strip set should measure 2½" high.

N
M
Make 3

Diagram 10

Step 2

Cut the strip sets into 1½-inch segments, as shown in **Diagram 11.** You will need a total of 40 segments.

1½"

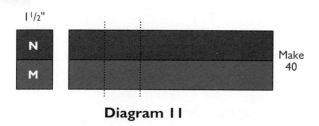

N
M
Make 40

Diagram 11

Step 3

Arrange the segments as shown in **Diagram 12.** Butt the seams, pin, sew, and press the segments as indicated by the arrow. Make ten of each Four Patch Unit.

❖ Four Patch Units should measure 2½" × 2½".

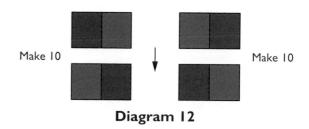

Make 10   Make 10

Diagram 12

Step 4

Sew together an O and a P triangle, as shown in **Diagram 13.** Trim the dog ears, and press toward O. Make a total of 16 OP Units.

❖ OP Units should measure 2½" × 2½".

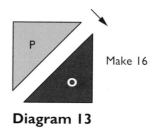

P

O

Make 16

Diagram 13

Step 5

Position the Four Patch Units and the OP Units into two mirror-image blocks, as shown in **Diagram 14.** Butt the seams, pin, sew, and press the units as indicated by the arrows. Make two of each block.

❖ Jacob's Ladder blocks should measure 6½" × 6½".

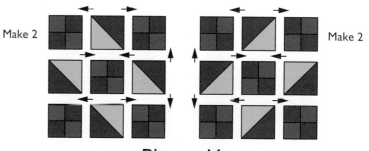

Make 2   Make 2

Diagram 14

Piecing the Nine Patch Blocks

Step 1

Sew together the black and dark green Nine Patch strips, as shown in **Diagram 15.** Sew the 13-inch strips into Strip Set 1 and the 7-inch strips into Strip Set 2, as shown. Press as indicated by the arrows after adding each strip.

❖ Strip sets should measure 3½" high.

Strip Set 1

Strip Set 2

Diagram 15

Step 2

Cut the strip sets into 1½-inch segments, as shown in **Diagram 16.**

❖ Cut eight segments from Strip Set 1.

❖ Cut four segments from Strip Set 2.

1½" **Strip Set 1**

1½" **Strip Set 2**

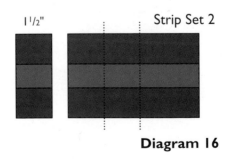

Diagram 16

Step 3

Arrange the segments into two different Nine Patches, as shown in **Diagram 17.** Butt the seams, pin, sew, and press as indicated by the arrows. Make two of each Nine Patch.

❖ Nine Patches should measure 3½" × 3½".

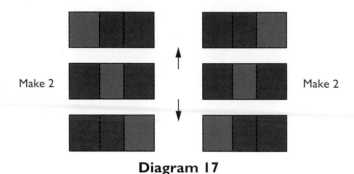

Make 2   Make 2

Diagram 17

Assembling the Top

Refer to the **Quilt Diagram** on the opposite page for the steps in this section.

Step 1

Orient the large star so the pink tips point up and down. Sew black lattice strips to opposite sides of the large star. Press toward the lattice. Place the Nine Patches as shown, and sew one to each end of the remaining two lattice strips. Press toward the lattice. Butt, pin, and sew these lattice units to the top and bottom of the large star. Press toward the lattice.

Step 2

Orient the small stars so the green tips point up and down. Sew a 6½-inch black background square to the top and bottom of two of the small Star blocks. Press toward the black. Sew one of these star units to each side of the large star unit. Press toward the large star.

Step 3

Lay out the Jacob's Ladder blocks, the remaining black background squares, and the remaining small Star blocks. Pay particularly close attention to how you position the Jacob's Ladder blocks. Butt, pin, and sew these units together. Press the seams away from the small Star blocks and toward the Jacob's Ladder blocks. Sew these units to the top and bottom of the large star unit.

Step 4

Measure the wallhanging for the side borders (page 103), and trim the border strips to fit. Pin and sew to the sides of the wallhanging (page 103). Press toward the border. Repeat for the top and bottom borders.

Finishing the Wallhanging

Step **1** Layer the backing, batting, and top. Quilt as desired. This wallhanging was machine quilted in the ditch around the blocks and with parallel diagonal lines and feather designs in the background and borders.

Step **2** Square up the wallhanging (page 104). Make and attach double-fold binding (page 107).

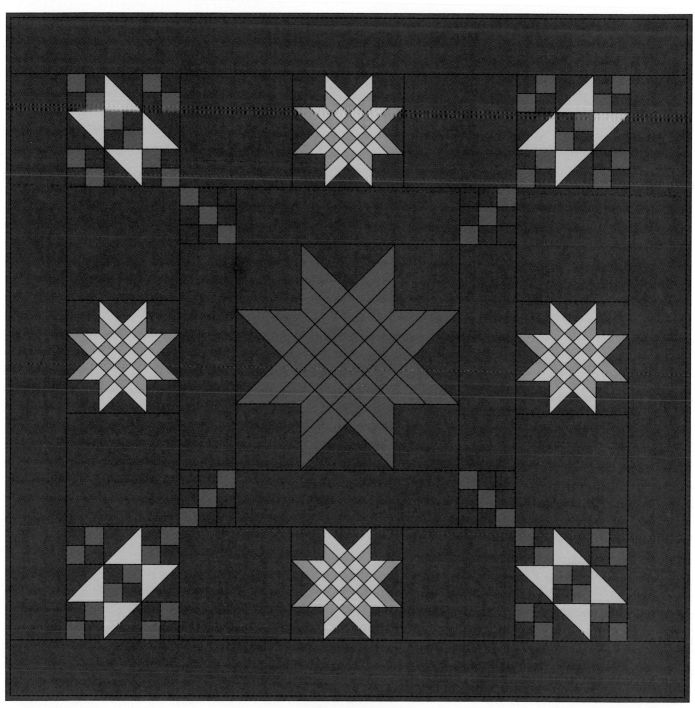

Quilt Diagram

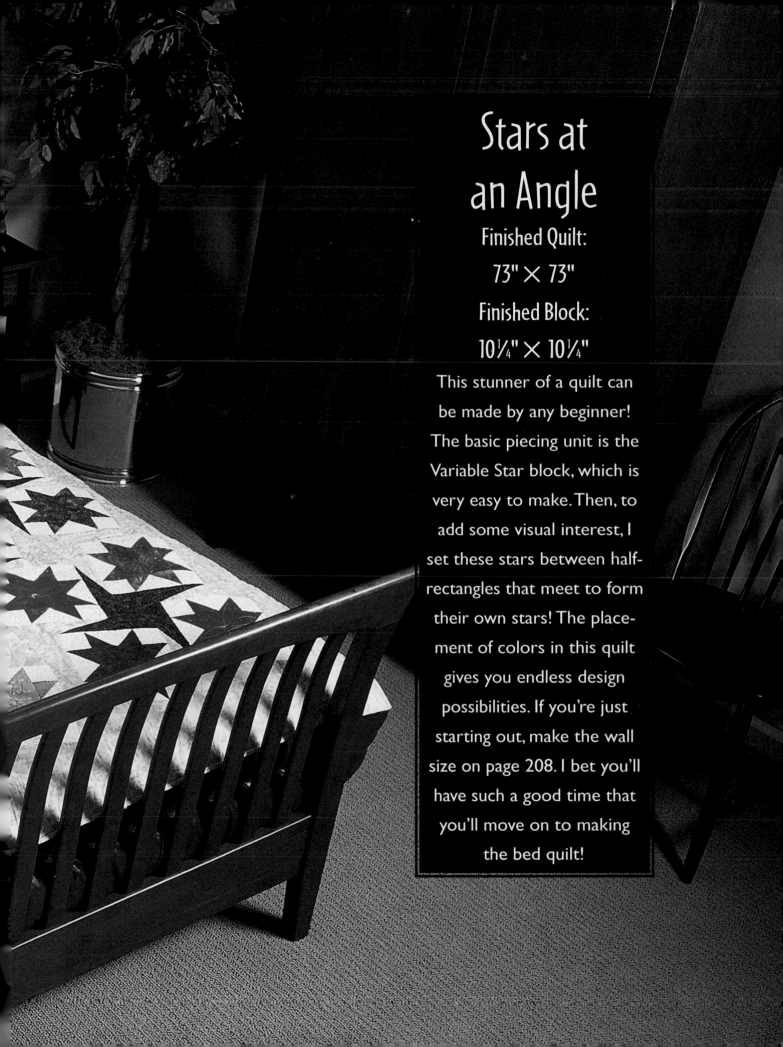

Stars at an Angle

Finished Quilt:
73" × 73"

Finished Block:
10¼" × 10¼"

This stunner of a quilt can be made by any beginner! The basic piecing unit is the Variable Star block, which is very easy to make. Then, to add some visual interest, I set these stars between half-rectangles that meet to form their own stars! The placement of colors in this quilt gives you endless design possibilities. If you're just starting out, make the wall size on page 208. I bet you'll have such a good time that you'll move on to making the bed quilt!

Materials and Cutting Chart

Fabric	Used For	Strips to Cut		First Cut			Second Cut	
		Number	Size	Number	Shape	Size	Number	Shape
Brights 8" × 12" scrap*	A	—	—	1	■ (37)	4½" × 4½"	—	—
	B	1	2⅞" × 12"	4	■ (37)	2⅞" × 2⅞"	8	◺ (38)
Light 2 yards	C	6	5¼" × 40"	36	■ (37)	5¼" × 5¼"	144	⊠ (39)
	D	9	2½" × 40"	144	■ (37)	2½" × 2½"	—	—
Medium Light 3⅜ yards	E1	12	3½" × 40"	46	▬ (44)	3½" × 9⅞"	92	◢ (45) (see **Diagram 5** on page 206 for cutting instructions)
	Border†	2	6" × 65"	—	—	—	—	—
		2	6" × 76"	—	—	—	—	—
Black ⅞ yard	E2	7	3½" × 40"	26	▬ (44)	3½" × 9⅞"	52	◢ (45) (see **Diagram 5** on page 206 for cutting instructions)

Batting 78" × 78"	Backing 78" × 78"	Binding ⅝ yard

Note: Yardages are based on 40-inch-wide fabric after preshrinking. Page numbers in parentheses indicate where to find instructions for rotary cutting individual shapes.

*Fabric amounts and cutting directions are for *one* star. Cut *thirty-six* different brights to make the quilt shown.

†Cut border strips on the lengthwise grain.

Stars at an Angle

This pattern would make a great scrap quilt—just make each variable star out of a different fabric. Try diagonal rows of color families for a more modern effect, or a one-color, many-fabric quilt for an antique look.

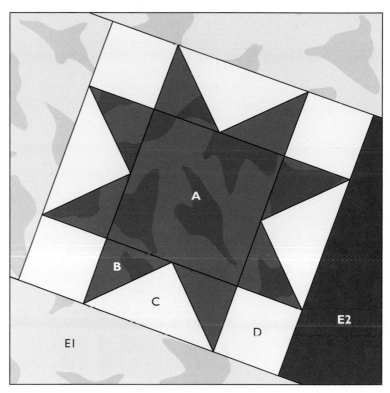

Block Diagram

Shapes Used

(page 37)
(page 38)
(page 39)
(page 44)
(page 45)

Techniques Used

Making Flying Geese
(page 89)
Squaring-Up Blocks
(page 90)

Piecing the Blocks

Step 1
Make BCB Flying Geese (page 89), as shown in **Diagram 1.** Press toward B, and trim the dog ears after adding each B triangle. Make four BC Flying Geese Units.

❖ BC Units should measure 2½" × 4½".

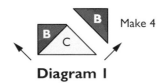

Diagram 1

Step 2
Sew a D square to each side of the BC Unit, as shown in **Diagram 2.** Press toward D. Make two BCD Units.

❖ BCD Units should measure 2½" × 8½".

Diagram 2

Step 3
Sew a BC Unit to each side of an A square, as shown in **Diagram 3.** Press toward A.

❖ Unit should measure 4½" × 8½".

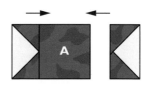

Diagram 3

Step 4
Butt (page 69), pin, and sew a unit from Step 2 to the unit from Step 3, as shown in **Diagram 4.** Press as indicated by the arrows. Repeat Steps 1 through 4 with different bright fabrics to make a total of 36 Star blocks.

❖ Block should measure 8½" × 8½".

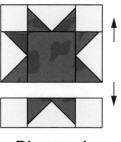

Diagram 4

Assembling the Quilt Top

Step 1

Cut the medium light E1 and black E2 rectangles into half-rectangles, as shown in **Diagram 5.** Make sure to cut from bottom right to top left, as shown. The right side of the fabric must face up.

Diagram 5

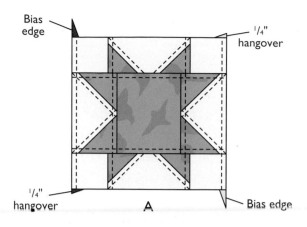

Step 2

Arrange the Star blocks on your design wall as you want them to appear in your quilt. Position the E1 and E2 half-rectangles in place around the stars, as shown in **Diagram 6.**

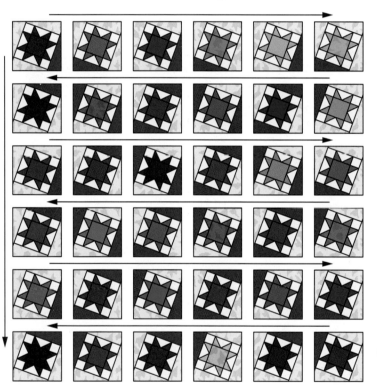

Diagram 6

Step 3

Pick up one Star block and one E1 or E2 half-rectangle. With the wrong side of the star facing you, align the long bias edge of the half-rectangle with the edge of the Star block, offsetting the fat tip by ¼ inch (the long thin tip will hang over the opposite end). See **Diagram 7A.** Pin in place and sew, then repeat on the opposite side. Press away from the Star block and trim the dog ears, as shown in **7B.** Repeat for the remaining two sides, then square up the block (page 90).

❖ Block should measure 10¾" × 10¾".

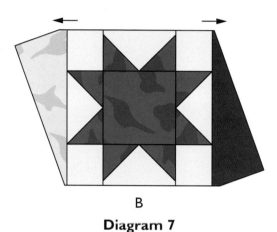

Diagram 7

Step 4

Sew the completed Star blocks into rows, pressing as indicated by the arrows in **Diagram 6.** Sew the rows together, pressing the seams as indicated by the arrow in the diagram.

Adding the Borders

Step 1

Measure the quilt for the side borders (page 103), and trim the two shorter border strips to fit. Pin and sew the borders to the sides (page 103), as shown in the **Quilt Diagram.** Press toward the borders.

Step 2

Measure for the top and bottom borders, and trim the remaining two strips to fit. Pin and sew the borders to the top and bottom. Press toward the borders.

Finishing the Quilt

Step 1
Layer the backing, batting, and quilt top. Quilt as desired. This quilt was quilted in the ditch around the stars, with stippling in the star background and a continuous-line flower inside the star. The border is filled with a leaf-and-vine pattern.

Step 2
Square up your quilt top (page 104). Make and attach double-fold binding (page 107).

Quilt Diagram

Stars at an Angle Wallhanging

Here's a smaller (52 × 52-inch), more country version of this quilt. To make it, I used 16 blue plaids for the stars and red for the half-rectangles. To add just a touch more country charm, I used the same red fabric for border cornerstones and one of the blues in the blocks for binding.

Make sure when making this version that you cut all four of your border strips to the exact same length. (This ensures that your quilt top is perfectly square!) Then, add the cornerstones to the ends of the top and bottom borders before you sew them on. You can also reduce your fabric yardages when you make this smaller version. Refer to the table below for the new fabric amounts.

Fabric	Amount	Used For
Red	½ yard	Half-rectangles and cornerstones
Blue	Sixteen 8" × 12" strips	Stars
Light	¾ yard	Star background
Medium light	1½ yards	Half-rectangles and border

Binding 3/8 yard	Batting 58" × 58"	Backing 58" × 58"

Resources

Alaska Dyeworks
300 W. Swanson Avenue
Wasilla, AK 99687
Hand-dyed fabrics

Big Board Enterprises
P.O. Box 748
Hughesville, MD 20637
Ironing boards

Cherrywood Fabrics, Inc.
P.O. Box 486
Brainerd, MN 56401
(218) 829-0987
Hand-dyed fabrics

Clotilde
2 Sew Smart Way B8031
Stevens Point, WI 54481-8031
(800) 772-2891
Fine silk pins

L. P. Sharp
HC 03, Box 48A
Emily, MN 56447
Sharpens rotary cutting blades

Quilting Creations International, Inc.
Box 512
Zoar, OH 44697
Quilting stencils

Sew Unique
40 Gulch Road
Sheridan, WY 82801
SlipNots and Bobbin Buddies

The Stencil Company
28 Castlewood Drive
Dept. C
Cheektowaga, NY 14227
Quilting stencils

Acknowledgments

The success of this book is due to many dedicated people working at a constant pace for months on end. I could not have written *Rotary Magic* without the unending support of my extraordinary family, my most valued old friends, and the talents of some new ones. Thank-yous go out to the following people who have touched and changed my life forever:

My husband, Frank, whose love and friendship make many things possible.

My children, Mark, Alan, and Karen, whose understanding and sacrifices for my career I deeply appreciate.

My mother, Ruby Johnson, who showed me at an early age the difference between quality and quantity.

Russ Tarlton, a friend and knowledgeable advisor.

Karen Brown and Georgia Adamitis, true friends who are always there, even though they aren't quilters!

Janet McCarroll, who always has time to listen and help. Marcella McCloskey, Marcia Rickansrud, Roxanne Sidorek, and Sandy Storz, who unflaggingly supported this project.

Carol Grossman, Ruth Lindhagen, and Erena Rieflin, whose invaluable help consisted of late nights and countless hours of proofing patterns.

Lea Wang, an incredible person who gets a special thank-you for rearranging her life in order to quilt the quilts in this book.

Gayle Snitselaar, whose sense of humor kept me going on days when things just wouldn't work out.

Sarah Dunn, my friend and editor, who gets a heartfelt thank-you for her soothing ways and creative energy that made this project a success.

Karen Coughlin, one of the best graphic designers I have ever worked with. Erana Bumbardatore, whose attention to detail and consistency contributed to the book's quality.

John Hamel, for a wonderful job with the photography.

Suzanne Nelson, a friend who believed in my talents.

Many companies supplied products for this book, and I appreciate each contribution. But special thanks go to the following companies who have really gone out of their way to provide me with products throughout the past few years:

American & Efird (Mettler thread, and for loaning us Stars at an Angle, page 202)
Benartex
Bernina of America
Mountain Mist
Omnigrid (and for loaning us Indian Puzzle, page 150)
The Stencil Company
Warm Products

Thanks go also to the following companies who graciously donated samples of their products for use and/or review in this book:

Big Board (Ironing board)
Cottage Tools (Mats and rulers)
EZ International (Mats and rulers)
Fairfield Processing Corp. (Batting)
Fasco/Fabric Sales Co. (Fabric)
Fiskars (Rotary cutters)
Hobbs Bonded Fibers (Batting)
Holiday Designs (Rulers)
June Tailor (Mats and rulers)
Master Piece (Rulers)
Mission Valley Textiles (Fabric)
Olfa (Rotary cutters, mats, and rulers)
P & B Textiles (Fabric)
Quilter's Rule (Rotary cutters and rulers)
Precision Quilting Rule (Rulers)
Prym-Dritz Corp. (Rotary cutters, mats, and rulers)
Salem (Rotary cutters, mats, and rulers)
Sew/Fit Company (Mats and rulers)

Index

Note: Page references in *italic* indicate illustrations. **Boldface** references indicate photographs.

METRIC CONVERSION CHART

mm=millimeters
cm=centimeters

Yards to Meters

YARDS	METERS	YARDS	METERS	YARDS	METERS	YARDS	METERS	YARDS	METERS
⅛	0.11	2⅛	1.94	4⅛	3.77	6⅛	5.60	8⅛	7.43
¼	0.23	2¼	2.06	4¼	3.89	6¼	5.72	8¼	7.54
⅜	0.34	2⅜	2.17	4⅜	4.00	6⅜	5.83	8⅜	7.66
½	0.46	2½	2.29	4½	4.11	6½	5.94	8½	7.77
⅝	0.57	2⅝	2.40	4⅝	4.23	6⅝	6.06	8⅝	7.89
¾	0.69	2¾	2.51	4¾	4.34	6¾	6.17	8¾	8.00
⅞	0.80	2⅞	2.63	4⅞	4.46	6⅞	6.29	8⅞	8.12
1	0.91	3	2.74	5	4.57	7	6.40	9	8.23
1⅛	1.03	3⅛	2.86	5⅛	4.69	7⅛	6.52	9⅛	8.34
1¼	1.14	3¼	2.97	5¼	4.80	7¼	6.63	9¼	8.46
1⅜	1.26	3⅜	3.09	5⅜	4.91	7⅜	6.74	9⅜	8.57
1½	1.37	3½	3.20	5½	5.03	7½	6.86	9½	8.69
1⅝	1.49	3⅝	3.31	5⅝	5.14	7⅝	6.97	9⅝	8.80
1¾	1.60	3¾	3.43	5¾	5.26	7¾	7.09	9¾	8.92
1⅞	1.71	3⅞	3.54	5⅞	5.37	7⅞	7.20	9⅞	9.03
2	1.83	4	3.66	6	5.49	8	7.32	10	9.14

Inches to Millimeters and Centimeters

INCHES	MM	CM	INCHES	CM	INCHES	CM
⅛	3	0.3	9	22.9	30	76.2
¼	6	0.6	10	25.4	31	78.7
⅜	10	1.0	11	27.9	32	81.3
½	13	1.3	12	30.5	33	83.8
⅝	16	1.6	13	33.0	34	86.4
¾	19	1.9	14	35.6	35	88.9
⅞	22	2.2	15	38.1	36	91.4
1	25	2.5	16	40.6	37	94.0
1¼	32	3.2	17	43.2	38	96.5
1½	38	3.8	18	45.7	39	99.1
1¾	44	4.4	19	48.3	40	101.6
2	51	5.1	20	50.8	41	104.1
2½	64	6.4	21	53.3	42	106.7
3	76	7.6	22	55.9	43	109.2
3½	89	8.9	23	58.4	44	111.8
4	102	10.2	24	61.0	45	114.3
4½	114	11.4	25	63.5	46	116.8
5	127	12.7	26	66.0	47	119.4
6	152	15.2	27	68.6	48	121.9
7	178	17.8	28	71.1	49	124.5
8	203	20.3	29	73.7	50	127.0